HOW TO USE THIS BOOK

The *A–Z Accounting Handbook* aims to provide a quick point of reference for students studying a wide variety of accounting courses. Each entry begins with a simple definition of the word or term in question and a more detailed explanation follows if necessary. In some cases a worked example is included and, depending on the type of course being studied, students may then wish to refer to a more detailed course text in order to determine the specific skill level required for their course.

This book is not an exhaustive list of all accounting terms but it does encompass the main terms and concepts currently employed by the majority of bodies validating accounting qualifications.

Accounting is studied at many different levels. For example, in the majority of GCE Advanced Supplementary (AS) examinations students are required to understand financial statements but do not need to know how to construct them. However, at GCE Advanced (A) level, some knowledge is required about how to construct financial statements and students must have a knowledge of the underlying accounting concepts and bookkeeping entries. However, those studying the subject at a professional level will need a much more detailed knowledge of very specific areas of accountancy such as taxation; a detail not required by A and AS level. The Association of Accounting Technicians course requires a practical knowledge of a wide variety of accounting activities, for example payroll and VAT. It is the intention of this book to give useful references for all these purposes and to aim the explanations at the 'general' reader rather than a specific one.

There are various ways in which students can benefit from this book. Some sections can be used to check the accepted format for certain aspects of accounting while others will help to develop understanding and the application of commonly used terms. In A-level examinations, written, rather than purely numerical, answers are increasingly being assessed and some of the definitions included in this book provide clear and precise explanations suitable for answering this type of narrative question.

In order to help the reader find their way around the book, entries have been cross-referenced where necessary.

At the end of the book a list of key words and terms has been included, together with some useful tips for examinations. This section is designed to pass on some valuable tips that will help students avoid the pitfalls that so many people fall into when taking examinations.

I hope that students will find this book useful to help them through their learning and as an invaluable time-saving reference during revision.

Ian Harrison

ACKNOWLEDGEMENTS

Writing a book of this type is obviously extremely time consuming and requires many hours of research. I must thank the team at Hodder and Stoughton, in particular Clare Smith, for the patience shown when awaiting my draft copies. Ian Marcousé cannot pass without mention as his comments and guidance were very much appreciated and helped me to ensure a consistent format throughout.

On a personal level, I must thank my wife, Sandra, for her proof-reading and most of all for her patience. I am also indebted to Stephen Irving who willingly shouldered some of my other responsibilities in order to allow me the time to complete this book.

Every effort has been made to be as accurate as possible but there may be occasions when a critical reader could feel that I have over-simplified some entries. I have done this in order to make the book as accessible to as many people as possible and therefore I hope that the 'experts' will be forgiving.

Ian Harrison

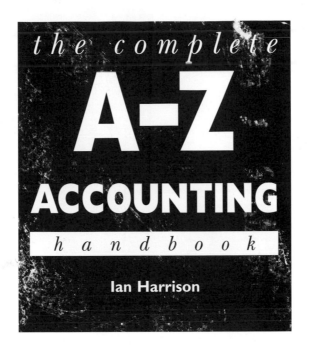

the complete
A-Z
ACCOUNTING
handbook

Ian Harrison

Hodder & Stoughton

A MEMBER OF THE HODDER HEADLINE GROUP

Order queries: please contact Bookpoint Ltd, 39 Milton Park, Abingdon, Oxon OX14 4TD. Telephone: (44) 01235 400414, Fax: (44) 01235 400454. Lines are open from 9.00–6.00, Monday to Saturday, with a 24 hour message answering service. Email address: orders@bookpoint.co.uk

British Library Cataloguing in Publication Data
A catalogue entry for this title is available from the British Library

ISBN 0 340 69124 7

First published 1998
Impression number   10 9 8 7 6 5 4 3 2 1
Year   2002 2001 2000 1999 1998

Typeset by GreenGate Publishing Services, Tonbridge, Kent.
Printed and bound in Great Britain for Hodder and Stoughton Educational,
a division of Hodder Headline plc, 338 Euston Road, London NW1 3BH,
by Redwood Books, Trowbridge, Wilts

AAT: see *Association of Accounting Technicians*

ABC classification of stocks: a method which classifies stocks held into categories of importance. Businesses can then apply the most elaborate procedures in the control of stock only to the items deemed to be most important. It is used when a business has large stocks of many different items.

abnormal losses are losses that occur during the production process but which should be avoided if normal efficient procedures are adopted and followed. They occur when a machine goes wrong or a worker wastes some material or component which ordinarily should not be wasted. The bookkeeping entries are:

Debit: Abnormal loss account   **Credit:** Process account

At the financial year end the abnormal loss account is treated as a *period cost*:

Debit: Profit and loss account   **Credit:** Abnormal loss account

above the line: income and expenditure that appear in the *profit and loss account* before the deduction of taxation.

absorption: when all *production overheads* have been allocated and *apportioned* to a product *cost centre*, the total has to be charged to specific units of production. This process is known as absorption. The main methods of absorption are:

- direct labour hour rate
- direct labour cost percentage rate
- machine hour rate

Worked example: Saluts are manufactured in department J of S M Neal & Co. Ltd. The budgeted overhead costs of department J are estimated to be £200 000 for the next accounting period.
Budgeted direct labour hours for department J for the next accounting period are expected to be 10 000 hours.
Budgeted costs of direct labour in department J for the next accounting period are expected to be £80 000.
Budgeted machine hours to be worked in department J for the next accounting period are expected to be 2450 hours.

Required:
Calculate the overhead absorption rate for department J using the following bases of absorption:
a) direct labour hour rate
b) direct labour cost rate, and
c) machine hour rate.

Solution:
a) direct labour hour rate: $\dfrac{£200\ 000}{10\ 000}$ = £20 per direct labour hour

b) direct labour cost percentage rate: $\dfrac{£200\,000}{80\,000}$ = 250% of direct labour cost

c) machine hour rate: $\dfrac{£200\,000}{2450}$ = £81.63 per machine hour

---

absorption costing: the system of absorbing factory overheads into the total product cost for each saleable unit produced in a factory. *CIMA* (the Chartered Institute of Management Accountants) defines absorption costing as '...the process which charges fixed as well as variable overheads to cost units'.

abstract: a shortened form, or an extract from a document or a report.

ACA: an Associate of the Institute of Chartered Accountants in England and Wales.

ACCA: an Associate of the Chartered Association of Certified Accountants.

accept a bill of exchange: to sign a *bill of exchange* indicating that the person signing will pay that bill when it falls due.

Access was a credit card system. In order to facilitate overseas acceptability the name has now been replaced by Mastercard.

account: a record of financial transactions. Financial data is initially entered into a *book of prime entry*. From there the information is recorded in the *double-entry bookkeeping* system in a book called the *ledger*. The ledger is made up of individual accounts which show in detail every financial transaction undertaken by the business. Generally, each account is shown on a separate page in the ledger. Every account has two sides: the *debit* (left side) and the *credit* (right side). Each piece of financial information is recorded in two accounts: one entry is made on the debit of one account, the other entry is made on the credit of another account.

Worked example: Mary purchases goods for resale paying cash £34.

Required:

Show this transaction in Mary's ledger.

Solution:

Purchases	Cash
Cash 34	Purchases 34

---

accountancy is the profession whose members are engaged in the collection of financial data, summarising that data and then presenting it to the *users of financial reports*.

accountant: a person compiling financial records. Anyone can call themselves an accountant and set up in business offering their services. However, some work undertaken by accountants is restricted to those who are members of one of the major accounting bodies.

accounting: the term applied to the use of financial information once it has been extracted from the basic *books of account*. The function of accounting is to record this information and classify it. The information is then summarised and prepared in a format which is designed to be accessible to the many *users of financial reports*.

The American Accounting Association describes accounting as '...the process of identifying, measuring and communicating economic information to permit informed judgements and decisions by users of the information'.

accounting bases: methods that have been developed in order to apply, generally, accounting concepts to particular accounting transactions. With the issue of *Statements of Standard Accounting Practice (SSAPs)* the number of alternative bases available has been reduced. (See also *accounting policies*.)

accounting concepts and conventions: assumptions which are generally recognised when *final accounts* are being prepared.

Final accounts are prepared on the assumption that:

- the business will continue to trade into the foreseeable future (*going-concern concept*)
- revenues and costs are recorded when they are incurred, not when the cash is received or paid (*accruals concept*)
- accounts are prepared following the same principles that were used in the previous sets of accounts (concept of *consistency*)
- only transactions that can be given a monetary value are recorded in the *books of account* (*money measurement concept*)
- as far as accounting is concerned, the business unit is distinct from all other units including the owner(s) (*business entity concept*)
- all financial transactions should be shown separately if a user of the accounts would be misled by not revealing that transaction (concept of *materiality*)
- if there is any doubt of the value of any transaction then a conservative approach should be adopted (concept of *prudence*)

accounting entity: this can be a *sole trader*, a *partnership*, a *limited company* or some form of non-trading organisation.

accounting equation: the accounting equation recognises that the assets owned by an organisation are always equal to the claims against the organisation.

One side of the accounting equation shows in monetary terms the resources (assets) that are owned by the organisation. The other side of the equation shows how these resources have been financed by funds provided by the owner(s) and borrowings.

The accounting equation can be stated as:

$$\text{FORMULA:} \quad \text{fixed assets} + \text{current assets} = \text{capital} + \text{long-term liabilities} + \text{current liabilities}$$

accounting for associated companies SSAP 1: if one company can significantly influence the business decisions of another company by holding equity shares in that company, then the full share of the profits due to that *holding company* should be shown in the *final accounts* rather than just the *dividends* accruing. This is known as *equity accounting*. The guideline to determine significance is a holding of 20 per cent of equity shares, or if the parent and associated company are engaged in a joint venture.

Worked example: Lyksop Ltd has an issued share capital of 500 000 ordinary shares of £1 each.

Kilton plc, a company with subsidiaries, acquires 100 000 of the £1 ordinary shares in Lyksop Ltd for £310 000.

Lyksop Ltd earns after-tax profits of £75 000. It declares a dividend of £35 000.

Required:

Journal entries showing how the results of Lyksop Ltd will be shown in:
i) the individual accounts of Kilton plc
ii) the consolidated accounts of Kilton plc.

Solution:

Journal

	Dr	Cr
i) Cash	7000	
Income from shares in associated companies		7000
ii) Investment in associated companies	8000	
Income from shares in associated companies		8000

Note:

Initially the investment in Lyksop Ltd would be shown in the balance sheet of Kilton plc at cost, i.e. £310 000.

After the results of Lyksop Ltd have been declared, the asset 'investment in associated companies' would be shown as £318 000, this being the cost of the investment plus the group share of post-acquisition retained profits. This asset will increase each year by the amount of Kilton plc's share of Lyksop's retained profits for the year.

accounting for capital instruments FRS 4: the main provisions of the standard are:

- If a liability falls due within one year then it should be shown as such. If a company shows a much longer maturity date of such a debt then investors may be misled into believing that the company has a much healthier liquid position than it in fact has.
- *Shareholders' funds* must be analysed into equity and non-equity interests.

accounting for contingencies SSAP 18 defines a contingency as 'a condition which exists at the *balance sheet date*, where the outcome will be confirmed only on the occurrence or non-occurrence of one or more uncertain future events. A contingent gain or loss is a gain or loss dependent on a contingency'.

If a contingent gain is:

- certain, it should be treated using the *accruals concept*
- probable, it should be disclosed as a note to the accounts
- possible, it should not be disclosed

If a contingent loss is:

- probable, it should be treated as an *accrued expense*
- a reasonable possibility, it should be disclosed as a note to the accounts
- a remote possibility, then it need not be disclosed.

accounting for deferred taxation SSAP 15 deals with the problem which arises because accounting profit is not the same as taxable profits.

Differences might be:

- permanent differences – certain *revenue expenditure* charged to the *profit and loss account* is not tax deductable
- timing differences – certain items included in the accounts may be attributable to another tax year

Deferred taxation is a means of smoothing out tax inequalities arising because of timing differences. The differences might be due to:

- short-term timing differences – arising because profits are calculated on the *accruals* basis but *tax liability* is calculated on a receipts and payments basis
- accelerated capital allowances – in some years *corporation tax* may be saved by using accelerated capital allowances. The deferred tax is charged to the profit and loss account and the provision is shown on the *balance sheet*. In years where the *provision for depreciation* is greater than the available *capital allowances*, the profit and loss account will be credited with the deferred tax and the provision shown on the balance sheet will be reduced accordingly.

accounting for depreciation SSAP 12: *depreciation* is defined in SSAP 12 as 'the measure of the wearing out, consumption or other reduction in the useful economic life of a *fixed asset* whether arising from use, effluxion of time or obsolescence through technological or market changes'.

The standard confirms the notion that depreciation is the allocation of the cost of the fixed asset, less any residual amount on disposal, spread over the *accounting periods* covering its useful economic life.

It also states that the managers of a business should select the method which is most appropriate to the type of asset and its use in the business.

The standard requires disclosure of:

- the method used
- the rates used
- the effect of any revaluations during the financial year

Changing the method of providing for depreciation is permissible if the change gives a fairer picture of the company's results and financial position. The change of method, the reasoning behind the change and the effects on the financial results should be disclosed by way of a note to the accounts.

accounting for goodwill SSAP 22: goodwill is the difference between the value of a business as a whole and the aggregate of the fair values of its separable net assets.

The main provisions of SSAP 22 are:

- Inherent (non-purchased) goodwill should never be recorded in the *books of account.*

- Purchased goodwill should normally be immediately written off to *reserves*.
- If goodwill is retained in the *balance sheet* it should be shown as an *intangible asset,* and *amortised* (written off) over its estimated useful life. The method used and the period involved should be disclosed and the reasons for the choice explained. It must never be revalued upwards.
- The treatment of goodwill in the accounts should be explained in a note to the accounts.
- Material acquisitions of goodwill should be disclosed.
- Movements in the goodwill account should be shown.
- Negative goodwill should be credited directly to reserve.

A recent *exposure draft* (1996) has recommended:

- Goodwill should be capitalised and not written off on acquisition.
- The life expectancy of goodwill should be reviewed annually.
- If the value of goodwill is expected to be maintained indefinitely it need not be written down.
- When goodwill is expected to have a limited life it should be amortised through the profit and loss account.
- Goodwill that has previously been written off may be reintroduced into the balance sheet.

accounting for government grants SSAP 4: if a government grant relates to *revenue expenditure* it should be credited to revenue in the same *accounting period* as when that revenue expenditure was incurred. If the grant relates to *capital expenditure* the grant should be credited to revenue over the expected useful life of the asset.

Worked example: A business receives a government grant of £100 000 to purchase a machine. The asset is expected to have a useful economic life of 4 years.

Required:

Show the cash account, grant received account and the profit and loss account extracts for the first two years of the asset's life.

Solution:

Cash			Grant received			
Year 0 Grant 100 000			Year1 P&L a/c	25 000	Year 0 Cash	100 000
			Year1 Bal. c/d	75 000		
				100 000		100 000
			Year 2 P&L a/c	25 000	Year 2 Bal. b/d	75 000
			Year 2 Bal. c/d	50 000		
				75 000		75 000
					Year 3 Bal. b/d	50 000

Profit and loss account Year 1	Profit and loss account Year 2
Grant 25 000	Grant 25 000

The grant would be shown as deferred income of £75 000 on the balance sheet as at the end of year 1. On the balance sheet as at the end of year 2 the balance would be £50 000.

Note:

The balance on the grant account must not be shown as part of the shareholders' funds in the balance sheet.

---

accounting for investment properties SSAP 19 defines the difference between properties held as an investment and other *fixed assets* held for general manufacturing or trading purposes. 'An investment property is an interest in land and/or buildings ... which is held for its investment potential'. As a result 'investment properties should not be subject to periodic charges for *depreciation* ... except for properties held on lease...'

Investment properties should be included in the company *balance sheet* at their open-market value.

Changes in the value of investment properties should be shown in an investment *revaluation reserve* – this reserve must never show a debit balance. To ensure that this is always the case, any permanent diminution in value of the investment property should be charged to the *profit and loss account* in the period in which it arises.

accounting for leases and hire-purchase contracts SSAP 21 was issued in 1984 to standardise the accounting treatment and disclosure of assets held under *lease* or *hire purchase.*

SSAP 21 recognised two types of lease:

- A finance lease transfers substantially all the risks and rewards of ownership of an asset to the *lessee.* Although the title to the asset has not passed from the *lessor* to the lessee, in substance the lessee may be considered to have acquired the asset.
- An operating lease is any lease which is not a finance lease.

In the books of the lessee:

- A finance lease should be recorded in the *balance sheet* of the lessee as an asset.
- Rental payments should be *apportioned* between finance charges and capital repayments.
- Assets leased under a finance lease should be depreciated over the lease term or useful life, whichever is shorter.
- An asset acquired under a hire-purchase contract should be depreciated over its useful life.

In the books of the lessor:

- Amounts outstanding from the lessee are recorded in the balance sheet as debtors.
- Operating leases should be recorded as assets, finance leases should not.
- Gross earnings under a finance lease should normally be allocated to *accounting periods* to give a constant periodic rate of return on the lessor's net cash investment in the lease in each period.

accounting for pension costs SSAP 24 standardises the treatment of pension costs in company accounts. The standard mainly deals with the method of allocating the costs of a defined benefit scheme.

(With a defined contribution scheme, the employer makes an agreed payment to a pension fund. The payments are easily measured. The employee's pension will depend on the investment performance of the fund.

A defined benefit scheme will pay the employee a stated pension, usually an amount depending on the employee's salary immediately before retirement. It is very difficult to anticipate how much the employer's contribution should be to guarantee the required final pension.)

The standard requires that an employer should select an actuarial method which recognises the increased future earnings and pensions in order to make good any deficiencies in their funding contributions.

accounting for post-balance-sheet events SSAP 17 defines *post-balance-sheet events* as 'those events, both favourable and unfavourable, which occur between the *balance sheet date* and the date on which the financial statements are approved by the *board of directors*'.

The standard states that 'events arising after the balance sheet date need to be reflected in financial statements if they provide additional evidence of conditions that existed at the balance sheet date and materially affect the amounts to be included'.

It goes on ...'To prevent financial statements from being misleading, disclosure needs to be made by way of notes of other material events arising after the balance sheet date which provide evidence of conditions not existing at the balance sheet date. Disclosure is required where the information is necessary for a proper understanding of the financial position'.

It further states ...'non-adjusting events are events which arise after the balance sheet date and concern conditions which did not exist at that time'.

accounting for research and development SSAP 13 defines *research and development expenditure* as:

- pure research – to obtain new knowledge which has no clear commercial end or application
- applied research – that with a practical aim or application
- development – the use of existing knowledge to produce new products in the future

The standard requires that:

- expenditure on pure and applied research should be written off in the year in which the expense occurred, but
- development expenditure may be capitalised and matched to future revenues

In order for a company to defer development expenditure:

- the project must be clearly defined and the related costs must be identifiable
- the project must be feasible and commercially viable
- the profits from the project should cover past and future development costs

- the company should have adequate resources to ensure completion of the project

accounting for subsidiary undertakings FRS 2 takes a broad view of how one company can influence another company. It introduced the concept of dominant influence; 'dominant influence' broadened the scope of what constitutes a *subsidiary undertaking*. The influence is not now restricted to share ownership.

The accounts of unincorporated businesses are now consolidated into group accounts as if the business is classified as a *subsidiary undertaking*.

accounting for value-added tax SSAP 5 deals with the treatment of *VAT* in the *final accounts* of *limited companies*.

- Reported turnover should be shown excluding VAT.
- Any material amount for VAT charged on *fixed assets* and other separately disclosed items should be included in their cost.
- Any net amounts due to or from Customs and Excise at the *balance sheet date* should be included in the total of debtors or creditors. (The figure need not be shown separately.)

accounting period: *final accounts* are prepared for a finite period of time – usually one year, although many businesses will also prepare final accounts monthly, quarterly or half yearly. The use of an accounting period enables final accounts of one accounting period to be compared with those of another accounting period for *stewardship* and *management accounting* purposes.

accounting policies: *accounting bases* that the managers of a business have selected to use because they are appropriate to their specific business, e.g. the managers of a quarry may choose to use the *depletion method* of depreciating their quarry; the managers of a fleet of delivery vans may decide to use a *reducing balance method* of depreciating their delivery vans. The name given to the fundamental *accounting concepts* used to prepare the financial statements of *limited companies* in the *Companies Act 1985*.

accounting rate-of-return method of capital investment appraisal (ARR) measures the profit earned on investment expressed as a percentage of the average investment. The formula for its calculation is:

$$\text{FORMULA: } \frac{\text{average annual profit}}{\text{average investment}} \times \frac{100}{1}$$

Note: the average annual profit is used, not *cash flows*. This may mean that a calculation of profit may need to be undertaken if the cash-flow figures are given.

Worked example: James & Co. Ltd requires a new piece of machinery. Two new machines are under consideration. They both require an initial investment of £200 000 and have an anticipated useful life of 4 years. The annual cash flow that each is expected to generate is given below:

	Machine LCJ	Machine HER
	£	£
Year 1	80 000	70 000
Year 2	60 000	60 000
Year 3	60 000	50 000
Year 4	40 000	50 000

Required:

Calculate the accounting rate of return for each machine.

Solution:

Average profits

	Machine LCJ			Machine HER	
	Cash flow – depreciation	£		Cash flow – depreciation	£
Year 1	80 000 – 50 000	30 000		70 000 – 50 000	20 000
Year 2	60 000 – 50 000	10 000		60 000 – 50 000	10 000
Year 3	60 000 – 50 000	10 000		50 000 – 50 000	–
Year 4	40 000 – 50 000	(10 000)		50 000 – 50 000	–
		40 000			30 000

Average profits (£40 000/4)		10 000	(£30 000/4)		7 500

Average investment (same for both machines)

	Cost	Accumulated depreciation	Net book value
	£	£	£
Year 1	200 000	50 000	150 000
Year 2		100 000	100 000
Year 3		150 000	50 000
Year 4		200 000	–
		Total	300 000

Annual average investment = £300 000/4 = £75 000

Accounting rate of return

Machine LCJ	Machine HER
$\dfrac{£10\ 000}{£75\ 000} \times 100 = 13.33\%$	$\dfrac{£7\ 500}{£75\ 000} \times 100 = 10\%$

This method can be used to decide between alternative capital projects when other factors are very similar. It is not particularly valuable as the only determinant, since it ignores the *time value of money* and the timing of the returns – average profits will remain the same whether profits are anticipated to be higher in the early years of the project or in the late years. For example, the average profits on the following three projects are the same over a three-year time period:

	Project A £	Project B £	Project C £
Year 1 profits	70 000	1 000	30 000
Year 2 profits	10 000	1 000	30 000
Year 3 profits	10 000	88 000	30 000
Average profits	30 000	30 000	30 000

Worked example: Douglas Ltd presently earns a return on capital employed of 15%. The managers are considering the purchase of a new machine costing £80 000. The machine is expected to yield additional profits of £18 000 per annum.

Required:

Calculate the accounting rate of return expected from the purchase of the new machine and advise the managers of Douglas Ltd whether or not they should purchase the new machine.

Solution:

$$ARR = \frac{18\ 000}{40\ 000} = 45\%$$

(the average capital employed in the new machine is half of £80 000)

On financial grounds the managers should purchase the machine, since the accounting rate of return (45%) is greater than the return they presently enjoy on capital employed (15%).

accounting standards: the rules applied in accounting practice that have been recommended by the *Accounting Standards Board*. These standards are 'concerned with principles rather than fine details'. The standards should be applied in the spirit of the standard rather than by strict observance of the actual wording; the emphasis is on 'substance over form'.

New standards are no longer called SSAPs – they are called *Financial Reporting Standards (FRS)*. Over time, all existing SSAPs will be replaced by FRSs.

Accounting Standards Board has drawn up *Financial Reporting Standards (FRSs)* and *Statements of Standard Accounting Practice (SSAPs)*. All professionally qualified accountants are required to apply the standards to the financial statements they prepare.

Accounting Standards Committee (ASC) developed *accounting standards* from 1970 until 1990 in order to ensure that all professional accountants prepared financial statements using common practices. In 1990 the ASC was replaced by the *Accounting Standards Board*.

accounting technician: a person who assists a fully qualified accountant to prepare financial statements. (See also *Association of Accounting Technicians*.)

accruals: amounts owed for services used by a business during its normal *accounting period*. (See *accrued expenses*.)

For example, a manufacturing business might pay the wages of its factory workers in the week following that in which the work was done. These wages must be included

11

in the end-of-year *manufacturing account*, even though they may be paid in the next financial year.

accruals concept: also sometimes referred to as the matching concept. Costs and revenues are matched so that the financial records refer to the same goods and services in the same time period.

Accountants are interested in accounting for the resources that a business has used during the financial year to generate the *revenue receipts* for that same year, rather than accounting for the money paid to acquire those resources.

The concept recognises the difference between the actual payment of cash and the legal obligation to pay cash. For example, the annual rent of Sybil's shop is £4800 per annum, payable quarterly in advance. At the end of her financial year she has only paid her landlord £3600. The amount shown on her *profit and loss account* is £4800 since she has had the use of £4800 worth of resource to help generate her revenues for that year.

The accruals concept also recognises the distinction between the receipt of cash and the right to receive that cash. For example, Sybil sublets the garage at the rear of her shop for a rental of £10 per week to Jack. At Sybil's financial year end Jack owes Sybil two weeks' rent. Sybil's profit and loss account would show 'Rent received £520' even though she has received only £500 from Jack.

Worked example: Yvonne rents business premises at a rental of £600 per calendar month, her financial year end is 31 December. Yvonne makes the following payments:

	£
7 January	1800
22 April	1800
13 July	1800
4 October	1800
6 December	1800

Yvonne sublets part of her premises to Tony at a rental of £300 per quarter, payable in advance on 1 January, 1 April, 1 July, 1 October. Tony makes the following payments to Yvonne:

23 February	300
8 June	300
6 December	300

Required:

The rent payable and rent receivable accounts as they would appear in Yvonne's general ledger.

Solution:

Rent payable				Rent receivable		
7 Jan Cash	1800				23 Feb Cash	300
22 Apl Cash	1800	31 Dec P&L a/c	7200	31 Dec P&L a/c 1200	8 Jun Cash	300
13 Jul Cash	1800				6 Dec Cash	300
4 Oct Cash	1800				31 Dec Bal c/d	300
6 Dec Cash	1800	31 Dec Bal c/d	1800	1200		1200
	9000		9000	1 Jan Bal b/d 300		
1 Jan Bal b/d 1800						

Both balances will appear as current assets on Yvonne's year-end balance sheet.

accrued expenses: those revenue expenses that remain unpaid at the financial year end. (See *accruals*.)

accrued income: that revenue income that remains unpaid at the end of the financial year. (See *accruals concept*.)

accumulated depreciation: the total amount of *depreciation* deducted from a *fixed asset* since its *acquisition*.

accumulated fund: the '*capital account*' of a non-trading organisation.

accumulated profits: the total profits earned by a business that have not been taken out of the business either as *drawings* (in the case of a *sole trader*) or as *dividends* (in the case of a *limited company*). They arc the profits retained in the business; the 'ploughed back' profits from this and all previous years.

accumulated reserves: the total *reserves* set aside out of profits by a *limited company*.

acid test ratio measures the immediate *liquidity* position of a business. It is sometimes called the quick ratio. The model (formula) is:

$$\text{FORMULA:} \quad \frac{\text{current assets} - \text{stock}}{\text{current liabilities}}$$

It should be expressed as 'something : 1'.

The immediate liquidity position excludes stock, since it can be quite difficult to dispose of stocks quickly. Even if stocks could be disposed of immediately the business could not continue to trade because it would have no stock to trade with.

If a business has a slow *stock turnover*, the acid test ratio should ideally be greater than one. With a fast *stockturn*, the ratio can be less than one without causing alarm.

When making an assessment, trends over a number of years should be observed rather than considering absolute figures. However, one should not be too pedantic about the ratio without referring to the nature of the business being observed. For example, many supermarkets will operate with an acid test ratio considerably lower than one.

Worked example: Raymond Yong has the following current assets and current liabilities:
Stock £12 509, debtors £3881, bank balance £578, creditors £3877.

Required:

Raymond's acid test ratio.

Solution:

$$\text{Raymond's acid test ratio} = \frac{\text{current assets} - \text{stock}}{\text{current liabilities}}$$

$$= 1.15 : 1 \ (3881 + 578 : 3877)$$

ACMA: an Associate (member) of the Chartered Institute of Management Accountants.

acquisition: the taking over of one business by another business, i.e. it acquires control or ownership. The acquisition may take the form of an aggressive *takeover* or be by consent of the managers or owners of the business being acquired.

acquisitions and mergers FRS 6 deals with the accounting treatment to be applied when one or more companies become subsidiaries of another company.

An acquisition usually takes place when a company acquires shares in another company by a cash purchase. In acquisition accounting, *pre-acquisition profits* are not available for distribution in the form of *dividends*.

A *merger* takes place when a company acquires shares in another company by issuing its own shares as the purchase consideration in exchange for the shares in that other company. Profits remain distributable if merger accounting techniques are used.

ACT: see *advance corporation tax*

activity-based costing (ABC): analyses an organisation's activities into groups of functions which lead to a particular output. Activity costing then seeks to identify factors that influence cost levels for those activities. Output is then costed according to the activities undertaken.

activity levels: a measurement of outcomes; the amount of work produced by a business in a set time period. Activity levels are usually used as a comparison when budgeting.

activity ratios measure a business's ability to meet its *current liabilities*. This depends on the rate at which debtors and stocks can be converted into cash. (See *rate of stock turnover* and *debtors' payment period*.)

actuary: a person employed, generally, by an insurance company to calculate the statistical likelihood of how often an occurrence will take place. The insurance company can then calculate the premiums necessary to cover such eventualities.

added value: see *value added*

additional depreciation charge was required by *SSAP 16* (*current cost accounting*). The depreciation charge on *fixed assets* was based on the replacement cost of the assets rather than on their historic cost.

additional voluntary contributions (AVC): extra payments made by a person in order to increase the benefits (i.e. lump sum and pension) they will receive on retirement.

adjusting events: see *accounting for post-balance-sheet events (SSAP 17)*

adjustment accounts: see *club accounts* and *incomplete records*

adjustments are made in *ledger* accounts (or to the figures on the *trial balance*), usually at the end of the financial year, to give the correct figure to be posted to the *trading* and *profit and loss accounts*.

The adjustments may be necessary to correct any errors discovered in the *double-entry bookkeeping* system or to take into account any *accruals* or *prepayments*.

administration expenses: expenses incurred in providing management of the affairs of the business.

administration overheads: expenses incurred in providing management and administration for the business.

All overheads need to be absorbed if a business is to cover its costs. It is very difficult to find a satisfactory way of absorbing administration overheads, as overheads in general are difficult to relate to levels of productive activity.

Administration overheads may be absorbed by using:

$$\text{FORMULA: } \frac{\text{total administration overhead}}{\text{total production cost}} \times 100$$

the result is then applied to the total factory cost of each unit produced; or:

$$\text{FORMULA: } \frac{\text{total administration overhead}}{\text{total sales revenue}} \times 100$$

the result is then applied to the selling price of each unit produced.

Worked example: the following information relates to Watton plc:

Total production cost	£720 000
Total sales revenue	£1 500 000
Total administration overhead	£120 000
Total number of units produced	1 000 000

Required:

Calculate the administrative overhead absorption rate for Watton plc using:
i) total production cost as the basis for absorption, and
ii) total sales revenue as the basis for absorption.

Solution:

i) administration overhead rate $= \dfrac{\text{total administration overhead}}{\text{total production cost}} \times 100$

$= \dfrac{120\ 000}{720\ 000} \times 100$

$= 16.67\%$

ii) administration overhead rate $= \dfrac{\text{total administration overhead}}{\text{total sales revenue}} \times 100$

$$= \frac{120\,000}{1\,500\,000} \times 100$$

$$= 8\%$$

Using total production cost as the basis for absorbing the administration overhead, each unit would absorb:

72 pence* × 16.67% = 12 pence   *(£720 000/1 000 000)

Using total sales revenue as the basis for absorbing the administration overhead, each unit would absorb:

£1.50* × 8% = 12 pence   *(£1 500 000/1 000 000)

---

administrator: a person appointed to try to rescue a company or to protect certain types of creditors when a company is in serious financial difficulties. If the rescue attempt fails it may have to be wound up (go out of business). Companies do not necessarily go into *liquidation* immediately.

admission of a new partner: a structural change to a business involving the addition of one or more new partners. This requires that the business be revalued immediately prior to the admission of the new partner(s), and that the 'old' partner(s) is credited with any increase in the value of the net assets shown on the *balance sheet* (or debited with any decrease) before the new partner(s) takes up office.

Worked example: George and Mildred have been in partnership for over 25 years sharing profits and losses in the ratio 2:1 respectively. They decide to admit Veronica as a partner with effect from 1 July 19*7. The new partners will share profits and losses equally.

The partnership balance sheet as at 30 June 19*7 was as follows:

	£			£
Premises at cost	46 000	Capital accounts	George	45 000
Fixtures and fittings at cost	14 000		Mildred	30 000
Vehicles at cost	9 000			
Stock	4 000			
Debtors	6 000	Creditors		6 000
Bank	2 000			
	81 000			81 000

The following asset values have been agreed between George, Mildred and Veronica:

Premises	£100 000
Fixtures and fittings	10 000
Vehicles	7 000
Goodwill	12 000

All other asset and liability values are agreed at book value.
Veronica is to introduce £20 000 cash.

Required:

The accounts in the partnership books of account to record the admission of Veronica as a partner and the partnership balance sheet as it would appear immediately after her admission as a partner.

Solution:

Revaluation account

Fixtures and fittings	4 000		Premises	54 000
Vehicles	2 000		Goodwill	12 000
Capital George	40 000			
Mildred	20 000			
	66 000			66 000

Capital accounts

	George	Mildred	Veronica		George	Mildred	Veronica
Goodwill	4 000	4 000	4 000	Bal. b/d	45 000	30 000	
				Reval. a/c	40 000	20 000	
Bal. c/d	81 000	46 000	16 000	Cash			20 000
	85 000	50 000	20 000		85 000	50 000	20 000
				Bal. b/d	81 000	46 000	16 000

Goodwill

Revaluation	12 000		Capitals	George	4 000
				Mildred	4 000
				Veronica	4 000
	12 000				12 000

George, Mildred and Veronica balance sheet as at 30 June 19*7 immediately after the introduction of Veronica as a partner

Premises at valuation	100 000	Capital	George	81 000
Fixtures and fittings at valuation	10 000		Mildred	46 000
Vehicles at valuation	7 000		Veronica	16 000
Stock	4 000			
Debtors	6 000	Creditors		6 000
Bank	22 000			
	149 000			149 000

Note:
The goodwill has been written off immediately (see *SSAP 22*).

advance corporation tax (ACT): company taxation that might be paid by a *limited company* that has paid out *dividends* during an *accounting period*. ACT is paid on a quarterly basis by reference to the date of payment to which the dividend relates.

The four quarterly return periods established by the Inland Revenue end on 31 March, 30 June, 30 September and 31 December. If a limited company's accounting period does not coincide with any of the quarterly dates, its return period will end on the *balance sheet date*. ACT is payable 14 days after the end of the return period.

The balance of the company's *tax liability* will be paid nine months after the end of the relevant accounting period as *mainstream corporation tax*.

adverse variances arise when actual results do not correspond to the results predicted. If the actual results reduce the profit that has been predicted in the budget, the variance is said to be an adverse variance. If, however, the variance increases the profit that was predicted in the budget then the variance would be a *favourable variance*. (See *standard costing, variance analysis*.)

Adverse variances arise when:

- actual revenue is less than budgeted revenue, or
- actual expenditure is greater than budgeted expenditure

advice note: used by the person in charge of receiving goods into stores to check that the goods received are the same as those described on the *invoice*.

after-hours dealing refers to buying or selling securities after a *stock exchange* has officially closed for the day. This is an increasingly common method of legitimate business which allows dealers to trade in other markets around the world, thus taking advantage of the different time zones.

ageing schedule of debtors: a list of all debtors categorised by the age of the debt. The longer a debt is outstanding the more likely it is that the debt will need to be written off as bad. An estimated percentage of doubtful debts in each age category is made and the total provision is calculated.

An ageing schedule for bad debts might look like this:

Period outstanding (months)	Amount £	Estimated percentage of potential bad debts	Provision for bad debt
0–1	20 000	1	200
1–2	16 000	2	320
2–3	7 000	3	210
3–6	4 000	4	160
6–12	3 000	5	150
over 12 months	500	50	250
	50 500		1 290

£1290 would be credited to the *provision for bad debts account* in the *general ledger*.

agent: a person who acts on behalf of another with their full authority and consent.

age profile of debtors: see *ageing schedule of debtors*

aggregate depreciation: the total *depreciation* deducted from the value of a *fixed asset*. The *published accounts* of a *limited company* must show this figure for each fixed asset.

AGM: see *annual general meeting*

algebraic method of apportioning reciprocal service department overheads: see *apportionment of reciprocal services*

allocation of overheads: the process of charging whole items of overhead to *cost centres* or *cost units*. The costs allocated are easily identified as deriving from the cost centre.

allottee: a prospective *shareholder* who has been allotted shares in a *limited company*.

allowable expenses: those expenses that can legitimately be included in the *profit and loss account* of a business and so are *tax deductible*.

amalgamation takes place when two or more businesses join together to form a new business.

amortise: the writing off of *intangible assets* such as *goodwill* and *leases*. According to *SSAP 22*, goodwill should be written off to the *profit and loss account* immediately on *acquisition*. When goodwill needs to be written off over a number of years, the process is known as amortisation. The process is similar to *depreciating* a *tangible fixed asset*.

The bookkeeping entries are:

      Debit: Profit and loss account   **Credit:** Goodwill account

analyse: to examine a subject in detail.

analysis involves detailed study of a subject and a report based on the findings of that study.

analyst: a person who studies a subject in fine detail and can then draw conclusions from their examination.

annual general meeting (AGM) of a *limited company* is the yearly meeting to which all *shareholders* are invited. The *directors* present the financial statements for the *financial year* which has just finished. The company's results can then be discussed with the *board of directors*.

The financial statements are approved at this meeting. The *dividends* are approved and *auditors* are appointed, and any vacancies on the board of directors are filled.

annual percentage rate (APR): the annual rate of *compound interest* charged on a *bank loan* or *hire-purchase* transaction which includes fees and management charges.

annual report and accounts: a summary of a company's activities which must be sent to *shareholders* in both *private* and *public limited companies* each year. The report must contain at least the minimum of information required by the *Companies Act 1985*. A copy must also be filed with the *Registrar of Companies* at Companies House. This document will contain:

- the *directors' report* on the previous year's financial results
- the *balance sheet* as at the end of the trading year
- the *profit and loss account*
- a *cash-flow statement*

The company's *auditors* will also report on whether the financial statements show a *true and fair view* of the company's financial position.

annual return: documents sent to the *Registrar of Companies* each year. The return gives particulars of *directors* and members plus a copy of the last *balance sheet* and *profit and loss account*.

annuity: the payment made to someone (usually a retired person) on an annual basis in return for a lump-sum investment. The annual payment made will depend on the amount invested and also the age of the person when the investment was initially made.

application and allotment account: the account to which monies are credited when prospective *shareholders* apply for shares (on application) and when shares have been allocated to them (on allotment).

When all monies are received on allotment, the account is closed by a transfer to the *ordinary share capital* account in the *general ledger*.

Worked example: Redorf plc offers 200 000 ordinary shares of £1 each for sale *at par* on the following terms:

on application 50 pence
on allotment 50 pence

Applications were received for 275 000 shares. The directors of Redorf plc rejected applications for 25 000 shares and the money was returned to the applicants. The remaining shares were allotted to the remaining applicants on a *pro rata* basis. The excess monies held by the company on application were used to reduce the amount due on allotment.

Required:

Journal entries (including those for cash transactions) to record the entries in the books of Redorf plc.

Solution:

Journal

	Dr	Cr
Cash	137 500	
Application and allotment		137 500
Monies received for 275 000 ordinary shares; 50 pence on application		
Application and allotment account	12 500	
Cash		12 500
Monies returned to unsuccessful applicants; 50 pence on 25 000 shares		
Cash	75 000	
Application and allotment		75 000
Balance of money paid by successful applicants who received 4 shares for every 5 they applied for. £100 000 should have been paid but the company is holding £25 000 that was overpaid when the applications were made.		
Application and allotment	200 000	
Ordinary share capital		200 000
Called-up capital being transferred to the ordinary share capital account		

(See also *calls on share issue*.)

application of funds: outlines the way that the managers of a business have spent the funds available to them during an *accounting period*.

apportion: to share. (See *apportionment of overheads*.)

apportionment of overheads: the process whereby some overhead costs are charged to *cost centres* on some rational basis chosen by the cost accountant (see *cost accounting*). The total rent of a factory, for example, will generally be apportioned according to the percentage of floor area occupied by each cost centre within the factory; the maintenance crew's wages might be apportioned according to the number of machines working within each cost centre; canteen facilities might be apportioned according to the numbers of personnel working in each cost centre.

apportionment of reciprocal service overhead costs: an internal transfer of costs between service departments that provide support services for each other. For example, the maintenance department workers may use the canteen for their breaks, and service and repair any kitchen machinery used in the canteen. The overhead costs incurred by each service department are *apportioned* in one of three ways:

- the elimination method, sometimes called the simplified method
- the continuous allotment method, sometimes called the repeated distribution method
- the algebraic method, sometimes called the simultaneous equation method

---

Worked example: Spellers manufacturing plc has three production departments (A, B and C) and two service departments (W and X).

Estimated overhead costs have been allocated and apportioned to each department as follows:

	Production departments			Service departments	
	A	B	C	W	X
	£	£	£	£	£
Estimated overheads	42 000	16 000	20 000	10 000	18 000

The service departments' overheads are to be apportioned as follows:

Department W	50%	30%	15%		5%
Department X	25%	40%	15%	20%	

Required:

Show how the overheads of the service departments W and X could be apportioned by using:

a) the simplified (elimination) method
b) the continuous allotment method
c) the algebraic method.

Solution:

a) the simplified method

	Production departments			Service departments	
	A	B	C	W	X
	£	£	£	£	£
Overheads	42 000	16 000	20 000	10 000	18 000
Apportionment of dept X costs	4 500	7 200	2 700	3 600	(18 000)
	46 500	23 200	22 700	13 600	–
Apportionment of dept W costs	6 800	4 080	2 040	(13 600)	680
	53 300	27 280	24 740	–	53 300

Department X's overheads are now ignored.

Always start with the service department with the largest overhead costs.

This simplified method is slightly inaccurate, but the estimated overheads themselves may be inaccurate since they are *estimates*; the accurate figures will only become available after the financial year end.

b) the continuous allotment method

	A £	B £	C £	W £	X £
Overheads	42 000	16 000	20 000	10 000	18 000
Apportionment of dept X's costs: 18 000 split 25:40:15:20	4 500	7 200	2 700	3 600	(18 000)
	46 500	23 200	22 700	13 600	—
Apportionment of dept W's costs: 13 600 split 50:30:15:5	6 800	4 080	2 040	(13 600)	680
	53 300	27 280	24 740	—	680
Apportionment of dept X's costs: 680 split 25:40:15:20	170	272	102	136	(680)
	53 470	27 552	24 842	136	—
Apportionment of dept W's costs: 136 split 50:30:15:5	68	41	20	(136)	7
	53 538	27 593	24 862	—	7
Apportionment of dept X's costs: 7 split 25:40:15:20	1	3	1	1	(6)
	53 539	27 596	24 863	1	1
				(ignore)	(ignore)

This is close enough without using pence.

The overheads of both service departments have been apportioned to the production departments repeatedly until (almost) all the service costs have been transferred in full to the production departments.

c) the algebraic method

let W = department W
let X = department X

ISLE COLLEGE
RESOURCES CENTRE

The amounts to be absorbed into production departments A, B and C is based on the following equations:

$$W = 10\,000 + 20\%X$$

(department W's overheads are £10 000 + 20% of X's overheads)　　　　[1]

$$X = 18\,000 + 5\%W$$

(department X's overheads are £18 000 + 5% of W's overheads)　　　　[2]

equation 1: $W = 10\,000 + 20\%X$

multiply equation 1 by 5:

$$5W = 50\,000 + X \qquad\qquad\qquad [3]$$

We know that $X = 18\,000 + 5\%W$ from equation 2, so if we substitute for X in equation 3 we get:

$$5W = 50\,000 + 18\,000 + 5\%W$$

$$5W = 68\,000 + 5\%W$$

$$5W - 5\%W = 68\,000$$

$$4.95W = 68\,000$$

$$W = \frac{68\,000}{4.95}$$

$$W = 13\,737$$

We now know the value of W, so we can substitute 13 737 for W in equation 3:

$$5W = 50\,000 + X$$

$$5 \times 13\,737 = 50\,000 + X$$

$$68\,685 = 50\,000 + X$$

$$X = 18\,685$$

These are the costs which need to be apportioned to the production departments in the ratios of the work done by the service departments.

50% of department W's overheads apportioned to department A, 30% to department B and 15% to department C:

50% of £13 737 to department A = £6868

30% of £13 737 to department B = £4121

15% of £13 737 to department C = £2060

25% of department X's overheads apportioned to department A, 40% to department B and 15% to department C:

25% of £18 685 to department A = £4671

40% of £18 685 to department B = £7474

15% of £18 685 to department C = £2802

So the total overheads to be allocated and apportioned to each of the production departments will be:

Department A = £53 539 (42 000 + 6868 + 4671)

Department B = £27 595 (16 000 + 4121 + 7474)

Department C = £24 862 (20 000 + 2060 + 2802)

apportionment of service cost centre overheads: each service department's overheads are charged to production departments according to how much each production department uses the service. Service departments (maintenance, canteen, stores, etc.) are not directly involved in the production process. For example, the cost of providing canteen facilities will be *apportioned* to each department according to the numbers of workers employed in each production department. (See *apportionment of reciprocal services.*)

appraisal: the process of determining the value of something. (See *capital investment appraisal* and *staff appraisal.*)

appreciation: an increase in the value of an asset. Under normal accounting procedures any appreciation in the value of *fixed assets* is ignored, since to use appreciated figures would contravene the concept of *prudence.* (See also *asset revaluation.*)

appropriation account: shows the *users of financial reports* what has happened to the profits of a business. If a business has more than one owner (*sole trader*), for example *partnerships* and *limited companies,* a profit and loss appropriation account is prepared.

Worked example: Linda and Mary are in partnership. Their capital account balances are:

Linda £30 000; Mary £20 000. Their partnership agreement allows Mary a partnership salary of £3500 per annum; it allows for interest on their capital accounts at 10% per annum; residual profits are shared in the ratios 3 : 2 respectively. The profits for the year ended 31 January 19*7 amount to £28 800.

Required:

The partnership profit and loss appropriation account for the year ended 31 January 19*7.

Solution:

Partnership profit and loss appropriation account for Rebe plc for the year ended 31 January 19*7:

		£	£
Net profit			28 800
Less salary – Mary			3 500
			25 300
Less interest on capital –	Linda	3 000	
	Mary	2 000	5 000
			20 300
Share of residual profits –	Linda	12 180	
	Mary	8 120	20 300

Worked example: Rebe plc has made a net profit for the year ended 30 July 19*7 of £23 400 000. Corporation tax due on these profits has been calculated to be £5 700 000. An interim ordinary dividend of £1 600 000 was paid earlier this year. The directors recommend a final ordinary dividend of £3 600 000 and a transfer to general reserve of £1 000 000.

Required:

The profit and loss appropriation account for Rebe plc for the year ended 30 July 19*7.

Solution:

Rebe plc profit and loss appropriation account for the year ended *****.

	£000	£000
Profit for year before tax		23 400
Less corporation tax		5 700
Profit for year after taxation		17 700
Less transfer to general reserve	1 000	
interim ordinary dividend	1 600	
final ordinary dividend	3 600	6 200
Retained profits for the year		11 500

APR: see *annual percentage rate*

area: the basis used to *apportion* certain *overheads* to various *cost centres* within a business, for example rent, rates, heating costs, lighting costs, etc. are generally apportioned according to the floor area occupied by the particular cost centre.

ARR: see *accounting rate of return method of capital investment appraisal*

arrangement fee: the amount charged by a bank or other financial institution to a client for arranging a loan or other type of credit facility.

Articles of Association: the document containing the rules which will govern the internal organisation of a *limited company*. This must be filed with the *Registrar of Companies* together with the *Memorandum of Association*.

The Articles of Association shows the company's rules regarding:

- organisation and control
- voting rights
- conduct of *directors'* meeting
- conduct of *shareholders' annual general meeting*
- directors' powers
- rights attached to the different classes of shares

ASC: see *Accounting Standards Committee*

A shares are ordinary shares with limited voting rights or, in some cases, no voting rights at all.

asset: see *current assets, fixed assets, intangible assets, liquidity, tangible fixed assets*

asset backed: a term generally applied to shares indicating that they are backed by the security of the company's assets.

asset disposal account is used when an asset is sold or scrapped. The asset must be removed from the *ledger* of the business. Any *depreciation* relating to the asset must also be removed from the ledger. An asset disposal account is used to calculate whether the asset was disposed of at a profit or a loss.

Worked example: Bluemore Ltd depreciates its machinery at 10% per annum and vehicles at 25% per annum, both using the straight-line method.

The following is an extract from the balance sheet of Bluemore Ltd as at the end of the last financial year:

Fixed assets	Cost	Depreciation	Net
	£	£	£
Machinery	135 000	64 000	71 000
Vehicles	98 000	48 000	50 000

Recently a machine which cost £38 000 was sold for £8000. The aggregate depreciation relating to the machine was £22 800.

Last week a vehicle which cost £20 000 was exchanged for a new vehicle costing £26 000. The aggregate depreciation on the vehicle traded in amounted to £10 000. Bluemore Ltd paid £15 000 in full settlement for the new vehicle.

Required:

The journal entries to record the disposal of the machine and the vehicle (show cash entries).

Solution:

Narratives have not been included.

Journal

	Dr £	Cr £
Disposal of machinery	38 000	
Machinery		38 000
Provision for depreciation of machinery	22 800	
Disposal of machinery		22 800
Cash	8 000	
Disposal of machinery		8 000
Profit and loss account	7 200	
Disposal of machinery		7 200
Disposal of vehicles	20 000	
Vehicles		20 000
Provision for depreciation of vehicles	10 000	
Disposal of vehicles		10 000
New vehicle	11 000	
Disposal of vehicles		11 000
Disposal of vehicles	1 000	
Profit and loss account		1 000

The vehicle account in the general ledger:

Vehicles

Balance b/d	98 000	Disposal	20 000
Disposal*	11 000		
Cash*	15 000	Balance c/d	104 000
	124 000		124 000
Balance b/d	104 000		

*£26 000 for new vehicle

asset replacement reserve: a *reserve* which is represented by a liquid asset (see *liquidity*) that can be converted into cash when it is necessary to replace a *fixed asset*.

asset revaluation will take place immediately before any structural change to the partnership (see *structural changes in partnerships*). Any overall increase in the value of the partnership assets will be credited to the partners' *capital accounts*; any overall decrease in the partnership assets will be debited to the partners' capital accounts.

Worked example: Norman, Olive and Peter are in partnership, sharing profits and losses in the ratios 3:2:1 respectively. The partnership has net assets that have a book value of £320 000. Norman has decided to retire from the partnership with effect from today. The partners have agreed that the net assets should be valued at £380 000.

Required:

The entries in the partnership books of account to record the increase in the value of the net assets.

Solution:

Net assets

Balance b/d	320 000
Revaluation	60 000

Revaluation

Capital Norman	30 000	Net assets	60 000
Capital Olive	20 000		
Capital Peter	10 000		
	60 000		60 000

Capitals

	Norman	Olive	Peter
Balances b/d	***	***	***
Revaluation	30 000	20 000	10 000

The managers of a *limited company* may have the assets of the company revalued by a professional valuer to reflect the current *market values* of the assets. The *unrealised profit* is recorded as a *capital reserve*.

Worked example: four years ago Irthing plc purchased land and buildings at a cost of £100 000. The directors of the company have recently had the asset valued. The land and buildings are currently valued at £170 000.

Required:

i) Entries in the books of Irthing plc to record the increase in the value of the land and buildings.

ii) Balance sheet extracts as they would appear after the revaluation of the land and buildings.

Solution:

i)

Land and buildings	Revaluation reserve
Balance b/d 100 000	Land & buildings 70 000
Reval. reserve 70 000	

ii) **Irthing plc balance sheet extract as at *****

	£
Fixed assets	
Land and buildings at valuation	170 000
Capital and reserves	
Revaluation reserve	70 000

associated company: a company that is partly owned by another and where the share-owning company can exert a significant influence over the associated company. Associated companies are referred to in the *Companies Acts* as *associated undertakings*. (See *accounting for associated companies*.)

associated undertakings: another term used to describe *associated companies*.

Association of Accounting Technicians was set up in 1980 by the four chartered bodies of accountants (the Institute of Chartered Accountants in England and Wales, the Chartered Institute of Management Accountants (*CIMA*), the Chartered Association of Certified Accountants and the Chartered Institute of Public Finance and Accountancy). It is a professional body for accounting-support staff such as clerks and accounting assistants. Membership of the Association is gained by proving competence in the field of accountancy and by passing central assessments set by the Association at three levels, foundation, intermediate and technician levels, and by completing one year's approved experience.

at arm's length is to treat a transaction as if there was no connection between the parties involved. For example, when a company purchases supplies or services from one of its own subsidiary companies the transaction is treated as if the purchase had been made from a totally unrelated other business.

at par: when shares are issued by a *limited company* at their *nominal* (face) *value* they are said to be 'issued at par'.

at sight: when a financial instrument is payable on presentation, it is said to be 'payable at sight'.

attainable standard is, according to the *CIMA* definition, 'a standard which can be attained if a standard unit of work is carried out efficiently, a machine properly operated or a material properly used. Allowances are made for normal losses, waste and machine downtime'.

Since these standards are achievable they can act as a powerful motivational factor. If staff are encouraged to beat the standard, this will benefit the business by increasing productivity.

audit is the process of checking the financial records of a business by an independent person, the *auditor*, in order to ensure that the records show a *true and fair view*. Internal audits are regular checks conducted by employees of the business to ensure that systems operating within the business are being adhered to. Internal auditors report to the management of the business.

auditors: people, usually trained accountants, who specialise in checking financial accounts that have been prepared by someone else. External auditors are appointed from outside the organisation to ensure objectivity. The auditors of a *limited company* are appointed by the *shareholders.*

auditors' remuneration: the amount paid to the *auditors* for the work done in checking the business's *final accounts.*

auditors' report: the auditors' report will indicate that the financial statements have been *audited* and it will also give the *auditors'* opinion about the financial statements. The report is usually quite brief and would normally contain very little information. (See *Companies Act 1985.*)

The auditors' report is attached to the main financial statements published by a *limited company* as a statutory requirement.

audit trail is used to verify information presented in the *final accounts* by tracing the passage of the information from its inception as a source document; through the *books of prime entry*; through the *ledger(s)* to the figure on the final accounts.

authorised share capital gives the details of the number, classes (i.e. *ordinary shares, preference shares*) and *nominal value* of the shares that a *limited company* may issue. The authorised share capital sets the upper limit to the number of shares the company can issue. This figure can only be exceeded with the approval of the existing *shareholders.* The authorised capital must be shown in the *published accounts* of a limited company. It is usually shown as a note.

AVC: see *additional voluntary contributions*

AVCO: see *methods of stock valuation*

average cost: see *weighted average cost method of stock valuation*

avoidable costs: costs which would disappear if the *cost centre* ceased to carry out its function. The classification is useful when calculating the *contribution* made by an activity. *CIMA* defines avoidable costs as 'the specific costs of an activity or sector of a business which would be avoided if that activity or sector did not exist'.

backer: a person(s) who provides financial support for someone else in business.

back office: where the paperwork involved in a broking firm is done.

bad debt relief: if a debt is more than two years old and has been written off in the accounts of the business, it is eligible for *VAT* relief.

bad debts: debtors that are unable to settle their debt. If it is impossible to collect the amount that is owed, it is necessary to write off that debt. If a debt cannot be collected it is no longer a *current asset*. The entries to write off a debt that has proved to be bad are:

> **Debit:** Bad debts account   **Credit:** The individual debtor

(See also *provision for bad debts, bad debts recovered account.*)

bad debts account: found in the *general ledger*, it is used when individual *bad debts* are written off. The bad debts account is itself written off to the *profit and loss account* at the end of the financial period.

Worked example: Arthur Benson owes £72. Charlotte Dixon owes £47. Ellis Fylde and Co. owes £93. These debts are now irrecoverable and need to be written off.

Required:

The bad debts account as it would appear in the general ledger at the financial year end. Transfer the appropriate amount to the profit and loss account.

Solution:

Sales ledger

Arthur Benson			Charlotte Dixon			Ellis Fylde & Co.		
Balance b/d	72	Bad debts 72	Balance b/d	47	Bad debts 47	Balance b/d	93	Bad debts 93

General ledger

Bad debts				Profit and loss account	
A Benson	72	Profit & loss account	212	Bad debts	212
C Dixon	47				
Ellis Fylde & Co.	93				
	212		212		

---

bad debts recovered account is used when a debt that has previously been written off will now be paid by the debtor. This event must be treated in a special way using the debtor's account in order to indicate that the debt has been recovered and that the debtor can once again be considered for credit facilities in the future.

Worked example: Graham Harris owed £49 in 1993 and the debt was written off to the bad debts account when it was thought to be irrecoverable. Harris repaid the £49 yesterday.

Required:

Write up the appropriate ledger accounts to show the entries relating to the recovered debt.

Solution:

Graham Harris				Bad debts recovered			
1 Bad debt recovered	49	2 Bank	49	3 Profit & loss	49	1 Graham Harris	49

Bank			Profit and loss account		
2 Graham Harris	49			3 Bad debt recovered	49

Note:

It is important to record the fact that Graham has now paid his debt by reinstating the fact in his personal account in the sales ledger. The £49 entered in the profit and loss account could be deducted from any debit entry for bad debts written off.

---

balance: the amount put in either the debit or credit column of an account to make the totals of the two columns equal to each other.

balance brought down (balance b/d): the balance used to open an account in the present *accounting period*. It is the closing balance on the account from the previous accounting period.

balance brought forward (balance b/fwd): another version of *balance b/d*.

balance carried down (balance c/d): the balance used to close an account at the end of an *accounting period*. It is used as the balance brought down at the start of the next time period.

balance carried forward (balance c/fwd): another version of *balance c/d*.

balanced budget: a budget where costs and revenues are equal.

balance sheet is a statement which shows the assets and liabilities of an organisation. It is generally prepared at the end of an *accounting period*. It is a 'sheet' showing all the balances remaining in the organisation's *ledgers* after the preparation of the *final accounts*.

The balance sheet can be prepared using a vertical format, for example:

Ken Sharpe plc balance sheet as at 31 December 1997

Fixed assets	Cost £	Depreciation £	Net £
Land and buildings	150 000	40 000	110 000
Machinery	180 000	30 000	150 000
Vehicles	90 000	45 000	45 000
	420 000	115 000	305 000
Current assets			
Stock		34 000	
Debtors		26 000	
Bank		12 000	
		72 000	

Creditors: amounts falling due within one year		
Trade creditors	18 000	
Taxation	19 500	
Dividends	12 500	
	50 000	
Net current assets		22 000
		327 000
Creditors: amounts falling due after more than one year		75 000
Net assets		252 000
Capital and reserves		
Called-up capital:		
Ordinary shares of 50p each		80 000
8% preference shares of £1 each		50 000
Share premium account		40 000
Profit and loss account		82 000
		252 000

Balance sheets for *sole traders* and *partnerships* can be prepared using a horizontal layout, for example:

Jeff Bellis Balance sheet as at 31 December 1997

Fixed assets	Cost	Dep	Net	Capital		
Premises	150 000	20 000	130 000	Balance as at 1 January 1997		105 000
Machinery	70 000	40 000	30 000	Add profit		67 500
Vehicles	47 000	28 000	19 000			172 500
	267 000	88 000	179 000	Less drawings		38 500
Current assets						134 000
Stock		27 000		Long-term loan		80 000
Debtors		13 000				
Bank		7 000	47 000	Current liabilities		
				Trade creditors	10 000	
				Accrued expenses	2 000	12 000
			226 000			226 000

balance sheet date: the date on which a *balance sheet* is drawn up. Although a balance sheet can be drawn up by extracting outstanding balances from the *ledgers* at any time, balance sheets are generally drawn up at the end of an *accounting period*.

balancing figure: the amount that needs to be inserted in the debit or credit column of an account to make the two totals equal. For example:

An Account		
58	42	176 is the balancing figure to be inserted into the
63		credit side of the account. When this is done
97		the account balances – both sides equal 218.

balancing item: see *balancing figure*

balancing the accounts makes the totals of the debit and credit sides of an account equal, usually at the end of an *accounting period*. This is achieved by entering a *balancing figure* on the debit side of the account and carrying it down to the credit side of the account to start the next accounting period, or by entering a balancing figure on the credit side of the account and carrying it down onto the debit side of the account to start the next accounting period.

bank: a business which holds money for its clients and lends money to clients.

bank account: an account that a customer has with a bank. The customer uses the bank account to deposit and to withdraw money.

bank balance: the amount of money that a bank owes a business. The balance in the *cash book* will be shown on the debit side. This is the balance that is shown on the debit of the *trial balance* and it will be shown as a *current asset* in the business's *balance sheet*. (See also *bank overdraft*.)

bank cash book: a *cash book* recording a business's payments made into and out of its bank account. In many businesses all receipts of cash and cheques will be banked on a daily basis. All cash transactions will be recorded in a *petty cash book*.

The bank cash book can be written in the traditional way with a debit side and a credit side. In a large business, the bank cash book might be divided into a bank receipts book and a bank payment book; each may be the responsibility of separate members of staff. The receipts book will have columns for *discounts allowed*, *VAT*, amounts received and totals banked. The payments side will have columns for *discount received*, VAT and cheques paid.

bank columns in a traditional *cash book* record *lodgements* made by a business into the bank account held for the business by its bankers, and *cheques* drawn by the business on the business bank account. Lodgements are recorded in the debit column while cheques drawn are recorded in the credit column of the cash book.

bank current account: an account at a clearing bank on which cheques can be drawn.

bank deposits: monies placed in a bank by its customers.

bank giro transfer: the method used by clearing banks to transfer money rapidly from one bank account to another.

bank identification number (BIN): a six-digit number which identifies a bank for *charge card* purposes.

bank loan: capital borrowed from a bank. The borrower must pay interest on the loan. This type of borrowing is generally used by a business to fund a specific project, for example the purchase of *fixed assets*. A bank loan will be shown on the *balance sheet* as a *long-term liability*.

The total interest charged annually by the bank is shown as an expense on the *profit and loss account*. Any *capital repayments* will reduce the long-term liability on the balance sheet.

Short-term borrowing to help fund a temporary shortage of funds is more likely to involve negotiation of a *bank overdraft*.

bank mandate: a written order from a potential customer addressed to a bank used to open a new account. It contains the customer's(s') specimen signature(s) and allows the customer(s) to sign cheques on behalf of the account holder.

ISLE COLLEGE
RESOURCES CENTRE

bank overdraft: an amount that is owed to a bank on a current account. An overdraft arises when cheques are drawn on an account that has insuffcient funds to cover that cheque. If there are insufficient funds to cover any cheque drawn, it cannot be assumed that the bank will honour (pay) the amount. The bank may well dishonour the cheque by referring it to *drawer.*

If a person or business believes that the current account will move into overdraft in the future, they should arrange overdraft facilities. This will ensure that the bank will honour cheques (up to the agreed limit), even though there are insufficient funds in the account to cover the value of cheques drawn. When a cheque is dishonoured and referred to drawer it is sometimes said to have '*bounced*'.

The balance in the *cash book* will be shown on the credit side. The balance is shown on the credit of the *trial balance* and as a *current liability* in the *balance sheet.*

bank paying-in slip: normally used when money and/or cheques are paid into a bank account.

bank reconciliation statement makes sure that an organisation's record of bank transactions agrees with the record of the organisation's bank transactions recorded in the bank's *ledger.* This rarely happens because of the difference in the time cheques are written and sent to a creditor and the time the creditor receives and pays the cheque into his/her bank account.

A copy of the bank's records are sent regularly to the organisation as a bank statement. Businesses will prepare a bank reconciliation statement on a regular basis, whenever a bank statement is received. The process is generally undertaken in two stages:

1 Making sure that the business bank *cash book* is written up to date. This is necessary since items may appear on the business bank statement which have not yet been entered in the business bank cash book, e.g. direct debit transfers, standing orders, bank charges, credit transfers, etc.

2 The actual reconciliation statement.

Worked example: the following details relate to Brian Tsen's business as at 31 December 19*7:

	£
Cash at bank as per the bank columns in Brian's cash book as at 31 December 19*7	196
Cheques drawn by Brian but not presented for payment	692
Direct debits, standing orders and bank charges entered on Brian's bank statement but not yet entered in the bank columns of his cash book	312
Credit transfers entered on Brian's bank statement but not yet entered in the bank columns of his cash book	87
Cheques received by Brian and paid into the bank but not yet entered on the bank statement	401
Cash at bank as per Brian's bank statement as at 31 December 19*7	262

Required:

Brian Tsen's business bank reconciliation statement as at 31 December 19*7

Solution:

Cash book (bank columns only)

	£		£
Balance b/d	196	Direct debits etc.	312
Credit transfers	87		
Balance c/d	29		
	312		312
		Balance b/d	29

Bank reconciliation statement as at 31 December 19*7

	£
Balance at bank as per Brian's cash book	(29)
Add unpresented cheques	692
	663
Less cheques not yet presented	401
Balance at bank as per bank statement	262

Alternatively:

Bank reconciliation statement as at 31 December 19*7

	£
Balance at bank as per bank statement	262
Less unpresented cheques	692
	(430)
Add cheques not yet presented	401
Balance at bank as per Brian's cash book	(29)

Bank reconciliations check:

- the accuracy of the entries in the bank cash book

- the accuracy of entries on the bank statement
- that unpresented cheques from previous reconciliation statements have been presented for payment

bankruptcy: a legal procedure applied to an individual giving him/her protection from his/her creditors. It occurs when the person is unable to pay his/her debts. The person's assets may be sold to pay off as many debts as possible.

Note that a *limited company* will go into *liquidation* if it is unable to discharge its liabilities.

bank statement: a copy of a bank account as it appears in the bank's *ledger*. When a deposit (*lodgement*) is made on behalf of a person, the bank owes that amount to the depositor. These deposits are shown on the bank statement as credits. When a cheque is drawn on the account, the amount is debited to the account and the balance is reduced by that amount.

Any Bank plc

UPPER DOWNING BRANCH
01999 123456

Statement of Account

CURRENT ACCOUNT –
INTEREST OPTION

REQUEST
13 JAN
POST NO.   52

Details		Payments	Receipts	Date	Balance
				1992	
BALANCE FORWARD				14DEC	330.14DR
	100220	25.00		15DEC	
CALOR LTD				15DEC	415.14DR
	DDR	60.00		15DEC	
	100222	28.74		18DEC	
	ATM		1312.80	18DEC	868.92
	100224	18.00		23DEC	850.92
	100223	70.00		24DEC	780.92
	100225	49.35		30DEC	
COL MUT LIFE ASSCE					
	DDR	83.32		30DEC	
SUN ALLIANCE LONDON					
	DDR	50.00		30DEC	598.25
N.A.T.F.H.E.					
	DDR	8.00		31DEC	590.25
				1993	
	100227	50.25		4JAN	
	100228	17.99		4JAN	
	100229	5.48		4JAN	
	100230	17.48		4JAN	
	100231	41.50		4JAN	
FRASERCARD SRV					
	STO	100.00		4JAN	
NORWEB					
	STO	5.00		4JAN	
XXXXXXXXXXXXXXXXXXXXXXXX					
UNAUTH O/D FEE £25.00					
	7DEC/3JAN	25.00		4JAN	327.55
XXXXXXXXXXXXXXXXXXXXXXXX					
	100232	988.60		5JAN	
HOMEOWNERS					
	DDR	27.00		5JAN	688.05DR
	100234	110.00		6JAN	798.05DR
COUNTER CREDIT			30.62	7JAN	767.43DR
	100233	54.40		8JAN	821.83DR

ABBREVIATIONS   DIV Dividend STO Standing Order BGC Bank Giro Credit DDR Direct Debit
DR Overdrawn Balance ATM Cash Dispenser Transaction

The bank will send a copy of the account, as a bank statement, as often as a person or business requires. The statement is used to check the entries in the *bank columns* of a business *cash book* prior to the preparation of a *bank reconciliation statement*.

bank statement balance shows the amount of cash a business has in its current account. This balance is used in a *bank reconciliation statement*, but it is not the balance used in the *trial balance* or the *current assets* section of the *balance sheet* of the business.

barter: the system whereby goods are given in exchange for other goods rather than in exchange for money.

basic pay: a person's normal gross wage before the addition of *overtime* or other additional payments.

basic standards: standards which once set are not changed. They are used as base figures in order to indicate trends in price levels and production methods. Managers may use basic standards as a means of extrapolating future movements in prices and production.

basis of assessment: the method of deciding into which year financial transactions should be included for the purposes of calculating tax liability.

batch costing: a method of costing used when a large number of identical products are to be produced either for a customer or as a component for another product being manufactured.

bear: a *stock exchange* speculator who believes that the price of shares that he/she has sold will fall and that he/she will be able to purchase them back at a lower price, thus making a profit.

bear market: a period when share prices in general are falling because *shareholders* are selling their shares in the belief that they will be able to purchase the shares later at a lower price.

bearer bond: indicates a debt to an unnamed party. When the bond matures the person holding the bond at that time will receive payment of the sum originally borrowed. (See *bond*.)

below the line refers to extraordinary financial transactions which are shown in the *profit and loss account*, but after the net profit after taxation figure has been calculated.

bill of exchange: a document drawn up by a business stating the amount owed by a debtor. It is sent to the debtor who will 'accept it' by signing it. The debtor then returns the signed bill. It is a commitment to pay a stated amount on a particular date.

There are three ways the business may treat the bill:

1 To settle a debt with an agreeable third party.
2 To deposit it with a bank. The bank will pay the business the value of the bill less an agreed discount rate. When the bill matures the bank will present it to the debtor for payment.
3 To hold the bill until it matures, when the business will present it to the debtor for payment.

bills payable: *bills of exchange* which a business will have to pay to its creditors when the bills mature. They are shown as a *current liability* in the *balance sheet*.

bills receivable: *bills of exchange* which are due to be paid to a business by a business's debtors when the bills mature. They are shown as a *current asset* on the *balance sheet.*

bin card: a name given to a *stock record card.*

black economy: trade in cash or by barter between suppliers and customers which is not recorded in the *books of account* and so will not be included in the business's *final accounts.* The profits on such transactions are therefore not declared for taxation purposes.

black market: the buying and selling of goods illegally. This type of market flourishes in times of war when certain types of goods are hard to come by or when certain types of goods are not legally available.

blank cheque: a cheque which the *drawer* has signed but has not indicated the amount to be paid.

blanket absorption of overheads: rather than calculate an absorption rate for individual *cost centres*, some manufacturing businesses calculate an overhead absorption rate for the factory as a whole.

Worked example: total factory overheads for the Bodbred Manufacturing Company plc for the year are £1 000 000. Direct labour hours worked in the factory during the year are 250 000 hours.

Required:

Calculate the blanket overhead absorption rate per direct labour hour for the factory.

Solution:

$$\text{blanket overhead absorption rate} = \frac{£1\ 000\ 000}{250\ 000} = £4 \text{ per direct labour hour}$$

so all units produced will be charged £4 per direct labour hour no matter how much time was spent in each individual section or department of the factory.

---

blue chip stocks: very low risk stocks or shares issued by a sound company with a record of paying good *dividends.*

board meeting: a meeting of the *board of directors* of a *limited company.*

board of directors: the group of people who run a *limited company.* They are elected by the *shareholders* of the company. (See *directors.*)

bond: a legally binding contract made by a company (or a government in the case of treasury bonds) promising to repay borrowed money at some date in the future. The holders of bonds receive interest from the issuer. The interest is generally paid half yearly.

bonded warehouse: a place where goods are stored until any duty due is paid.

bonus shares: shares issued to existing *shareholders* without payment. The shares are given in proportion to the shareholder's holding by using the company's *reserves.* For this reason the issue is also referred to as a capitalisation issue.

The company's reserves provide permanent finance for a company. The transfer from reserves to *share capital* by a book entry has no effect on the capital structure of the company.

A bonus issue is also known as a scrip issue.

The *directors* may propose a bonus issue if:

- the company has large reserves
- the bulk of the reserves are *capital reserves*
- the payment of a cash *dividend* could cause *liquidity* problems

---

Worked example: the following is an extract from the balance sheet of Pocklinton plc.

Share capital and reserves	£
Ordinary shares of £1 each	4 000 000
Share premium	500 000
Revaluation reserve	200 000
Profit and loss account	653 000

The directors propose a scrip issue on the basis of one bonus share for every four shares already held. It is company policy to maintain reserves in the most flexible form.

Required:

Journal entries to record the scrip issue.

Solution:

Journal

	Dr	Cr
	£	£
Share premium	500 000	
Revaluation reserve	200 000	
Profit and loss account	300 000	
Bonus account		1 000 000
Bonus account	1 000 000	
Ordinary share capital account		1 000 000

Note:

The two *capital reserves* are used first. The remainder of the required sum is transferred from the profit and loss account. The profit and loss account is used last because it is the most flexible of the company's reserves.

---

bookkeeper: a person employed to record the financial transactions undertaken by his/her employer.

bookkeeping: the recording of all financial transactions undertaken by a business (or an individual). (See *single-entry bookkeeping, double-entry bookkeeping*.)

books of account: the generic name given to the *ledgers* and *books of prime entry* in which all business transactions are recorded.

books of prime entry: see *purchase day book, purchase returns day book, sales day book, sales returns day book, journal, cash book*.

book value: the net value of a *fixed asset* as it appears in the *general ledger* of a business. It is calculated by taking the *aggregate depreciation* of the fixed asset from the value in the asset account. The book value is also known as the net book value or the written-down value.

Worked example: the following accounts have been extracted from the general ledger of Tomlok plc:

Premises	Motor vehicles
Balance b/d 100 000	Balance b/d 89 000
Reval. reserve 75 000	

Depreciation of premises	Depreciation of motor vehicles
Balance b/d 24 000	Balance b/d 64 000

Required:

Calculate the book value of Tomlok plc premises and motor vehicles.

Solution:

book value of premises   = £151 000 (£175 000 − 24 000)
book value of motor vehicles = £25 000 (£89 000 − 64 000)

bottom line: literally, the last line in the *final accounts* of a business. It will indicate whether the business has made a profit or a loss in the financial year under review.

bought day book: also known as the *purchase day book* or purchase journal.

bought ledger: see *purchase ledger*

bounced: a colloquial expression indicating that a bank has dishonoured a cheque. The cheque will be referred to *drawer*, that is, it will be returned to the person who tried to cash it or deposit it in their bank account.

brackets are used in some financial statements to indicate a negative figure.

branch: an outlet in an area away from head office or the main part of a business.

branch accounts: the accounts that show the transactions undertaken by the branch(es) of a business. The accounting records may be kept centrally at the head office or the branches may keep their own.

   1 **Branch accounts maintained at head office**. Head office will usually maintain all financial records when administration for the whole business is centralised. The system is used as a control mechanism since the purchase and issue of stock will be administered from head office. All moneys received by the branch will be banked daily and credited to the head office account at the bank.

   The accounts may be drawn up using either a double column for branch stock (method 1) or a branch stock adjustment account (method 2).

Worked example: method 1 – Trinkets Ltd operates a branch at Walton. Head office is in Netton. All goods are purchased by head office and invoiced to and sold by the branch at cost plus 100%.

Credit customers are required to pay any outstanding balances on their accounts to head office direct. All transactions are recorded in the books at head office.

The following transactions relate to the branch during the year ended 31 March 19*7:

	£
Stock at cost 1 April 19*6	4 000
Debtors 1 April	750
Goods sent to Walton from head office during the year at invoice price	24 000
Cash sales	12 000
Credit sales	10 000
Cash remitted to head office by debtors	9 500
Stock at cost 31 March 19*7	5 000
Debtors 31 March 19*7	1 250

Required:

The following ledger accounts for the year ended 31 March 19*7:
i) branch stock
ii) branch debtors
iii) goods sent to branch
iv) cash.

Solution:

Branch stock

	Selling price £	Memo- randum £		Selling price £	Memo- randum £
Stock b/d	8 000	4 000	Sales – cash	12 000	12 000
Goods sent to branch	24 000	12 000	– credit	10 000	10 000
Gross profit to P&L a/c		11 000	Stock c/d	10 000	5 000
	32 000	27 000		32 000	27 000
Stock b/d	10 000	5 000			

Note:

If the selling price column on the credit side of this account needs a balancing figure, this would represent a stock loss which might require investigation if the deficiency is outside acceptable parameters.

Branch debtors

Balance b/d	750	Cash	9 500
Branch sales	10 000	Balance c/d	1 250
	10 750		10 750
Balance b/d	1 250		

Goods sent to branch

Transfer to head office trading account	12 000	Branch stock	12 000

Cash		
Branch debtors	9 500	
Branch stock	12 000	

Worked example: method 2 – using the same information as above:

Branch stock (at selling price)				
Balance b/d	8 000	Sales – cash	12 000	
Goods sent to branch	24 000	– credit	10 000	
		Balance c/d	10 000	
	32 000		32 000	
Balance b/d	10 000			

Branch stock adjustment (profit loading)				
Gross profit				
to profit and loss account	11 000	Unrealised profit b/d	4 000	
Unrealised profit c/d	5 000	Goods sent to branch	12 000	
	16 000		16 000	
		Unrealised profit b/d	5 000	

2 **Branch maintains its own accounting records.** This is normally the case when a business has a small number of branches. Head office and the branch will have current accounts showing the relationship each has with the other. The relationship between head office and the branch is the usual debtor/creditor one.

Transactions between head office and the branch are recorded in the same way as transactions between unconnected businesses.

Worked example: Stumper & Co has its head office at Currock. A branch of the business is situated at Arraby. The manager at Arraby maintains the branch accounting records.

On 1 February 19*6 the current accounts at head office and the branch show balances of £6430. The following transactions took place during the year ended 31 January 19*7:

	£
Goods sent to branch	38 760
Cheques received from the branch	47 280
Returns from the branch	600
Assume branch profit for the year	£9 200

Required:

The Arraby branch current account as it would appear in the head office ledger.
The head office current account as it would appear in the ledger at Arraby.

Solution:

Head office ledger

Arraby branch current account

	£		£
Balance b/d	6 430	Returns from branch	600
Goods sent to branch	38 760	Cheques received from branch	47 280
Branch net profit	9 200	Balance c/d	6 510
	54 390		54 390
Balance b/d	6 510		

Branch ledger

Head office current account

	£		£
Returns to head office	600	Balance b/d	6 430
Cheques sent to head office	47 280	Goods received from head office	38 760
Balance c/d	6 510	Net profit	9 200
	54 390		54 390
		Balance b/d	6 510

As one would expect, the two accounts mirror each other.

There may be a difference in the two current account final balances at the time the *final accounts* are being prepared. This may be caused by goods sent to the branch, returns from the branch to head office and cash being in transit between the branch and head office.

Worked example: details as before for Stumper & Co. However, £760 goods sent by head office to the branch have not yet arrived at Arraby.

Required:

The Arraby branch current account as it would appear in the head office ledger. The head office current account as it would appear in the ledger at Arraby.

Solution:

Head office ledger

Arraby branch current account

	£		£
Balance b/d	6 430	Returns from branch	600
Goods sent to branch	38 760	Cheques received from branch	47 280
Branch net profit	9 200	Goods in transit c/d	760
		Balance c/d	5 750
	54 390		54 390
Balance b/d	5 750		
Goods in transit b/d	760		

The head office account in the Arraby branch ledger is the same as that shown in the solution above.

---

brand name: the name of a particular make of product, for example 'Coke' and 'Pepsi' are brand names of two makes of cola.

break-even analysis: the calculation of the level of output and/or sales revenue at which a business makes neither a profit nor a loss.

break-even chart: a graphical representation showing the point at which a business breaks even. The limitations of a break-even chart include:

- the assumption that all data used behaves in a linear manner
- the assumption that all production is sold
- charts, generally, only relate to a single product
- the chart does not show clearly the amount of profit or loss made by the product

(For a worked example, see *break-even point.*)

break-even point: the lowest level of sales or units sold at which total revenue received by a business is equal to the business's total costs. It can be ascertained by:

1 The unit contribution method

$$\text{FORMULA: break-even} = \frac{\text{total fixed costs}}{\text{contribution per unit}} = \frac{\text{number of units}}{\text{required to be sold}}$$

Worked example: the following information relates to the production and sales of 40 000 puttles.

	£ per unit
Selling price	40
Raw material costs	8
Direct labour costs	14
Fixed costs	11

Required:

i) the break-even point in units for sales of puttles
ii) the margin of safety in units for puttles

Solution:

	£	
Contribution per puttle	18	[SP – VC, 40 – (8 + 14)]
Total fixed costs	440 000	[11 × 40 000]

$$\text{i) break-even} = \frac{\text{total fixed costs}}{\text{contribution per unit}} = \frac{440\ 000}{18}$$

$$= 24\ 445 \text{ puttles (always round-up)}$$

ii) margin of safety = forecast sales – break-even sales = 40 000 – 24 445
$$= 15\ 555 \text{ puttles}$$

2 The contribution/sales method. Some text books refer to this as the profit/volume method

$$\text{FORMULA: break-even} = \frac{\text{total fixed costs}}{\text{total contribution/sales}} = \frac{\text{total sales}}{\text{revenue required}}$$

**ISLE COLLEGE
RESOURCES CENTRE**

Worked example: use the information above relating to the production and sales of puttles.

Required:

i) Calculate the total revenue required from the sales of puttles in order to break even.

ii) Calculate the margin of safety for puttles (answer required in sales revenue).

Solution;

i) $\dfrac{\text{contribution}}{\text{sales revenue}} = \dfrac{1\ 600\ 000 - 880\ 000}{1\ 600\ 000} = \dfrac{720\ 000}{1\ 600\ 000} = 0.45$

$\text{break-even} = \dfrac{\text{total fixed costs}}{\text{total contribution/sales}} = \text{total sales revenue required}$

$\text{break-even} = \dfrac{440\ 000}{0.45} \qquad = £977\ 777.78$

ii) margin of safety = forecast sales revenue − break-even level of sales revenue
= £1 600 000 − £977 777.78 = £622 222.22

This method is more useful if some form of income statement is available. It is also useful to determine the break-even sales revenue if a number of products are being sold by a business.

3 The algebraic method

FORMULA: break-even occurs when total costs = total revenue

Worked example: use the information given above relating to the production and sales of puttles.

Required:

Calculate the break-even point in units for sales of puttles.

Solution:

Let Q = the number of puttles to be sold in order to break even.
break-even =

total costs = total revenue
fixed costs + variable costs = total revenue
440 000 + 22Q = 40Q
440 000 = 40Q − 22Q
440 000 = 18Q
Q = 440 000/18

number of puttles to be sold in order to break even = 24 445

4 The graphical method

Worked example: use the information given above relating to the production and sales of puttles.

Required:

A break-even chart showing the break-even point and the margin of safety for sales of puttles.

Solution:

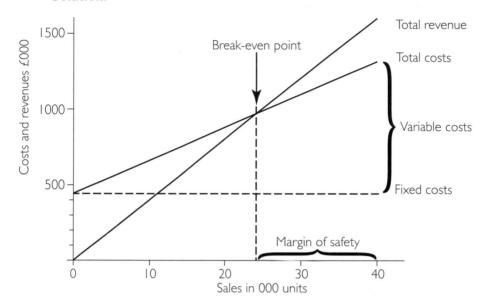

broker: a person who acts as an intermediary between a buyer and a seller. Examples include stockbrokers who buy and sell shares or *bonds* on behalf of their clients, and insurance brokers who sell insurances to clients.

brokerage: the *commission* charged by a *broker*.

B shares: ordinary shares with special voting rights. They are often owned by the original owner(s) of a business and his/her family.

budget: a short-term financial plan. *CIMA* defines a budget as 'a plan expressed in money.'

It is prepared in advance of a defined period of time, generally a year (although monthly and quarterly budgets are often prepared). Budgets are based on the objectives of the business and they show how policies are to be pursued during that time period in order that business objectives can be achieved. (See *business objectives, capital expenditure budget, cash budget, creditors' budget, debtors' budget, flexible budget, production budget, sales budget.*)

budgetary control delegates financial planning to managers. It evaluates the performance of managers by continuous comparison of actual results achieved by their department against those set in the budget. This process allows remedial action to be taken. It also ensures that all departmental decision making is related to the corporate plan (see *strategic planning*).

budgeting: the preparation of budgets.

budget period: the time covered by a particular budget. The budget period can be broken down into smaller time periods called *control periods* in order that managers may exercise greater control over their departments.

buffer stocks: stocks held to ensure that there will always be stocks available for production purposes no matter what eventualities are encountered. (See *stock reorder level.*)

bull: a *stockmarket* speculator who purchases shares in the belief that their market price will rise and that the shares can be sold in the future at a higher price.

bull market: a period when share prices in general are rising on the *stockmarket*. The increase in prices reflects general optimism in the economy, causing people to purchase shares.

business cycle: the rise and fall in trade within the economy that tends to be repeated on a regular basis. Boom times are followed by *recession*, then slump, which later gives way to recovery and another boom.

business entity concept states that only transactions affecting the financial position of a business are recorded in the business *books of account*. The owner's(s') private financial affairs are not recorded.

If, for example, the owner of a business wins £9 000 000 on the national lottery this would not be recorded in the business books of account. Only if he decided to inject part of his winnings into the business as capital introduced would the business accounts be affected.

business objectives set out what the managers of a business hope to achieve. The objectives may be short term (e.g. to introduce a new product line in the next few months) or they may be long term (e.g. the strategic plan for the next ten years).

Whatever the business objectives are, managers must plan for their implementation. These plans take the form of budgets.

business plan: a document that is drawn up to show interested parties how a business is to progress in the future. It usually comprises:

- a *marketing* strategy in the short and long run
- a *cash budget*
- a projected *profit and loss account* and *balance sheet*
- details of financial needs of the business
- details of staffing needs
- details of capital equipment needs

An *entrepreneur* will generally be asked to prepare a business plan when seeking funding from a bank or other financial institution, either when first starting in business or when seeking extra finance to expand.

business rates: a form of local taxation levied on business premises.

business review: a section of the *directors' report* presented to the *shareholders* at the *annual general meeting* of a *limited company*, outlining in general terms the business carried out by the company over the last financial year.

bust: a colloquial expression indicating that a business has gone into *liquidation* or that a person has been declared *bankrupt*.

buyer: the person responsible for purchasing materials or products for a business.

buyers' market occurs when there are few buyers but many sellers. This usually results in goods or services being sold more cheaply than on previous occasions.

buying department: the department responsible for the purchase of raw materials or components to be used by a business.

by-product is defined by *CIMA* as the 'output of some value produced incidentally in manufacturing something else'.

calls in advance: monies received from *shareholders* before a company has actually made the call. (See *calls on share issue.*)

calls in arrears: calls on share capital for which the money has not yet been received from the *shareholders*. (See *calls on share issue.*)

calls on share issue: any instalments due to be paid after application and allotment monies have been paid. Many share issues now require the prospective *shareholder* to pay for the shares by instalments.

The instalments are monies paid on:

- application
- allotment
- call(s)

(See *issue of shares.*)

called-up capital: the part of the total amount to be paid on a share issue that has been requested by a *limited company*. Further calls are to be made at a later date. The amount asked for is known as the called-up capital.

For example, a company has received £562 500 on application and allotment from an issue of 750 000 ordinary shares of £1. This is shown on the balance sheet thus:

	£
Issued capital:	
750 000 ordinary shares of £1 each	750 000
Called-up capital:	
750 000 ordinary shares of 75 pence each	562 500
Paid-up capital:	
750 000 ordinary shares of £1 each 75 pence paid	562 500

(so the uncalled capital is £187 500.)

capital represents the investment made by the owner(s) of a business. It is the excess of assets over liabilities. It comprises the initial investment made by the owner(s) plus any *retained profits*, less any profits withdrawn from the business as *drawings* in the case of a *sole trader* or a *partnership*, or as *dividends* in the case of a *limited company*. (See also *loan capital.*)

capital account records the dealings that the proprietor(s) of a business has with the business. It records what the proprietor(s) has initially contributed to the business out of his/her private resources; it also records the profits that have been left in the business.

Worked example: Yoon Ling has invested £35 000 in a business. During the first year of trading:

i) the business made a profit of £9307
ii) Yoon Ling withdrew £6411 in cash and £456 in goods from the business.

Required:

Yoon Ling's capital account as it would appear at the end of her first year's trading.

Solution:

Yoon Ling capital account

Drawings	6 411	Cash	35 000
Drawings	456	Profit and loss account	9 307
Balance c/d	37 440		
	44 307		44 307
		Balance b/d	37 440

Partners' capital accounts are prepared in a similar way, although, obviously, there will be a capital account for each partner. (See *fluctuating capital accounts, fixed capital accounts.*)

Generally, the only entries shown in partners' capital accounts are injections of capital. Entries regarding the division of profits and partners' drawings are usually entered in *partnership current accounts.*

capital allowances: statutory tax allowances based on *capital expenditure* which can be set off against business profits, thus reducing the business's *tax liability.* The allowances are based on the *depreciation* that has arisen from wear and tear or diminution in the value of *fixed assets.*

capital budgeting: the process of appraising proposed *capital expenditure.* The major evaluation techniques used by UK businesses are *payback, accounting rate of return, internal rate of return* and *net present value.*

capital employed: the total of *fixed assets* and *current assets* used in a business, less *current liabilities.* The accuracy of this figure depends on the accuracy of the valuation of the fixed assets shown in the *balance sheet.*

There are a number of different measures of capital employed, so when making *inter-firm comparisons* it is essential to compare like with like. It may be necessary to adjust the data to take into account any differences in *accounting policies.*

capital expenditure: money spent on *fixed assets* or their improvement. It includes any costs that are necessary in preparing the fixed assets for use within a business. For example, if land and buildings were purchased the amount of capital expenditure would include estate agents' fees, legal costs, etc. If a new machine were purchased the capital cost would include transport costs associated with delivery and any installation costs.

capital expenditure appraisal: see *capital investment appraisal*

capital instrument: any contractual document issued by a *limited company* to raise finance. Ordinary shares, *preference shares, debentures,* corporate *bonds, convertible loan stock, loans* and options or warrants to subscribe for shares are all types of capital instrument.

FRS 4 applies to all financial statements that are intended to give a *true and fair view* of a business's financial position and profit or loss. The standard addresses the treatment of capital instruments in the accounts. They should be treated in a 'clear, coherent and consistent manner'.

Capital instruments must be reported as:

- *liabilities* if they contain an 'obligation to transfer economic benefit'
- *shareholders' funds*; the *balance sheet* must show the total amount of shareholders' funds analysed into equity and non-equity interests

capital investment appraisal: the process of determining the future *net cash flows or profitability* of a capital project. (See *accounting rate of return, payback method of capital investment appraisal, net present value method of capital investment appraisal* and *internal rate-of-return method of capital investment appraisal.*)

capital investment budget: the plans for future *capital expenditure*. The items included in the budget will normally have been subjected to various methods of *capital investment appraisal*. The capital investment budget is a vital part of the *strategic plan* because:

- it often involves large sums of money
- once undertaken, the business could be committed to particular business strategies for many years

capitalisation issue: see *bonus shares*

capital maintenance reserve: see *current cost reserve*

capital reconstruction: see *capital reduction* and *bonus shares*

capital redemption reserve: created when a *limited company* redeems shares or buys back some of its own shares without issuing new shares to fund the redemption. The company must protect its creditors by replacing the redeemed shares, which have not been funded by a new issue of shares, with a *capital reserve* transferred out of profits that would otherwise have been available for distribution as *dividends.*

The capital redemption reserve is available to issue *bonus shares*.

Worked example: the following is an extract from the balance sheet of Dibson plc:

	£
Cash	140 000
Ordinary share capital	400 000
8% redeemable preference shares	80 000
Share premium	100 000
Profit and loss account	370 000

Dibson plc redeems all the redeemable preference shares at a premium of 20%. There is an issue of £45 000 ordinary shares at par for the purpose. The preference shares had originally been issued at a premium of 15%.

Required:

Show the journal entries to record the above transactions in the books of Dibson plc.

Solution:

Narratives have not been used. Explanations of some entries are included in brackets.

Dibson plc: Journal

	Dr £	Cr £
8% redeemable preference shares	80 000	
Redemption account		80 000

(The redemption account is used to 'collect' the shares and the premium.)

Share premium account	12 000	
Redemption account		12 000

(Only £12 000 of the £16 000 premium to be paid to the preference shareholders can be taken from the share premium account since this is the amount that was raised when the shares were originally issued. The remainder of the £16 000 premium must be transferred out of the company's retained profits.)

Profit and loss account	4 000	
Redemption account		4 000
Redemption account	96 000	
Cash		96 000
Cash	45 000	
Ordinary share capital		45 000
Profit and loss account	35 000	
Capital redemption reserve		35 000

(Only £45 000 was raised by a new issue of shares, so £35 000 has to be transferred out of distributable reserves into a capital reserve.)

capital reduction: a revaluation of both assets and liabilities at a lower level than previously recorded. It might be necessary when the share capital of a *limited company* is not represented by the assets of the company. This generally happens when a company has suffered poor results over a number of years leading to a debit balance on the *profit and loss account*.

A capital reduction scheme needs the support of *shareholders* and other interested parties and must receive the consent of the Court. This support will only be forthcoming if the *directors* of the company can give assurances that the same situation will not occur again in the future.

Worked example: Seok Chin plc has the following balance sheet as at 31 December 19*7:

	£
Net asset	270 000
Capital and reserves	
500 000 ordinary shares of £1 each	500 000
Less debit balance – profit and loss account	230 000
	270 000

The following scheme of capital reduction has been agreed by the shareholders and sanctioned by the Court:

The ordinary shares are to be reduced to 50 pence per share.
The net assets are to be written down to £250 000.

The profit and loss account balance is to be written off.

Required:

i) journal entries to record the above transactions in the company's books

ii) the balance sheet of Seok Chin plc after the scheme has been completed

Solution:

i) **Seok Chin plc journal**

	Dr £	Cr £
Ordinary share capital	250 000	
Capital reduction account		250 000
Capital reduction account	250 000	
Net assets		20 000
Profit and loss account		230 000

The principles involved in a reconstruction can be seen very clearly if we construct our balance sheet using a horizontal layout:

	£		£
Net assets	270 000	Share capital	500 000
Profit and loss account	230 000		
	500 000		500 000

The left-hand side of the balance has to be reduced by £250 000, so the right-hand side must also be reduced by £250 000.

ii) Seok Chin plc balance sheet after the capital reduction scheme has been implemented

	£
Net assets	250 000
Capital and reserves	
500 000 ordinary shares of 50 pence each	250 000

capital repayments are deducted from the outstanding balance owed on a long-term loan. They reduce the amount shown as owing in the *balance sheet*. Interest payments are *revenue expenditure* and as such they are shown as an expense on the *profit and loss account*.

capital reserves: amounts set aside out of profits that are not *provisions*. They are not created by setting aside amounts out of operating profits. They are not available for transfer to the company's *profit and loss appropriation account*, so they are not, therefore, available for cash dividend purposes. They may be distributed in the form of *bonus shares*.

Examples of capital reserves are:

- *share premium account*
- *revaluation reserve*
- *capital redemption reserve*

carriage, insurance and freight (CIF): the estimate of a price inclusive of the charge for insurance cover and any transport costs incurred.

carriage inward: *revenue expenditure* incurred in the transporting of raw materials or products for resale into a business. Sometimes delivery charges are included in the total purchase price, at other times a separate charge is made. This separate charge is termed carriage inwards. Any such carriage charges should be debited to the carriage inwards account in the *general ledger*. At the end of the *accounting period* the carriage inward account will be written off to the *prime cost* section of the *manufacturing account* (if the carriage charge was incurred in transporting raw materials to the factory) or to the *trading account* (if the carriage charge was incurred in transporting goods for resale in a retail outlet).

carriage on sales: see *carriage outward*

carriage outward: *revenue expenditure* incurred in delivering goods or raw materials to a customer. These costs are debited to the carriage outward account in the *general ledger*. Since this cost is incurred after the goods have been made ready for sale, the account is written off to the *profit and loss account* at the end of the *accounting period*. Carriage outwards is sometimes referred to as carriage on sales.

cash: money in notes and coins.

cash and cash equivalents: for the purposes of FRS 1:

- cash is cash in hand and deposits payable on demand
- cash equivalents are short-term, highly liquid investments that can be converted easily into cash without notice and which were acquired within three months of their maturity; less any advances from banks that are repayable within three months from the date of their maturity.

cash book: a *book of prime entry* in which all cash and bank transactions are recorded. It contains two *general ledger* accounts:

- the business cash account
- the business bank account

Since it is part of the general ledger it follows that it is part of the double-entry system. The *cash book* for a *VAT*-registered business will have four columns on the debit side and four columns on the credit side:

Debit	Credit
Discount (1) VAT (2) Cash (3) Bank (4)	Discount (1) VAT (2) Cash (3) Bank (4)
1 Discount allowed to customers for prompt payment	1 Discount received for prompt payment to suppliers
2 VAT collected from customers on behalf of the Customs and Excise	2 VAT paid to suppliers on goods and services received
3 Cash receipts	3 Cash payments
4 Cheque receipts	4 Cheque payments

cash budget shows estimates of future cash incomes and cash expenditure for revenue and capital transactions. It is drawn up to help management aware of any potential shortages or surpluses of cash resources that could occur, thus allowing management to make necessary financial arrangements.

A cash budget deals only with transactions involving the movement of cash; it does not include non-cash expenses such as *depreciation*.

Banks often request the preparation of a cash budget when a business person seeks financial support in the form of a business loan or an *overdraft* facility.

A cash budget layout is shown below:

Cash budget for the three months ending 30 September 19*7:

	July £	August £	September £
Receipts:			
Cash sales	4 000	5 000	5 000
Receipts from debtors	23 000	37 000	35 000
	27 000	42 000	40 000
Payments:			
Payments to creditors	16 000	18 000	17 000
Cash purchases	2 300	2 700	2 400
Rent		16 000	
Wages	8 000	8 000	8 800
other expenses	1 750	3 560	3 100
	28 050	48 260	31 300
Balance b/fwd	1 450	400	(5 860)
Receipts	27 000	42 000	40 000
	28 450	42 400	34 140
Payments	28 050	48 260	31 300
Balance c/fwd	400	(5 860)	2 840

This cash budget shows that the business requires an overdraft facility during August and September.

cash columns in a traditional *cash book* record cash received on the debit side, and cash payments on the credit side.

cash discount: an allowance that can be deducted from the total amount shown on an *invoice* if the debt is settled within a time specified by the supplier of the goods. (See *discount allowed* and *discount received.*)

cash flows: cash movements in and out of a business. Since *liquidity* is vitally important for the short-term survival of a business, it is important that cash inflows (receipts of cash and cheques) are greater than cash outflows (expenditure in cash and cheques).

Cash flows need to be calculated for use in:

- *cash budgets*
- *cash-flow statements FRS 1*
- *capital investment appraisal*

cash-flow statements FRS 1 shows how cash has been generated by a *limited company* and how cash has been spent. It '... forms an essential element of the information required ... to give a *true and fair view* of the state of affairs of large companies ...'. This was the view of the *Accounting Standards Board* in 1991.

The standard sets out the structure of a cash-flow statement using the following standard headings:

ISLE COLLEGE
RESOURCES CENTRE

- operating activities
- returns on investments and servicing of finance
- taxation
- investing activities
- financing

A total cash inflow or outflow must be shown for each heading, plus a total cash inflow or outflow before financing.

The standard requires companies to produce:

- a note to the statement reconciling the operating profit as shown in the *profit and loss account* with the *net cash flow* from operating activities
- a reconciliation of the amounts shown in the *balance sheet* with the equivalent figures in the previous year's balance sheet, regarding the items shown in the financing section of the cash-flow statement

FRS 1 shows information which is not available from scrutiny of the profit and loss account and balance sheet. It concentrates on *liquidity*, which is important for business survival. The inability to generate cash resources is the single biggest reason for many businesses going into *liquidation*. (Remember that the profit generated by a business is not necessarily the same as the cash generated by that business.)

Worked example: The following are the balance sheets as at 31 December 19*6 and 31 December 19*7 for Mose and Catt plc:

	19*6			19*7	
	£000	£000		£000	£000
Fixed assets at cost	3478			4368	
Less depreciation	1060	2418		1045	3323
Current assets:					
Stock	1481			1534	
Debtors	639			596	
Bank	846			1121	
	2966			3251	
Less creditors – less than one year:					
Trade creditors	720		745		
Taxation	240		316		
Dividends	300	1260	1706	308	1369	1882
			4124			5205
Less creditors – more than one year:					
8% debentures			1000			800
			3124			4405
Capital and reserves:					
Issued share capital			1750			2000
Share premium account			875			1000
Profit and loss account			499			1405
			3124			4405

Note:

During the year, fixed assets costing £600 000, which had been depreciated by £375 000, had been sold for £300 000. An interim dividend of £100 000 was paid during the year. Debenture interest of £70 000 was also paid during the year.

Required:

A cash-flow statement for Mose and Catt plc for the year ended 31 December 19*7.

Solution:

Mose and Catt plc cash flow statement for the year ended 31 December 19*7

	£000	£000
Net cash inflow from operating activities		2000
Returns on investments and servicing of finance:		
Interest paid	(70)	
Dividends paid	(400)	
Net cash outflow from returns on investments and servicing of finance		(470)
Taxation:		
Corporation tax paid	(240)	
Taxation paid		(240)
Investing activities:		
Payments to acquire tangible fixed assets	(1490)	
Receipts from the sale of fixed assets	300	
Net cash outflow from investing activities		(1190)
Net cash inflow before financing		100
Financing:		
Issue of ordinary share capital including premium	375	
Redemption of debenture stock	(200)	
Net cash inflow from financing		175
Increase in cash and cash equivalents		275

Reconciliation of operating profit to net cash inflow from operating activities:

	£000
Operating profit	1700
Depreciation	360
Profit on disposal of fixed assets	(75)
Increase in stock	(53)
Decrease in debtors	43
Increase in creditors	25
	2000

Calculation of operating profit:

Change in retained earnings	906
Provision for corporation tax	316

Proposed dividend	308
Interim dividend paid	100
Debenture interest paid	70
	1700

Analysis of cash and cash equivalents:

	£000
Balance at 1 January 19*7	846
Net cash inflow	275
Balance at 31 December 19*7	1121

A cash-flow statement shows:

- how cash flows (positive and negative) have been generated during the year
- major financing activities for the year
- how the company met its obligation to service loans and pay *dividends*
- why reported profits differ from related cash flows during the year

cash in hand: money and notes not banked but kept within a business to make necessary cash payments. The balance at the year end is shown in the *balance sheet* as a *current asset.*

cash in transit: cash sent by a branch to head office or vice versa. The cash is an asset of the business and so must be included as part of the business's *cash in hand.*

cash on delivery (COD): cash that must be paid for goods when they are delivered.

certification of work done: an interim valuation of work completed by a professional quantity surveyor or architect. The valuation will include an element of profit and forms the basis of the contractor's interim *invoices.*

When a *long-term contract* takes many years to complete it would be unreasonable to expect the contractor to wait until the contract is complete before the client pays. It would also be unreasonable to expect the client to pay for the whole contract before the contract is started. *Progress payments* are made by the client, based on interim valuations of work completed. (See *contract costing.*)

chairman of the board of directors: the person who presides over the *board meetings* of a *limited company.*

chairman's statement: a general comment on the performance of the company made by the *chairman of the board of directors.*

Limited companies usually include a statement written by the chairman in the *annual report.* The statement is not a statutory requirement, but it can be used as a vehicle for comments on outside influences which might have affected the company over the time covered by the annual report.

charge card: a credit card whose balance must be paid off at the end of each month.

checking cash: checking the balance of cash shown in the *cash columns* of the *cash book* and *petty cash book* against the cash in the till. Checks should be conducted regularly, at least once per day.

cheque: an instruction to a bank to pay or transfer a sum of money to a named person. The instructions are written on a preprinted form (the cheque) supplied by the bank.

- The person filling in the cheque and who signs it is the *drawer*.
- The *drawee* is the bank on which the cheque is drawn.
- The person to whom the cheque is payable is the *payee*.

Cheques are out of date six months after the date specified.

cheque book: a booklet issued by a bank to its customers which contains blank cheques.

cheque crossings are made in order to restrict the use of a cheque. If a cheque is uncrossed the *payee* can cash the cheque at the bank.

An uncrossed cheque is also known as an open cheque.

The main crossings in use are:

1 general crossing – the cheque must be paid into another bank account
2 not negotiable – the holder of the cheque cannot have a better claim to it than the previous holder
3 a/c payee only – the cheque must be paid into the payee's account
4 special – the cheque can only be paid into the payee's account at the bank named on the crossing

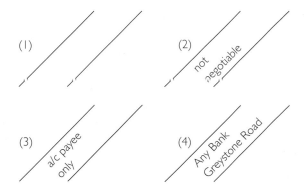

cheque guarantee card: this guarantees that a bank will honour a cheque up to the value of £50 (recently it has been possible to have a guarantee of £100 or £250). When a cheque is offered by a cash customer in settlement of a debt, it is usual to accept the cheque only when it is supported by a cheque guarantee card. The card has a specimen of the holder's signature.

cheque signatories: the people who are authorised to sign cheques on behalf of a business. Their signatures will appear on the *bank mandate*.

CIF: see *carriage, insurance and freight*

CIMA: Chartered Institute of Management Accountants.

circulating assets: another name for *current assets*.

clock cards: a record of the time of arrival and departure of employees to and from their place of work. They are often issued to production staff in order to record the time they spend on the business premises.

Each worker is given a clock card. When the card is inserted into a time recorder the card is stamped with the time. The clock card provides the wages department with a record of:

- how long the employee has spent on the business premises
- whether the employee has been late
- whether the employee has been absent from work

(See *time sheet.*)

closing stock: this value is obtained by a physical stocktake at the end of the financial year of a business when the other accounts relating to stock have been closed. The bookkeeping entries to record the introduction of stock into the final accounts are:

	Debit	Credit
Purchases account is closed by	Trading account	Purchases account
Sales account is closed by	Sales account	Trading account
A stock account is opened.		
Since stock is an asset it should be recorded as such.		
Stock account is opened by	Stock account	Trading account

Worked example: Mary McDougal completed her first year of trading on 30 November 19*7.
The entries on the debit side of her purchases account total £26 000.
The entries on the credit side of her sales account total £48 000.
Mary values her stock on 30 November 19*7 at £4500.

Required:

The trading account and the stock account as they would appear in the general ledger of Mary McDougal at the end of her first year of trading.

Solution:

Mary's stock is an asset.
A stock account is opened and the stock debited.
The double-entry system requires a credit entry – so the trading account is credited.
Mary's general ledger would show the following two accounts:

Trading account for the year ended 30 Nov. 19*7				Stock	
	£		£		£
Purchases	26 000	Sales	48 000	Trading acc. 4 500	
Gross profit c/d	26 500	Stock	4 500		
	52 500		52 500		
		Gross profit b/d	26 500		

Many trading accounts are presented using a vertical format. In this case the closing stock is deducted from the purchases to give a cost of sales figure.

Trading account for the year ended 30 November 19*7

	£	£
Sales		48 000
Less cost of sales:		
Purchases	26 000	
Less closing stock	4 500	21 500
Gross profit		26 500

club accounts are the *final accounts* of clubs and societies. They differ from those of business organisations in a number of respects:

Club and society accounts	Business accounts
Income and expenditure account	Profit and loss account
Surplus of income over expenditure	Profit
Excess of expenditure over income	Loss
Accumulated fund	Capital account

There are four key stages in preparing the final accounts of clubs and societies:

- prepare an opening *statement of affairs* (similar to an opening *balance sheet*)
- prepare a *receipts and payments account* (summary of the *cash book*); this is often given as part of the information in an examination question)
- prepare *adjustment accounts* (to take into account the *accruals concept*)
- prepare the final accounts

Worked example: the following is the receipts and payments account of the Stanegate badminton club for the year ended 31 October 19*7:

	£		£
Cash and bank balances b/fwd	211	Secretarial expenses	141
Subscriptions	824	Rent of village hall	700
Competition entry fees	72	Dinner dance expenses	200
Dinner dance receipts	248	Stationery and printing	48
Balance c/fwd	78	Other expenses	224
		Competition prizes	120
	1433		1433

The following additional information has been given:

	19*6	19*7
	£	£
Equipment at valuation	210	180
Subscriptions paid in advance	48	64
Subscriptions in arrears	32	16
Amount owing to Matthews & Co. for stationery	29	37

Required:

Prepare an income and expenditure account for the Stanegate badminton club for the year ended 31 October 19*7 and a balance sheet as at that date.

Solution:

Stage 1: prepare an opening statement of affairs.

Statement of affairs as at 1 November 19*6

	£
Equipment at valuation	210
Subscriptions in arrears (members owe club = debtor)	32
Cash and bank balances in hand	211
	453
Subscription in advance (club owes members = creditors)	48
Creditor for printing – Matthews and Co.	29
Accumulated fund (missing figure)	376
	453

Stage 2: prepare receipts and payment account. Already done – given in the question.

Stage 3: important stage. Prepare adjustment accounts. One for each item on statement of affairs.

Equipment				Matthews and Co.			
Balance b/fwd	210	Missing figure (1)	30	Cash	48	Balance b/fwd	29
		Balance c/fwd	180	Balance c/fwd 37		Missing figure (2)	56
	210		210		85		85
Balance b/fwd	180					Balance c/fwd	37

Cash and bank	Accumulated fund
Already done – stage 2!	Will be adjusted on closing balance sheet.

The most testing account when preparing club accounts is the subscriptions account:

Subscriptions			
Balance b/fwd		Balance b/fwd	
(subscriptions in arrears)	32	(subscriptions in advance)	48
Missing figure (3)	792	Cash	824
Balance c/fwd	64	Balance c/fwd	16
	888		888
Balance b/fwd		Balance b/fwd	
(subscriptions in arrears)	16	(subscriptions in advance)	64

Missing figure (1) is the annual depreciation charge on the club's equipment. Missing figure (2) is the actual printing done during the year by Matthews & Co. Missing figure (3) is the subscriptions figure for the year.

Stage 4: preparation of the final accounts.

Stanegate Badminton Club income and expenditure account for the year ended 31 October 19*7

	£	£
Incomes:		
Subscriptions		792
Profit on dinner dance (it is usual to show activities that		
are not central to the purpose of the club as 'net' figures)		48
		840
Less expenditure:		
Secretarial expenses	141	
Rent	700	
Loss on competitions	48	
Stationery and printing	56	
Other expenses	224	
Depreciation: equipment	30	1199
Excess of expenditure over income		359

Balance sheet as at 31 October 19*7

	£	£
Equipment at valuation	210	
Less depreciation	30	180
Subscriptions in arrears		16
		196
Accumulated fund	376	
Less excess of expenditure over income	359	17
Bank overdraft		78
Stationery creditor		37
Subscriptions in advance		64
		196

COD: see *cash on delivery*

collective bargaining: the process of negotiation between employers and employee representatives covering wage rises and working conditions for a whole group of workers.

columnar day books allow a business to analyse its purchases and sales into different categories.

Worked example: Robert Caffrey is a sole trader who sells kitchen and bedroom furniture. The following invoices in respect of goods for resale have been received:

6 May Kwality Kitchens	£963 + VAT	
13 May Snoozabed Ltd	£1673 + VAT	
26 May Kitchen Fans plc	£450 + VAT	£50 + VAT
	(kitchens)	(bedroom fittings)
27 May Headboards Ltd	£875 + VAT	

The following sales invoices in respect of credit sales have been sent to customers:

14 May Howard Sellers for fitted kitchen   £1698 + VAT

23 May Bill Blakemore for bedroom furniture £765 +VAT
30 May Louise Harrison for fitted kitchen   £4300 + VAT

VAT = 17.5%

Required:

The purchase day book and the sales day book for Robert Caffrey.

Solution:

Purchase day book

Date Details	Kitchens	Bedrooms	Net	VAT	Gross
	£	£	£	£	£
6 May Kwality Kitchens	963		963	169.52	1132.52
13 May Snoozabed Ltd		1673	1673	292.77	1965.77
26 May Kitchen Fans plc	450	50	500	87.50	587.50
27 May Headboards Ltd		875	875	153.12	1028.12
	1413	2598	4011	702.91	4713.91

The ledger accounts for the entry on 26 May would be:

Debit (in general ledger)   Kitchen purchases   £450
                             Bedroom purchases   £50
                             VAT   £87.50

(These amounts would not be posted individually but would be included in the totals posted at the month end.)

Credit (in purchase ledger) Kitchen Fans plc   £587.50

Sales day book

Date Details	Kitchens	Bedrooms	Net	VAT	Gross
	£	£	£	£	£
14 May Howard Sellers	1698		1698	297.15	1995.15
23 May Bill Blakemore		765	765	133.87	898.87
30 May Louise Harrison	4300		4300	752.50	5052.50
	5998	765	6763	1183.52	7946.52

The ledger accounts for the entry on 14 May would be:

Credit (in general ledger) Kitchen sales   £1698

VAT   £297.15

(These amounts would not be posted individually but would be included in the totals posted at the month end.)

Debit (in sales ledger) Howard Sellers   £1995.15

Many businesses use columnar day books to record all non-cash transactions. The following is an example of how this type of analysis book may be written up:

Purchase day book

		Net	VAT	Gross	Purchases	Stationery	Motor exp.	Rates etc
		£	£	£	£	£	£	£
7 April	Gladstone Ltd	38	6.65	44.65	38			
12 April	Easton CBC	78		78				78
15 April	Todd plc	125	21.87	146.87		125		
23 April	Jeff's garage	651	113.92	764.92	—	—	651	—
		892	142.44	1034.44	38	125	651	78

At a convenient time the following postings will be made to the general ledger:

Totals of the purchases column to the debit of the purchases account

stationery column to the debit of the stationery account

motor expenses column to the debit of the motor expenses account

rates column to the debit of the rates account

and any other analysis columns to the debit of the respective accounts

VAT column to the debit of the VAT account

The following postings will be made to the purchases ledger:

Credit Gladstone Ltd	£44.65
Credit Easton CBC	£78
Credit Todd plc	£146.87
Credit Jeff's garage	£764.92

columnar presentation of final accounts is a useful source of financial information with regard to the profitability of different departments or sections of a business.

An analysis of purchases and sales must be made (see *columnar day books*).

A departmental stocktake must be undertaken in order to prepare a *trading account* for each department. The *final accounts* might be presented like this:

Robert Caffrey departmental trading account for the year ended 30 June 19*7

		Kitchen department		Bedroom department		Total
		£		£		£
Sales		126 000		93 000		219 000
Stock 1 July 19*6	8 000		4 500		12 500	
Purchases	74 000		28 000		102 000	
	82 000		32 500		114 500	
Less						
Stock 30 June 199*	7 500		5 200		12 700	
Cost of goods sold		74 500		27 300		101 800
Gross profit		51 500		65 700		117 200

The final accounts can be extended to include departmental *profit and loss accounts*.

Each department must be charged with its share of the business's expenses. This can present problems. Expenses that can easily be identified with a department should be allocated accordingly, e.g. bedroom fitters' wages are easy to identify and can therefore be charged to the bedroom department. Other expenses should be *apportioned* using some rational basis, e.g. rent, business rates, heating costs, electricity charges, etc. can be apportioned according to the floor area occupied by each department. Administration expenses, sales assistants' salaries, advertising, etc. can be apportioned according to the proportion of total sales generated by each department.

Robert's profit and loss account for the year ended 30 June 19*7 might look like this:

	Kitchen department £		Bedroom department £		Total £
Gross profit		51 500		65 700	117 200
Less expenses					
Wages and salaries	21 800		27 400		49 200
Rent and rates	7 000		14 000		21 000
Admin. expenses	13 808		10 192		24 000
Electricity charges	3 333		6 667		10 000
Depreciation	3 500		3 500		7 000
		49 441		61 759	111 200
Net profit		2 059		3 941	6 000

commercial banks offer banking services to the general public. (See *merchant bank*.)

commission: a payment made to another party for business done or for sales revenue achieved. The amount is generally a percentage based on the *agent's* or salesperson's performance.

Commission payable is an expense and appears on the debit side of the *profit and loss account* in the *final accounts*. Commission receivable is income earned by a business and is shown on the credit side of the profit and loss account in the final accounts.

commission error: see *errors not affecting the balancing of the trial balance*

common costs: costs incurred in the production of more than one product. They must therefore be *apportioned* between joint products. The following are the usual methods used:

- Sales value at the stage when joint products are recognisable as individual products (the split-off point or point of separation) in their own right. For example, product P and product Q incur joint costs of £35 000. At the split-off point, product P has a saleable value of £36 000 and product Q has a saleable value of £24 000. The joint costs will be apportioned:

$$\text{product P} = \frac{36\,000}{60\,000} \times 35\,000 = £21\,000$$

$$\text{product Q} = \frac{24\,000}{60\,000} \times 35\,000 = £14\,000$$

- Sales value after further processing has taken place. For example, using the data given above:

After the split-off point, product P incurs additional expenses of £8000, the saleable value rises to £45 000; product Q incurs additional expenses of £1000, the saleable value rises to £27 000.

	Product P	Product Q
Sales value after further processing	£45 000	£27 000
Additional processing costs incurred	£8 000	£1 000
Contribution value (sales − additional costs)	£37 000	£26 000
The total contribution value − £63 000		

The joint costs are apportioned according to the contribution value of each product expressed as a proportion of the total contribution value.

product P is apportioned with $\dfrac{37\ 000}{63\ 000} \times 35\ 000 = £20\ 556$ of the joint costs

product Q is apportioned with $\dfrac{26\ 000}{63\ 000} \times 35\ 000 = £14\ 444$ of the joint costs

- Units produced method. For example, using the data given above:

  At the point of separation, 5400 units of product P were produced and 3200 units of product Q were produced. The joint costs are apportioned according to the number of units of each product produced, expressed as a proportion of total production.

  Product P is apportioned with $\dfrac{5400}{8600} \times 35\ 000 = £21\ 977$ of the joint costs

  Product Q is apportioned with $\dfrac{3200}{8600} \times 35\ 000 = £13\ 023$ of the joint costs

Companies Act 1985: the main piece of legislation governing the activities of *limited companies* in England, Scotland and Wales.

Limited companies are required to prepare and publish accounts annually. The Act sets out the legal requirements with regard to the information that must be shown in the company's *annual report*. The annual report must contain:

1 A *directors' report* giving information:
   - about the business activities
   - allowing the *shareholders* to assess the asset backing of their shares
   - making shareholders aware of material changes in the ownership of the *issued share capital*
   - indicating the company's activities in the community
   - recommending a *dividend*
2 The criteria for information appearing in the published *profit and loss account*:
   - financial statements are required to present a *true and fair view* of the profits, assets and liabilities of the company
   - statements are required to comply with fundamental *accounting concepts*
   - presentational format is prescribed (see *format 1 and format 2 layouts for the published profit and loss accounts of a limited company*)

- sensitive information is required to be disclosed by way of a note to the accounts

3 The criteria for information appearing in the published *balance sheet*:
  - presentation of the format is prescribed
  - rules for asset valuation
  - disclosure of accounting policies (see *accounting principles, accounting bases* and *accounting policies*)

4 The *auditors' report*, which explains the work that the *auditors* have completed. In most cases the report will state that the *audit* has been carried out according to auditing standards and that in the auditors' opinion the accounts show a true and fair view and have been properly prepared in accordance with the Act. The auditors may qualify their report if they disagree with the *directors* of the company on a matter of principle or if they are not satisfied that the accounts do show a true and fair view.

Companies Acts rule how companies should conduct their financial affairs.

company accounts are the *final accounts* of a *limited company*. They are drawn up by the *directors* of the company in the way that best suits their own purposes as managers of the business.

However, when the directors publish the company's accounts to send to the *shareholders* and to the *Registrar of Companies*, schedule 4 of the *Companies Act 1985* lays down the information that must be shown in the accounts and how it should be shown.

comparability of financial statements: it is important that the users of accounting information can make valid *inter-firm comparisons* and *trend analysis* over a number of years. In order to make such comparisons meaningful, accounts are prepared in accordance with guidelines laid down by the *Companies' Acts, Statements of Standard Accounting Practice* and *Financial Reporting Standards*.

compensating errors occur when a number of different errors cancel each other out.

competing courses of action: when faced with having to choose between competing courses of action, managers need to consider only the *marginal costs* incurred for each option.

Worked example: Mandy Carruthers has started a small furniture manufacturing business. She specialises in producing only one product. She will produce either kitchen tables, armchairs or sideboards. She provides her accountant with the following information:

	Table	Armchairs	Sideboards
	£	£	£
Selling price per unit	460	180	290
Direct material costs per unit	110	65	90
Direct labour costs per unit	85	70	105
Total fixed costs £35 000			

Required:

Advise Mandy which product she should produce.

Solution:

Since the fixed costs will be incurred whichever product is produced, it can be disregarded in your decision making.

Tables make a positive contribution of £265.
Armchairs make a positive contribution of £45.
Sideboards make a positive contribution of £95.

Mandy should produce tables since they will earn her the greatest net profit. Once this decision has been made all costs must be included in any revenue statement.

---

competitive pricing means taking the price of competitors' products into account when setting the price of one's own.

complete reversal of entries: see *errors not affecting the balancing of the trial balance*

compound interest is interest calculated on the capital sum plus any interest that has accrued since the previous interest calculation was made.

Worked example: Sean O'Hare deposited £1000 in a bank deposit account three years ago today. Interest rate payable on the account is 10% per annum.

Required:

Calculate the value of Sean's deposit today.

Solution:

Value of Sean O'Hare's bank deposit account

	£	
Year 0 (time of original deposit)	1000	
Year 1	1010	(£1000 + 10% interest)
Year 2	1111	(£1010 + 10% interest on £1010)
Year 3	1222.10	(£1111 + 10% interest on £1111)

Today Sean's bank deposit account will have a balance of £1222.10.

For examination purposes, assume that interest will be calculated on a compound basis unless the question indicates otherwise.

---

computerised accounts: many businesses now use computers to process substantial amounts of their accounting information.

Computers are extremely useful where large quantities of data need to be processed. They are used extensively in *financial accounting* in:

- the preparation of *sales invoices* and the posting of these to the *sales ledger*
- posting *invoices* received to the *purchase ledger*
- maintaining the *general ledger* (*nominal ledger*)
- maintaining *stock control* records
- maintaining payroll records and preparing wages slips
- maintaining a record of receipts and payments

- the preparation of reports to managers
- the preparation of *final accounts*
- maintaining *credit control*

Computers are equally useful in the fields of *cost* and *management accounting*, for example:

- the preparation of budgets
- the preparation of other forecast statements, e.g. forecast final accounts, estimates for clients
- the construction of *capital investment appraisals*
- keeping costing records

Advantages of using computers in accounting:

- data is processed extremely quickly
- one entry of data will update all relevant parts of the system
- large quantities of data can be processed simultaneously
- very complex information using different data banks can be produced and analysed easily (previously, preparation of such information was time consuming and therefore expensive)
- *software* packages allow information to be presented in a wide variety of forms, e.g. graphics, tables, drawings, graphs, etc., thus making complex information more user friendly
- they are very accurate (the vast majority of errors are operative errors)
- grouping of similar data can be achieved quickly
- dissimilar data can be identified easily
- exception reports can be compiled easily; this aids *management by exception*
- reduction in staff, therefore saving on wage costs

Disadvantages of using computers in accounting:

- sophisticated equipment is expensive
- staff need training and regular skill updating when new packages are introduced
- some staff may feel threatened if they lack confidence in using computers
- if there has been a reduction in staffing there may be a lowering of morale in the remaining workforce
- it may be expensive to adapt a system to an individual manager's needs

concepts and conventions of accounting are the assumptions, or basic rules, that are applied to accounting procedures. Since 1971 the accountancy profession has issued a series of guidelines to encourage uniformity in the preparation of financial statements.

Until 1990 the guidelines were known as *Statements of Standard Accounting Practice (SSAPs)*. Since then the standards have been issued as *Financial Reporting Standards (FRSs)*.

(See *accruals concept, business entity concept, consistency, dual aspect concept, going concern concept, materiality, money measurement concept, prudence, realisation concept*.)

conservatism: see *prudence*

consistency: once a business adopts a policy for use in recording financial transactions, it should continue to use the same methods in subsequent years. This means that year-on-year figures can be compared, safe in the knowledge that any changes that occur in the results are due to the performance of the business and not to a change in the *accounting policies.*

Changes can be made in policy if the circumstances of the business change. When changes of this nature are made and profits are affected by a material amount, then the effect of the change should be stated clearly in the accounts so that any comparative figures can be adjusted accordingly by the users of the accounts.

consolidated accounts: the combination of the financial statements of a group of companies. (See *consolidated balance sheet* and *consolidated profit and loss account.*)

consolidated balance sheet: all resources of a *holding company* and its *subsidiary companies* are included in the group *balance sheet.* Since the holding company has a majority of the shares in the subsidiary company it has control of all the resources of the subsidiary.

Worked example: Thryp plc balance sheet as at 30 June 19*7:

	£
Fixed assets	20 000
Investment in HGP plc	6 000
Net current assets	12 000
	38 000
Ordinary share capital	25 000
Profit and loss account	13 000
	38 000

HGP plc balance sheet as at 30 June 19*7:

	£
Fixed assets	9 000
Net current assets	4 000
	13 000
Ordinary share capital	10 000
Profit and loss account	3 000
	13 000

Thryp plc purchased 60% of the issued ordinary share capital of HGP plc at par.

Required:

The consolidated balance sheet as at 30 June 19*7 for the group.

Solution:

Thryp plc consolidated balance sheet as at 30 June 19*7

	£	
Fixed assets	29 000	(20 000 + 9000)
Net current assets	16 000	(12 000 + 4000)
	45 000	
Share capital	25 000	(of the holding company)
Profit and loss account	14 800	(13 000 + 60% of 3000 HGPs reserves)
Minority interest	5 200	(40% of ordinary shares not owned by Thryp plc + 40% of 3000 HGPs reserves)
	45 000	

Worked example: Thryp plc balance sheet as at 30 June 19*7

	£
Fixed assets	20 000
Investment in HGP plc	18 000
Net current assets	12 000
	50 000
Ordinary share capital	26 000
Profit and loss account	24 000
	50 000

Thryp plc purchased 60% of the issued ordinary share capital of HGP plc for £18 000. Balance sheet of HGP plc is as shown above.

Required:

The consolidated balance sheet as at 30 June 19*7 for the group.

Solution:

Thryp plc consolidated balance sheet as at 30 June 19*7

	£	
Fixed assets	29 000	(20 000 + 9000)
Goodwill	10 200	(18 000 investment − 7800 Thryp's interest 6000 + 1800)
Net current assets	16 000	(12 000 + 4000)
	55 200	
Ordinary share capital	26 000	
Profit and loss account	24 000	
Minority interest	5 200	(40% of ordinary shares not owned by Thryp plc + 40% of HGP's reserves)
	55 200	

consolidated profit and loss account shows the profit or loss of a group of companies as if it was a single entity. If the *subsidiary company*(ies) is wholly owned then the *profit and loss account* is added to that of the *holding company* to form the consolidated profit and loss account.

If there is a minority interest in the subsidiary company(ies) the total profit is calculated, total *corporation tax* is deducted, and then the share of profit attributable to the minority interest is deducted. This results in the group profit for the year.

Worked example: Ventro plc owns 80% of the issued ordinary share capital of Redco plc.

The following are the profit and loss accounts of Ventro plc and Redco plc for the year ended 31 October 19*7:

	Ventro plc £	Redco plc £
Profits for the year before taxation	740 000	610 000
Less corporation tax	190 000	150 000
Profits for the year after taxation	550 000	460 000

Required:

Prepare the consolidated profit and loss account for the year ended 31 October 19*7.

Solution:

Ventro plc consolidated profit and loss account for the year ended 31 October 19*7

	£	
Profits for the year before taxation	1 350 000	(740 000 + 610 000)
Less corporation tax	340 000	(190 000 + 150 000)
Consolidated profits for the year after taxation	1 010 000	
Less minority shareholders' interest	92 000	(20% of Redco's profit after tax)
Group profit for the year	918 000	

When the group profits have been determined an appropriation account must be prepared.

Any dividends paid or proposed by the subsidiary company(ies) are eliminated for the purposes of consolidation.

Worked example: Wallace plc owns 60% of the issued ordinary share capital of Wastell plc. The following are the profit and loss accounts for the year ended 30 April 19*7 of Wallace plc and Wastell plc:

73

	Wallace plc	Wastell plc
	£000	£000
Turnover	2000	950
Cost of sales	750	200
	1250	750
Administration expenses	360	175
	890	
Dividend from Wastell plc	72	
Profit on ordinary activities before taxation	962	575
Less tax on profit on ordinary activities	210	150
Profit on ordinary activities after taxation	752	425
Dividends paid and proposed	200	120
Retained profit for the year	552	305

Required:

Prepare the consolidated profit and loss account for the year ended 30 April 19*7.

Solution:

Wallace consolidated profit and loss account for the year ended 30 April 19*7:

	£000	
Turnover	2950	(2000 + 950)
Cost of sales	950	(750 + 200)
	2000	
Administrative costs	535	
Profit on ordinary activities before tax	1465	
Taxation on profit on ordinary activities	360	(210 + 150)
Profit on ordinary activities after tax	1105	
Minority interest	170	(40% × 425 Wastell profit after tax)
Profit for financial year	935	
Proposed dividend	200	(Holding company only)
Retained profit for the year	735	

consumables: goods that are used up during the everyday administration of a business, e.g. stationery.

contingencies: see *accounting for contingencies SSAP 18*

contingent liabilities: a potential liability which exists when a *balance sheet* is drawn up, the full extent of which is uncertain. The *Companies Act 1985* requires that the following details be given in respect of any contingent liability:

- the amount (or estimated amount) of the liability
- its legal nature
- whether any valuable security has been provided by the company in connection with the liability and if so, what

(See *accounting for contingencies SSAP 18.*)

continuous allotment method: see *apportionment of reciprocal services*

contra items occur in a *cash book* when money is paid out of cash takings into a bank or when money is drawn out of a bank and put into the till. Both the debit entry and the credit entry appear in the same book.

The business is neither better nor worse off because of the transaction; it is rather like a person taking a £10 note from their wallet and putting the money in a pocket.

Contra entries are identified by placing a 'C' alongside each entry.

Worked example: George has cash sales for the day amounting to £834. He pays £750 into the business bank account.

Required:

Show how the entries given above would be entered in the two-column cash book.

Solution:

Cash book

	Cash £	Bank £		Cash £	Bank £
Cash sales	834		Bank C	750	
Cash C		750			

Worked example: Carol withdraws £4352 from the business bank account in order to have sufficient cash to pay her staff wages the next day.

Required:

Show how the entries given above would be entered in the two-column cash book.

Solution:

Cash book

	Cash £	Bank £		Cash £	Bank £
Bank C	4352		Cash C		4352
The following day …					
			Wages	4352	

contract: a legally binding agreement between two parties.

contract account: similar to a *trading* and *profit and loss account* for the *contract*. (See *contract costing*.)

contract costing: when a job spans several *accounting periods*, a *contract account* is opened for that job. All *direct costs* incurred on the contract and all overheads allocated to the contract are debited to it.

The client will usually make a number of payments as the contract progresses, based on a *certification of work done*. These are credited to the contract account.

Worked example: Fretley plc commenced work on contract 5641 for Durber District Council on 1 October 19*6. In the year ended 30 September 19*7 the following items had been charged to the contract:

	£
Materials	160 000
Site wages	97 000
Sub-contractors charges	13 500
Plant purchased for contract 5641	24 000
Hire of specialist machinery	21 000
Expenses incurred on site	48 500
Head office administrative expenses allocated to contract 5641	19 500

At the 30 September 19*7:

	£
Materials on the site were valued at	18 000
Plant on the site had a net book value of	75 000

Fretly plc received an architect's certificate relating to work completed up to 30 September 19*7. Durber DC has paid £360 000, having retained 10% of the value of the certificated work.

Required:

The account for contract 5641 for the year ended 30 September 19*7 as it would appear in the books of Fretley plc

Solution:

Contract 5641

	£		£
Materials sent to site	160 000	Architect's certificate	400 000
Site wages	97 000	Stock of materials on site c/d	18 000
Sub-contracting charges	13 500	Value of plant c/d	7 500
Purchases of plant	24 000		
Machine hire	21 000		
Site expenses	48 500		
Head office administration charges	19 500		

There is a credit balance of £109 500 on this contract account. This would appear to be the profit made on the contract so far.

The concept of *prudence* dictates that we should not anticipate profits. If we were to follow this concept to the letter when considering *long-term contracts*, some business-es would report large losses over a number of years and extremely large profits in the odd years when long-term contracts were completed.

Attributable profit is that part of the total profit of a contract that fairly reflects the profit earned on the work done up to the accounting date. The formula to calculate attributable profit is:

FORMULA:

$$\text{work certified} - \text{cost of work certified} \times \frac{2}{3} \times \frac{\text{cash received on account}}{\text{value of work certified}}$$

$$\text{The attributable profit on contract 5641} = £109\ 500 \times \frac{2}{3} \times \frac{360\ 000}{400\ 000}$$

$$= £65\ 700$$

The incomplete contract account from above can now be completed:

	£		£
Profit and loss account –		Balance b/d	109 500
recognised profit	65 700		
Reserve – profit not yet			
recognised as earned	43 800		
	109 500		109 500
Profit not yet recognised as earned			43 800

(See also *stocks and long-term contracts SSAP 9.*)

contribution: the difference between selling price and *variable costs.* Contribution should correctly be named 'contribution towards *fixed costs* and profit'. It is available to pay the fixed costs of a business; once they are covered contribution becomes profit.

Contribution can be calculated in total or per unit.

Contribution is a key element in using *marginal costing* as a management tool.

contribution accounting focuses on identifying *fixed* and *variable costs* and calculating the total *contribution* generated by a business. The total fixed costs are then deducted to arrive at the net profit.

Worked example: Gronk Ltd is a small manufacturing business. The following information relates to the year ended 31 May 19*7:

	£
Direct wages	210 000
Direct materials	100 000
Factory overheads	80 000
Administration overheads	60 000
Total sales revenue	503 000

Assume direct wages are a variable cost and that all overheads are fixed costs.

Required:

A revenue statement showing clearly contribution and net profit for the year ended 31 May 19*7 for Gronk Ltd.

Solution:

Gronk Ltd revenue statement for the year ended 31 May 19*7

		£	£
Sales			503 000
Less variable costs	– direct wages	210 000	
	– direct materials	100 000	310 000
Contribution			193 000
Less fixed costs	– factory overheads	80 000	
	– administrative overheads	60 000	140 000
Net profit			53 000

contribution graph: the name given to an alternative presentation of a *break-even chart.* Sales revenue is graphed from the origin as in a traditional break-even chart.

ISLE COLLEGE
RESOURCES CENTRE

Variable costs are also graphed from the origin, and then *fixed costs* are built onto the variable costs.

Worked example: Andre Baget produces and sells one product – a 'nont'. The following information relates to the production and sales of 25 000 'nonts'.

	£ per unit
Selling price	13
Fixed costs	6
Variable costs	3

Required:

i) a traditional break-even chart for sales of 'nonts'
ii) a contribution break-even chart for sales of 'nonts'

Solution:

i)

ii)

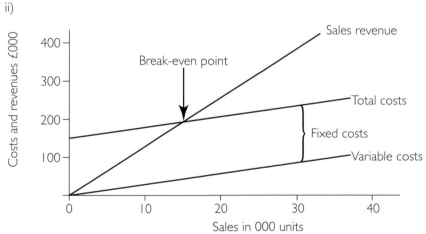

This graph emphasises the total contribution earned by the product at every level of sales.

---

contribution pricing sets the selling price of a product at a value below total *unit cost* but one that will cover *variable costs*. As long as the selling price of the product is set at a level that gives a positive *contribution*, short-term profits will increase (or short-term losses will be reduced).

Worked example: Mitzon & Co. produces 'gugs' which sell at a price of £14 each. Total fixed costs amount to £37 500 per annum. The variable costs of producing a gug are £6.50. The factory currently has spare capacity.

A Korean retailer wishes to purchase 4000 gugs but is only prepared to pay £10 per unit.

Required:

Advise the management of Mitzon & Co. whether they should accept or reject the Korean order.

Solution:

The order should be accepted; it makes a positive contribution per unit of £3.50.

Contribution per unit = selling price per unit − variable costs per unit
= £10.00 − £6.50
= £3.50

£14 000 (4000 × £3.50) will go towards covering fixed costs. If fixed costs are already covered, then £14 000 extra profit will be earned.

(See *marginal costing*.)

contribution/sales ratio expresses *contribution* as a fraction or a percentage of the sales figure. It can be used to find:

- profit at various levels of business activity
- the break-even level of sales

The contribution/sales ratio is calculated using the formula:

FORMULA: $\dfrac{\text{sales} - \text{variable costs (total contribution)}}{\text{sales}}$

Worked example: Griffiths Ltd produces 'pilts'. The following data refer to the production of 20 000 pilts:

	£
Budgeted sales	720 000
Variable costs	324 000
Fixed costs	134 000

Required:

Calculate:
i) the profit if sales reached £400 000
ii) the break-even point for sales of pilts.

Solution:

i) contribution/sales ratio $= \dfrac{\text{sales} - \text{variable costs}}{\text{sales}} = \dfrac{396\ 000}{720\ 000}$

$= 0.55$ or 55%

so contribution is $0.55 \times £400\ 000 = £220\ 000$

profit $=$ contribution $-$ fixed costs
$ = £220\ 000 - £134\ 000$
$ = £86\ 000$

ii) break-even sales revenue $= \dfrac{\text{fixed costs}}{\text{c/s ratio}} = \dfrac{£134\ 000}{0.55} = £243\ 637$

control accounts are used as a method of checking the accuracy of the entries in the *purchase ledgers* and the *sales ledgers*.

Control accounts are prepared by using totals from the *books of prime entry*. Individual *personal accounts* in the ledgers are prepared from the individual entries in the books of prime entry. Because control accounts and the individual accounts are prepared from the same source, they should agree in every respect.

A control account should be prepared for each sales ledger and each purchase ledger each month. In this way it can be ascertained precisely which ledger(s) contains the error(s) and in which month it(they) occurred.

The balances brought down when the sales ledger control accounts have been prepared should be the same as the totals of the schedule of debtors extracted from all the accounts in the sales ledgers. Similarly, the balances brought down when the purchase ledger control accounts have been prepared should be the same as the totals of the schedule of creditors extracted from all the accounts in the purchase ledgers. If either of these conditions is not satisfied, the matter should be investigated.

Control accounts can be part of the double-entry system (integrated) or they might be used merely as proof of arithmetic accuracy of the ledger. In both cases the control account is prepared in the same way.

Worked example: the following information has been extracted from the books of Rashid Ltd for the month of August:

		£
1 August	Sales ledger balances	6 184
	Purchase ledger balances	4 197
Totals for August:		
	Sales day book	62 491
	Purchase day book	51 773
	Returns inwards	1 067
	Returns outward	450
	Cheques and cash received from credit customers	56 415
	Cheques paid to suppliers	46 004
	Discounts allowed	764
	Discounts received	1 570
	Bad debts written off	143

Dishonoured cheque   549
Balance in sales ledger set off against balance in purchase ledger   720

Required:

Prepare a sales ledger control account and a purchase ledger control account for the month of August for Rashid Ltd.

Solution:

Sales ledger control account for August

	£		£
1 August balances b/d	6 184	31 August cash and cheques	56 415
31 August credit sales	62 491	31 August discount allowed	764
31 August dishonoured cheque	549	31 August returns inward	1 067
		31 August bad debts written off	143
		31 August transfer to purch. led.	720
		31 August balance c/d	10 115
	69 224		69 224
1 September balance b/d	10 115		

Purchase ledger control account for August

	£		£
31 August cheques paid to suppliers	46 004	1 August balances b/d	4 197
31 August discount received	1 570	31 August credit purchases	51 773
31 August returns outward	450		
31 August transfer from sales ledger	720		
31 August balances c/d	7 226		
	55 970		55 970
		1 September balances b/d	7 226

The uses of control accounts are as follows:

- location of errors
- help to make fraud more difficult – generally the person preparing the control accounts will not be the same person writing up the ledger
- can give management quick, up-to-date information on total debtors and creditors

controllable costs: costs that can be regulated by the manager of a *cost centre*, and for which he/she is responsible. Control of such costs may well form part of a manager's performance criteria. It would be wrong to assess performance on costs that are outside a manager's control – these are known as *non-controllable costs*.

control period: see *budget period*

convertible loan stock gives the holder the opportunity to exchange the loan into ordinary shares of a company at some specified time in the future.

corporate name: the name of a large company.

corporation tax: the tax paid by *limited companies*. All individuals are liable to pay tax on their incomes, after the deduction of certain *tax allowances*. Since, in the eyes of the law, limited companies are *legal entities*, they too must pay tax on their earnings. A company's taxable profits are its net profit before *dividends* and certain costs which attract special tax treatment.

Corporation tax is charged at different rates according to the level of each individual company's profits. Corporation tax rates are set annually in the *Finance Act*. Currently, companies with small profits pay corporation tax at a rate of 24 per cent, whilst companies with larger profits pay corporation tax at 33%.

Companies must pay their *tax liability* nine months after the relevant *accounting period*. If a company pays dividends during the accounting period, then it may be required to pay *advance corporation tax (ACT)*. The balance of the tax due would then normally be paid nine months after the relevant accounting period.

correction of errors: when errors in a bookkeeping system are found they must be corrected. Errors in a *double-entry bookkeeping* system should be discovered fairly quickly if the accountant has checked the system on a regular basis. The checks that should be used are as follows:

- the *cash columns* in the *cash book* and *petty cash book* should be checked frequently by comparing *cash in hand* with the actual cash in the till and petty cash float
- the *bank columns* in the cash book should be checked against the bank statements when they are received
- each individual *ledger* should be checked by preparing a *control account* for each ledger each month
- the arithmetic accuracy of the whole double-entry system should be checked by extracting a trial balance. Some errors in the system will not be revealed by extracting a trial balance (see *errors not affecting the balancing of a trial balance*).

The *book of prime entry* used when correcting errors is the *journal*.

cost accounting is an essential element in the decision-making process of a business. It is a branch of management accounting which records all costs (past costs, present costs and estimated future costs) and uses these as a basis to determine prices, prepare budgets and to provide the information necessary to calculate profitability.

cost centre: the *CIMA* definition is 'a production or service location, function, activity or item of equipment whose costs may be attributed to *cost units*'.

cost classification may be:

- into elements of cost – materials, direct labour, other direct expenses, overheads
- according to function – manufacturing, distribution, selling, administration, financing
- according to whether they are *product costs* (materials, direct labour) or *period costs (fixed costs)*
- by behaviour – fixed costs, *variable costs*
- by the amount of control over the costs
- according to whether they are *avoidable* or *unavoidable*

For decision-making purposes costs can be classified as:

- *future differential costs*
- *relevant costs*
- *sunk costs*
- *opportunity costs*

cost concept: assets are normally shown in a *balance sheet* at cost. This is an objective valuation, therefore it removes subjectivity. (But see *asset revaluation*.)

cost driver are activities that cause costs to be incurred.

cost of borrowing: the interest rate charged by a lender of money.

cost of capital: the discounting factor to be used in *net present value* calculations. It is generally based on a weighted average cost of capital available to a business.

In order to make a meaningful comparison between the original investment in a project (or in capital equipment) and the future returns of cash from the investment, there is a need to discount the *cash flows* so that they are equivalent in value to a cash flow now. A comparison of 'like with like' is then possible.

Worked example: Victor Abutu Ltd has the following capital structure:

	£
Ordinary shares (currently paying a dividend of 10%)	700 000
8% preference shares	300 000
9% debenture stock	200 000
Bank loan (current rate of interest payable 11%)	50 000

Required:

Calculate the weighted average cost of capital for Victor Abutu Ltd.

Solution:

	Nominal value	Rate of return paid	Cost of capital per annum
Ordinary share	700 000	10%	70 000
Preference shares	300 000	8%	24 000
Debenture stock	200 000	9%	18 000
Bank loan	50 000	11%	5 500
	1 250 000		117 500

$$\text{average cost of capital} = \frac{\text{cost of capital per annum}}{\text{nominal value of capital}} = \frac{£117\,500}{£1\,250\,000} = 9.4\%$$

This shows that it would cost Victor Abutu Ltd an average of 9.4% to raise the required amount of capital to fund the new project.

Note:

This example is correct in principle, but taxation has been ignored in considering interest on debenture stock and bank loan interest. In reality, the £18 000 and £5500 would be reduced by the current rate of corporation tax being paid by Victor Abutu Ltd. Both are tax deductible as profit and loss expenses.

---

cost of goods sold: also known as *cost of sales*.

cost of living allowance: an additional payment given with wages to cover increased living costs due to inflation.

cost of sales is deducted from net sales to calculate the gross profit of a business. The cost of sales calculation is:

> FORMULA: opening stock + net purchases − closing stock = cost of sales

This calculation is necessary because the *trading account* is prepared on the *accruals* basis. The sales generated in the financial period need to be matched with the cost of those same sales. Consider this example:

Trading account for the year ended 30 April 19*7

£

Stock 1 May 19*6	10 740	This is the stock left in the shop at the end of last year.
Purchases	99 640	These are the goods purchased to be sold during the year.
	110 380	These are the goods that we could have sold during the year, but they were not all sold because we have stock left ...
Stock 30 April 19*7	8 450	... at the end of the year. If we deduct this closing stock it will tell us the value of our sales ...
Cost of sales	101 930	... but at cost price!

If the net sales figure for the year ended 30 April was £200 000 then the business gross profit was £98 070 (200 000 − 101 930).

cost-of-sales adjustment was required by SSAP 16 (*current cost accounting*) and took into account price changes as they affected *stock valuations*. The adjustment required that *opening* and *closing stocks* should be adjusted to a value which represented the average value of stock for the period. This meant that both opening and closing stock were valued using the same base as the purchases made during the period.

cost-plus pricing takes total *unit cost* of production and adds a percentage on as profit. If the set price makes the product uncompetitive, too few units may be sold to recover total costs out of sales revenue.

cost unit: a unit of production (or a unit of a service provided) which absorbs the *cost centre's* overhead costs. It could be, for example, a CD player, a CD or a passenger-mile.

Cost units are often used for comparative purposes. The cost of one unit of production is calculated and can then be compared with alternative production methods or even the purchase of the same unit from a third party.

cost-volume-profit analysis (CVP): see *break-even analysis*

'creative accounting' is the practice of manipulating figures in the accounts to present a better picture than the correct one. This might be done in order to make a business more attractive to a potential purchaser. It could be done by reducing or cutting out certain expenditure like building maintenance or some advertising expenditure.

credit is the right-hand side of an account. An entry on the credit side indicates:

- a decrease in *assets*
- a decrease in *expenses*
- an increase in *liabilities*
- an increase in *revenue,* or
- an increase in *capital*

credit balance on an account indicates that the credit side of the account is greater than the debit side. For example:

An Account	
31	216

The balancing figure is 185. This figure is inserted on the debit side of the account as the balance carried down (c/d)

An Account	
31	216
Balance c/d 185	___
216	216

At the start of the next accounting period it is shown on the credit side of the account as the balance brought down (b/d)

An Account	
	Balance b/d 185

Credit balances in the *purchase ledger* (and sometimes in the *sales ledger*) are creditors.

credit control: if a business sells goods on credit, the managers should make sure that the amounts outstanding from individual debtors do not get out of control. This will mean the establishment of a system covering:

- individual credit limits
- collection of outstanding balances
- sending statements and other reminders

Poor credit control will make the working capital position of the business worse and could make the possibility of *bad debts* more likely.

credit limit: the maximum that a customer can owe at any one time.

credit note: a document that details the amount of the allowance to be made when a purchaser returns faulty goods to the supplier. The credit note is often printed in red and is sent to the customer, who will set it off against the next purchase made. The supplier records the credit note(s) in the *sales returns day book.*

creditor: a person or business that is owed money for goods or services supplied on credit. (See *credit sales.*)

creditors: amounts falling due after one year is the term used by the *Companies Act 1985* for *long-term liabilities.* The following would be shown under this heading on the *balance sheet* of a *limited company*:

- *debentures*
- long-term bank loans

creditors: amounts falling due within one year is the term used by the *Companies Act 1985* for *current liabilities*. The following would be shown under this heading on the *balance sheet* of a *limited company*:

- *trade creditors*
- *bank overdraft*
- *bills payable*
- *accruals*
- *corporation tax* for the current year less *ACT*
- proposed *dividends*
- *ACT* on proposed dividend

creditors' budget: a forecast of the amounts that will be owed at the end of each month to creditors. It will be linked to the raw materials budget (and any other relevant budgets e.g. capital expenditure budget) and the cash budget.

The creditors' budget could look similar to the following example:

Creditors' budget

	February £	March £	April £
Balance b/fwd			
(*creditors end of January)	*4 563	4 863	5 455
Credit purchases	16 432	16 712	18 051
	20 995	21 575	23 506
Cash paid to creditors	15 823	15 661	15 968
Discounts received	309	459	901
Balance c/fwd	4 863	5 455	6 637

creditors' ledger: another name for the *purchase ledger*.

creditors' payment period measures the average time a business takes to pay its creditors. The calculation is:

$$\text{FORMULA: creditors' payment period} = \frac{\text{creditors} \times 365}{\text{credit purchases}}$$

so if credit purchases for the year were £89 567 and creditors at the year end were £7894, the creditors' payment period would be:

$$\frac{7894 \times 365}{89\ 567} = 32 \text{ days}$$

Whether this is good or bad will depend on:

- trend – is this a longer or shorter time than in previous years?
- debtors – are debtors paying sooner or later than creditors are being paid?

Generally, the longer this time period the better for the business, however care must be taken not to alienate suppliers.

credit rating: the amount that a credit rating agency feels that a customer should be allowed to borrow. The agency will research information and keep a history of a person's or business's record of settling debts. This record enables a business to determine whether a new client should be given credit facilities.

credit sales: sales made without an immediate payment in cash being made by the purchaser. The entries in the *ledger* are:

General ledger		Sales ledger	
Sales		**A Customer**	
A Customer	613	Sales	613

(See *sales day book*.)

cumulative preference shares: if a company fails to pay the preference *dividend* in any year, the dividend deficiency is carried forward until profits are sufficiently large to pay off the arrears. These arrears are payable before the ordinary shareholders receive a dividend. (See *preference shares*.)

current account (bank): a bank account on which a customer of the bank can withdraw money by writing a cheque. The other current account services include:

- transfer of monies by standing order or direct debit
- transfer of monies by credit transfer
- overdraft facilities
- bank loan facilities
- night safe facilities
- banker's draft facilities

current account (partnership): see *partnership current accounts*

current assets are cash or assets that will be turned into cash in the near future. The term 'current' means within the next twelve months. They are used for the day-to-day expenses of running a business.

Current assets are listed in reverse order of l*iquidity*, that is, with the most difficult to change into cash heading the list, and ending with cash itself. They include:

- *closing stocks* at the end of the *accounting period*
- *trade debtors*
- prepayments on expense accounts (see *prepayments of expenses*), e.g. *business rates* paid in advance
- *bank balances*
- *cash in hand*

They are sometimes known as trading assets or circulating assets.

current cost accounting: a method of accounting which takes changes in the price level into account. It replaced *current purchasing power accounting* (CCPA) when that method lost favour. This version of current value accounting became mandatory in 1980 by the issue of SSAP 16, but it became so unpopular that it was withdrawn at the end of 1985.

SSAP 16 tried to reduce the the level of historic cost profit to allow for increases due to inflation. The standard required four adjustments to be made to the historic *profit and loss account* and two to the *balance sheet*:

- *cost-of-sales adjustment (COSA)*
- *additional depreciation charge (ADA)*
- *monetary working capital adjustment (MWCA)*
- *gearing adjustment (GA)*
- *fixed assets* to be included in the balance sheet at net replaceable cost – that is, gross replacement cost less *depreciation* based on replacement cost
- *closing stocks* to be included in the balance sheet at their replacement cost as at the *balance sheet date*

current cost reserve was required when preparing a balance sheet using *current cost accounting.* It was credited with surpluses arising out of the revaluation of *fixed assets* and stock. The surpluses due to the *monetary working capital adjustment* and the *gearing adjustment* were also credited to this *reserve.* It is also known as capital maintenance reserve.

current liabilities are short-term debts which a business has to pay within the following *accounting period.* They include:

- *trade creditors,* for debts incurred in the normal course of trade
- *accrued expenses,* e.g. wages due but unpaid, rent due but unpaid
- *bank overdrafts*

In the case of a *limited company,* current liabilities also include:

- provision for taxation
- proposed dividends

The term 'current' means within the next twelve months.

The *Companies Act 1985* requires the term '*creditors: amounts falling due within one year*' rather than 'current liabilities' to be used in the *balance sheets* of limited companies.

current purchasing power accounting (CCPA): model of inflation accounting resulting from SSAP 7. This standard required:

- The continued use of *historic cost accounting* as the basis of the *annual report and accounts,* supplemented by CPPA *profit and loss account,* CCPA *balance sheet* (both adjusted to take into account the effects of inflation) and a statement reconciling the historic cost profit with the profit revealed in the CCPA profit and loss account.
- The use of the *retail price index* to assess movements in prices.
- Identification of gains and losses of purchasing power through the business holding monetary items.

This method of inflation accounting was rejected by the Sandilands Committee Report issued in September 1975.

current ratio compares assets which will become liquid in less than twelve months with liabilities which fall due within the same time period. The current ratio is sometimes called the working capital ratio.

The calculation is:

FORMULA: $\dfrac{\text{current assets}}{\text{current liabilities}}$

ISLE COLLEGE
RESOURCES CENTRE

The ratio is expressed as 'something':1, e.g. 2.3:1. There is no ideal ratio. Generally the ratio should be greater than unity (i.e. greater than 1:1) although some businesses prosper with a ratio of less than this unity.

Worked example: Raymond Yong has the following current assets and current liabilities:

Stock £12 509, debtors £3881, bank balance £578, creditors £3877.

Required:

Calculate Raymond's current ratio.

Solution:

Raymond's current ratio = 4.38:1 (12 509 + 3881 + 578 : 3877).

---

current replacement price values assets at their replacement cost to a business. This method of valuation takes into account changes in prices which are specific to the business.

CVP: see *break-even analysis*

data: information.

database: a store of information held in a computer. Once data has been inputted (stored) it is available to be used in any process. For example, when goods are sold on credit, this information will be inputted to the database. It can then be used to:

- update stock records
- create a *sales invoice*
- debit the customer's account in the *sales ledger*
- debit the sales ledger *control account*
- credit the *sales account* in the *general ledger*
- prepare costings
- prepare management accounts
- prepare statistical information

data processing: the organising and processing of information. By using a computer to process data, much detailed, selective information can be obtained quickly from the data bank.

Data Protection Act 1984 regulates organisations in their use of the information that they hold on computer databases. The Act seeks to guarantee that the personal data stored is accurate, and it gives the individual the right to access his/her personal file.

Organisations holding personal information have to register with the Data Protection Registrar.

day books: see *subsidiary books*

day rates calculate gross pay by multiplying the hours worked by the wage rate per hour, so if an employee works 38 hours one week and the hourly rate for the job is £6.00, the gross pay for the week is 38 × £6.00 = £228.00. Also known as hourly rates or weekly rates.

DCF: see *discounted cash flow*

debenture discount: see *discount on debentures*

debenture interest: the annual payment made to the holders of *debentures*. This is a fixed payment and is specified in the title, e.g. '8 per cent debentures 2019' (the annual rate of interest to be paid by the *limited company* is 8 per cent). This interest must be paid whether the company makes a profit or a loss. The interest is debited to the *profit and loss account.*

debenture issue: the bookkeeping entries are similar to those used for the *issue of shares*. The word 'debenture' should be substituted for the words 'share capital'.

debentures: *bonds* recording a long-term loan to a *limited company*. The company pays a fixed rate of interest on debentures. They may be repayable at some date in the future (e.g. '8 per cent debentures 2019' pay 8 per cent interest to the lender and are redeemable in the year 2019) or they may be irredeemable, that is, the holder will only be repaid when the company is liquidated.

Some debentures have the loan secured against specific assets or all of the company's assets; these are known as mortgage debentures. If the company was wound up or the company failed to pay the interest due, the holders of mortgage debentures can sell the assets and recoup the amount outstanding.

debit is the left side of an account. An entry on the debit of an account indicates:

- an increase in *assets*
- an increase in *expenses*
- a decrease in *liabilities*
- a decrease in *revenue,* or
- a decrease in *capital*

debit balance on an account indicates that the debit side is greater than the credit side. For example:

An Account

| 199 | 54 |

The balancing figure is 145. This figure is inserted on the credit side of the account as the balance carried down (c/d)

An Account

| 199 | 54 |

At the start of the next accounting period it is shown as the balance brought down (b/d) on the debit side of the account.

| | Balance c/d 145 |
| 199 | 199 |

An Account

Balance b/d 145

debit note: a note sent to a customer when an *invoice* is undercharged. Some customers send debit notes to suppliers when they return goods.

debt factoring: see *factoring*

debtor: a person or organisation that owes money to a business.

debtors' budget: a forecast of amounts owed to a business at the end of each month. It will be linked to the *production budget* and the *cash budget*.

The debtors' budget could look similar to the following example:

| | Debtors' budget | | |
	June £	July £	August £
Balance b/fwd (*debtors at end of May)	*16 731	20 137	25 333
Credit sales	43 789	58 051	49 003
	60 520	78 188	74 336
Cash received from debtors	39 875	51 980	47 435
Discounts allowed	508	875	761
Balance c/fwd	20 137	25 333	26 140

debtors' ledger: another name for the *sales ledger.*

debtors' payment period (collection period): a measurement of the average time that debtors take to pay outstanding balances. It is also known as debtor days. The calculation is:

FORMULA: debtors' payment period $= \dfrac{\text{debtors} \times 365}{\text{credit sales}}$

So if credit sales for the year were £604 722 and the debtors at the year end were £51 493 the debtors' payment period would be:

$$= \frac{51\ 493 \times 365}{604\ 722}$$

$$= 31 \text{ days}$$

This appears to be acceptable, although many businesses would like outstanding debtor balances to be cleared in 30 days.

Whether the payment period is acceptable will depend on:

- trend – is this a longer or shorter time than in previous years?
- creditors – are creditors being paid more or less quickly than debtors are settling their debts?

Generally, the shorter this time period the better. However, this calculation gives an average collection time which could mask the fact that some debtors' balances may have been outstanding for some considerable time.

deferred shares: shares usually issued to the person who started a *limited company.* They often carry a disproportionately large voting right. These shares only receive a *dividend* after all other dividends have been paid.

deferred taxation: see *accounting for deferred taxation SSAP 15*

delivery note: a note signed by a purchaser when goods are delivered as proof that the goods have been received. The delivery note is taken back to the accounts department by the carrier and an *invoice* is raised.

departmental accounts: see *columnar presentation of final accounts*

departmental budgets are prepared showing projected income and expenditure for each department. Departmental budgets may form part of an overall system of *budgetary control.*

depletion method of providing for depreciation: a method of *depreciation* based on the purchase price of an exhaustible asset. It can be used when the value of a physical asset, for example a gravel pit or a quarry, is being reduced in value by an extractive process.

Worked example: Digem Ltd purchases a limestone quarry for £10 000 000. It is estimated that the quarry contains 2 500 000 tonnes of limestone.

Required:

Calculate the annual depreciation charge in a year when 450 000 tonnes of limestone have been extracted from the quarry.

Solution:

Depreciation charge for year $= £1\,800\,000$ (450 000 tonnes extracted $\times £4$)

Workings $\dfrac{£10\,000\,000}{2\,500\,000} = £4$ per tonne

deposit account: a bank account in which surplus cash that is not needed immediately is deposited. Individuals and businesses can use deposit accounts. Balances attract interest and, theoretically, notice must be given to withdraw money from a deposit account, but banks generally waive the notice required. However, they may penalise the depositor by charging interest on the sum withdrawn. Deposit accounts do not usually carry the right to use a cheque book.

depreciation: the *apportioning* of the cost of an asset over its useful economic life. All assets with a finite life should be depreciated (*Companies Act 1985*), so the only asset that is not subject to depreciation is land. The calculation of depreciation should conform to the *accruals* (or matching) *concept* and the *consistency* concept of accounting. (See *accounting for depreciation SSAP 12*.)

despatch note: a note kept by a storekeeper noting the date on which goods are sent out to a customer. The note is retained in case there is a query regarding the goods.

destroyer pricing: see *penetration pricing*

development costs: see *accounting for research and development SSAP 13*

differential costs: see *future differential costs*

differential piece work: see *piece work*

direct costs are defined by *CIMA* as 'expenditure which can be economically identified with a specific saleable cost unit'. Examples of direct costs include direct labour charges and direct materials.

direct labour: workers whose work can be identified clearly with converting raw materials or components into the final product. It might include machine operatives, assembly workers and packers.

direct labour costs: the labour costs that are directly attributable to a unit of production. They form part of the *prime cost* in a *manufacturing account*. Direct labour costs are made up of workers' gross pay and related *on-costs*. They can be traced easily to the finished product.

direct labour efficiency variance is favourable when the direct workforce saves time and therefore money for a business. A *favourable variance* could be due to:

- higher skilled workers being employed
- workers using good machines suited to the job
- good conditions in the workplace
- good working methods being employed
- good quality control

An *adverse variance* will occur if the opposite conditions apply.

For a worked example, see *direct labour variance*.

direct labour hour rate method of absorbing overheads: see *absorption*

direct labour rate variance: the difference between the budgeted labour rate and the actual labour rate. This will be adverse when the direct workforce wages are increased (see *adverse variances*). This could be due to:

- use of a more highly skilled workforce
- wage inflation since the standard was set
- overtime or premium rates being paid

A *favourable variance* could be due to workers with a lower level of skill being employed and being paid at a lower rate than the standard.

For a worked example, see *direct labour variance*.

direct labour variance is the difference between standard *direct labour cost* and actual direct labour cost. The variance is made up of:

- *direct labour efficiency variance*
- *direct labour rate variance*

Worked example: A business produces 'clords'. The standard direct labour costs involved in the production of 'clords' were set at 46 hours at a cost of £8.00 per hour. The actual direct labour costs were 50 hours at £7.50 per hour.

Required:

Calculate:
a) direct labour efficiency variance
b) direct labour rate variance
c) total direct labour cost variance.

Solution:

One way of calculating all three variances is to use the following grid. If you are comfortable using it, you can also apply it to materials and sales.

standard quantity × standard price)

actual quantity × standard price)   = quantity variance

actual quantity × actual price   = price variance

total variance

So: £   £
sq × sp 46 × 8.00 = 368.00
                                = 32.00 adverse labour efficiency variance
aq × sp 50 × 8.00 = 400.00
                                = 25.00 favourable wage rate variance
aq × ap 50 × 7.50 = 375.00
total labour variance   7.00 adverse

---

direct material costs: the costs involved in the acquisition of materials that can be identified clearly as being part of a finished product. They form part of the prime cost in a *manufacturing account*.

direct material price variance: the difference between the budgeted or standard cost of materials and the actual cost of materials used. The variance will be favourable if the materials cost less than was set in the standard, thus saving the business money. A *favourable variance* could be due to:

- the supplier charging less
- change in quantity being purchased, so losing bulk prices
- use of a cheaper alternative material
- currency movement if materials were purchased abroad

An *adverse variance* could be due to the opposite conditions applying, plus general or specific inflation.

For a worked example, see *direct material variance*.

direct materials: the materials that can be identified as being used in a specific product. They might include timber in a furniture manufacturing business, or cloth in clothes manufacturing.

direct material usage variance will be favourable if fewer materials are used than was set in the standard, thus saving the business money. A *favourable variance* could be caused by:

- use of better materials than those budgeted for
- use of well-trained workers
- use of good machinery suited to the job

An *adverse variance* could be due to the opposite conditions applying plus:

- theft of materials
- deterioration of materials

For a worked example, see *direct material variance*.

direct material variance is the difference between the standard *direct material cost* and the actual direct material cost. The variance is made up of:

- *direct material usage variance*
- *direct material price variance*

Worked example: a business produces 'gritos'. The standard direct material costs involved in the production of 'gritos' were set at 16 square metres at a cost of £3.00 per square metre. The actual direct material costs were 18 square metres at £2.60 per square metre.

Required:

Calculate:
a) the direct material usage variance
b) the direct material cost variance
c) the total direct material cost variance.

Solution:

Using the grid shown in *direct labour cost variance:*

$$
\left.
\begin{array}{l}
\text{standard quantity} \times \text{standard price)} \\
\\
\text{actual quantity} \times \text{standard price)} \\
\\
\text{actual quantity} \times \text{actual price}
\end{array}
\right\}
\begin{array}{l}
= \text{ quantity variance} \\
\\
= \text{ price variance} \\
\hline
\text{total variance}
\end{array}
$$

So:

	£	£
sq × sp 16 × 3.00 = 48.00		
aq × sp 18 × 3.00 = 54.00	= 6.00	adverse direct material usage variance
aq × ap 18 × 2.60 = 46.80	= 7.20	favourable direct material usage variance
total direct material cost variance	1.20	favourable

---

directors are appointed by, and are accountable to, the *shareholders* of a *limited company,* and help manage the company. Executive directors are actively involved with the day-to-day running of the company. They usually head a large division or section of the company. Non-executive directors are not company employees. They attend *board meetings* but only act as independent advisors.

Although accountable to the shareholders, directors exert a great deal of influence over the affairs of the company because of the diffusion of shares among large numbers of shareholders.

The board of directors reports annually to the shareholders of the company.

directors' emoluments are payments made to the *directors* of a *limited company* for the work that they do on behalf of the company. Also known as directors' fees or directors' remuneration.

directors' report: a summary, prepared by the *directors*, of the main activites undertaken by a business during the year. It is a requirement of the *Companies Act 1985*. It should deal with:

- the principal activities of the company during the year and significant changes in those activities
- *dividend* payments recommended
- future developments in the business of the company
- *research and development* activities of the company
- significant changes in the company's *fixed assets* during the year
- names of directors who have served the company during the year, also their interests in shares or *debentures* in the company
- donations to political parties or charities in excess of £200 in the year
- information regarding the health, safety and welfare of the workforce
- policy regarding the employment of disabled persons if the company employs more than 250 people

disclosure of accounting policies SSAP 2 identifies four fundamental *accounting concepts*. These are:

- *going-concern concept*
- *accruals concept*
- *consistency* concept
- *prudence* concept

The *Companies Act 1985* recognises the same four concepts (the Act uses the term 'accounting principles') and adds separate valuation principles. (See also: *business entity concept, money measurement concept, cost concept.*)

discount allowed may be given to a customer if the outstanding debt is settled in a time specified by the creditor. It is treated as an expense on the *profit and loss account.*

discount columns of the cash book: cash discounts allowed to and received by a business are listed in the discount columns of a *cash book.* They are totalled independently. The 'discount allowed' column is then posted to the debit side of the discount allowed account in the *general ledger.* The total of the 'discount received' column is posted from the credit side of the cash book to the credit side of the discount received account in the general ledger.

It may seem that the posting is debit to debit and credit to credit, but clearly this cannot be so in a *double-entry bookkeeping* system. Both discount columns in the cash book are memorandum columns, that is, they are not part of the double-entry system – they are merely there as reminders. The double entry is:

Debit:	Discount allowed account	**Credit:**	The customers' accounts
Debit:	The suppliers' accounts	**Credit:**	Discount received account

discounted cash flow: methods of *capital investment appraisal* recognising the *time value of money.* The various methods compare future *net cash flows* which accrue over the life of a project, at their present value, with the value of the initial investment.

(See *payback method of capital investment appraisal, internal rate-of-return method of capital investment appraisal,* and *net present value method of capital investment appraisal.*)

discounted payback method of capital investment appraisal: see *payback method of capital investment appraisal*

discount on debentures allows an investor to purchase *debentures* at a price lower than par. Debentures are usually issued in multiples of £100. If some 9 per cent debentures were to be issued at a 3 per cent discount, the price would be quoted as '9 per cent debentures at 97'.

The total discount on the issue is treated as a capital loss and is shown separately on the *balance sheet* until it is written off.

Interest paid on the debentures is calculated on their nominal value, not their discounted value.

discount received might be given by a supplier if the outstanding debt is settled in a time specified by the supplier. It is credited to the *profit and loss account,* thus increasing the net profit of the business.

dishonoured cheque: if a cheque is presented for payment and the *drawer* has insufficient funds in his/her account to cover the cheque, it will be returned to the *payee* marked 'refer to drawer'.

When a supplier (payee) receives a cheque from a customer (drawer) the supplier's *cash book* is debited and the customer's account in the *sales ledger* is credited with the amount of the cheque.

A dishonoured cheque is shown in the debit column of the bank statement. It should be entered in the credit side of the supplier's cash book and the debit side of the customer's account in the sales ledger.

distributable profits are the profits of a *limited company* that are available for distribution to the *shareholders* as *dividends*. This is the *revenue reserves*, including the *profit and loss account*.

distribution overheads are the costs involved in storing, packing and sending goods to a customer.

dividend cover measures how many times a company's total *dividend* could have been paid out of the current year's profits after tax and interest. The result gives an indication of the company's potential to maintain dividends in the future.

The calculation is:

$$\text{FORMULA:} \quad \frac{\text{profit after tax and interest}}{\text{ordinary dividend paid}}$$

Worked example: Ginalatti plc has paid an ordinary dividend of £75 000 out of total profits after tax and interest of £460 000.

Required:

Calculate the dividend cover for Ginalatti plc.

Solution:

$$\text{dividend cover} = \frac{\text{profit after tax and interest}}{\text{ordinary dividend paid}} = \frac{£460\ 000}{£75\ 000} = 6.13 \text{ times}$$

---

dividend yield measures the actual percentage rate of return that an investor in *ordinary shares* is receiving on the investment made. The calculation is:

$$\text{FORMULA:} \quad \frac{\text{dividend per share}}{\text{market price per share}}$$

Investors who require an annual income should compare the yield on many different alternative investment opportunities before committing themselves to one in particular.

Worked example: Croft plc has an issued ordinary share capital of 500 000 £1 shares. The total dividend for the year is £140 000. The current market price per share is £4.80.

Required:

Calculate the dividend yield on Croft plc's ordinary shares.

Solution:

$$\text{dividend per share} = \frac{140\ 000}{500\ 000} = 0.28$$

$$\text{dividend yield} \; = \; \frac{\text{dividend per share}}{\text{market price per share}} \; = \; \frac{0.28}{4.80} \; = \; 5.83\%$$

dividends: the rewards paid to *shareholders* out of the profits of a *limited company*. The dividends are paid to individual shareholders in proportion to the size of their shareholding. They are usually paid annually, but there may be an interim (half-year) dividend.

Ordinary shares do not entitle the shareholder to a specific dividend; this will vary according to the level of company profits. Holders of *preference shares* will normally receive a fixed dividend. In years when profits are too low to pay a dividend, the cumulative preference shareholders' dividends accrue until such time as company profits are large enough to pay the arrears.

All dividends are dependent on the availability of:

- profits
- cash to pay the dividends

All dividends appear as appropriations in the company *profit and loss appropriation account.*

division of the ledger: all financial transactions of a business using a *double-entry bookkeeping* system are recorded in the l*edger*. In a small business, it may be feasible to use only one ledger. From a practical point of view, it makes more sense for a larger business to segregate parts of the ledger according to the entries:

- Since the bank and cash accounts are used more frequently than any other accounts, they are kept separate in a *cash book.*
- All credit suppliers' accounts are kept in the *purchase ledger.*
- All credit customers' accounts are kept in the *sales ledger.*
- All real and nominal accounts are kept in the *general ledger.*

In addition, some business people will keep a *private ledger* in which confidential financial information can be recorded, for example *capital accounts*, proprietor's *drawings, loan accounts, profit and loss accounts*, etc.

dominant influence: see *accounting for subsidiary undertakings FRS 2*

double-entry bookkeeping requires that there must always be a debit entry and a credit entry when recording financial transactions which affect the business. The system works on the principle that whenever value is given, value must also be received. The system ensures that the *dual aspect concept* of accounting is adhered to.

drawee: see *cheque*

drawer: see *cheque*

drawings: the resources that are withdrawn from a business by the proprietor(s) for private use outside the business. Drawings can be cash, goods or services taken from the business. (See *drawings account.*)

drawings account is used to record all resources withdrawn from a business by the proprietor(s) for private use. At the end of the *accounting period* the total of the drawings account is transferred to the debit side of the proprietor's *capital account.*

ISLE COLLEGE
RESOURCES CENTRE

The total of partners' drawings accounts are transferred to the debit side of the partners' current accounts.

Worked example: Sahera and Bhupesh are in partnership. The following is a list of the resources they withdrew from the partnership during the year for their own private use:

	Sahera	Bhupesh
	£	£
Cash	10 463	14 761
Goods	869	301
Private telephone calls	177	106
Private motoring expenses	618	799
Tax paid	3 002	3 244

Note:

Sole traders and partnerships are not legal entities and therefore do not pay tax. However, the owners of the business do pay tax on their earnings. If they use the business bank account to settle their tax liability to the Inland Revenue then this is a withdrawal of cash and is therefore drawings.

Required:

The partnership drawings account showing clearly the transfer to the partners' current accounts.

Solution:

Partnership drawings account

	Sahera	Bhupesh		Sahera	Bhupesh
	£	£		£	£
Cash	10 463	14 761	Current accounts	15 129	19 211
Purchases	869	301			
Telephone	177	106			
Motor expenses	618	799			
Bank – tax	3 002	3 244			
	15 129	19 211		15 129	19 211

Remember that the narrative in an account shows where the 'other' entry is.

There will be a credit entry in the cash book every time the partners withdrew cash during the year.

There will be two credits in the purchases account (£869 and £301), telephone account (£177 and £106), motor expenses account (£618 and £799) and bank account (£3002 and £3244) in the business cash book.

drawings of goods: see *goods for own use*

dual aspect concept states that there are always two ways of looking at every accounting transaction. One considers the assets of the business, the other considers the claims against them.

The concept is clearly shown in the accounting equation:

FORMULA:

fixed assets + current assets = capital + long-term liabilities + current liabilities.

the assets = the claims against the assets

The *double-entry bookkeeping* system ensures that the concept is upheld.

E & O E is the abbreviated form of 'errors and omissions excepted'. This is generally printed on an *invoice* to indicate that the business issuing the invoice takes no responsibility for any mistakes printed on the invoice.

earnings per share measures the amount of profits earned by a company attributable to each issued share. It is widely used by investors or potential investors as a measure of a company's performance. It can be used to compare:

- the results of one particular company over a number of years
- the performance of one company's *ordinary shares* against the performance of another company's ordinary shares
- the earnings against the return obtainable from alternative investments

It is also used as part of the *price/earnings ratio* of a *limited company.*

SSAP 3 earnings per share applies only to companies listed on a recognised *stock exchange.* It is calculated using the profit attributable to *ordinary shareholders* after tax, minority interest, *extraordinary items*, preference *dividends* and other appropriations in respect of *preference shares*. The calculation is:

$$\text{FORMULA: earnings per share} = \frac{\text{earnings in pence}}{\text{number of issued ordinary shares}}$$

Worked example: Pomfret plc has an issued capital of 10 000 000 ordinary shares of 50 pence each. Profits for the year after tax amounted to £1 751 000. Preference dividends for the year are £600 000.

Required:

Calculate the earnings per share for Pomfret plc.

Solution:

$$\text{earnings per share} = \frac{\text{earnings in pence}}{\text{number of issued ordinary shares}}$$

$$= \frac{175\ 100\ 000 - 60\ 000\ 000}{20\ 000\ 000} = 11.51 \text{ pence}$$

---

economic order quantity attempts to calculate the most cost-effective quantity of stock to order from a supplier. The calculation attempts to find a compromise between the cost saving made by ordering large quantities and the extra costs incurred when holding large quantities of stock.

It is more cost effective to order large quantities of stock from a supplier. It involves lower administration costs and lower delivery charges, but the costs of holding large stocks is obviously greater than the costs involved in holding smaller levels of stock.

The calculation is:

$$\text{FORMULA: economic order quantity} = \sqrt{\left(\frac{2 \times \text{annual consumption} \times \text{cost per order}}{\text{annual holding cost per item}}\right)}$$

efficiency variance: see *labour efficiency variance*

elasticity of demand: see *price elasticity of demand*

elasticity of supply: see *price elasticity of supply*

elements of cost are the individual costs that make up the final cost of the product. They are:

- manufacturing costs
- distribution costs
- sclling costs
- administration costs
- research and development costs

Each of these can be further subdivided into their component parts (elements). The elements of cost within the manufacturing process are:

- raw materials
- direct labour costs
- other direct expenses
- royalties
- factory overheads

elimination method of apportioning overhead costs of reciprocal service departments: see *apportionment of reciprocal services*

employee buy out: the purchase of a business by its employees.

entertainment allowance: additional cash given to staff to enable them to entertain prospective customers.

entity concept: see *business entity concept*

entrance fees are often charged when a member first joins a club. Since these fees are 'extraordinary' they should not be entered in the annual *income and expenditure account*. The fees should be credited to an entrance fees account which is capitalised. Each year a proportion of the account should be transferred to the annual income and expenditure account.

Worked example: The Bunkerhill golf club charges new members an entrance fee of £500 when they join the club. The club committee transfers each member's entrance fee to the club income and expenditure account over a five year period.

During the year ended 30 April 19*7 entrance fees paid by new members amounted to £6500. The balance on the entrance fees account at 30 April 19*6 was £23 700. The amount to be transferred to the club income and expenditure account for the year ended 30 April 19*7 is £1600.

Required:

The entries in the income and expenditure account and entrance fees account of the Bunkerhill golf club for the year ended 30 April 19*7.

Solution:

Bunkerhill golf club income and expenditure account for the year ended 30 April 19*7

Income:			£
Entrance fees			1 600

Entrance fees account

	£		£
I & E account	1 600	Balance b/d	23 700
Balance c/d	28 600	Cash	6 500
	30 200		30 200
		Balance b/d	28 600

entrepreneur: a person who is prepared to take the risk of starting a new project or starting up a new business when the opportunity presents itself.

EPS: see *earnings per share*

equity accounting is the term used to describe the accounting methods used to deal with an *associated undertaking*. (See *accounting for associated companies SSAP 1.*)

equity share capital: the name given to the *ordinary share capital* of a *limited company*.

error of commission: see *errors not affecting the balancing of the trial balance*

error of omission: see *errors not affecting the balancing of the trial balance*

error of original entry: see *errors not affecting the balancing of the trial balance*

error of principle: see *errors not affecting the balancing of the trial balance*

errors: see *errors not affecting the balancing of the trial balance*

errors not affecting the balancing of the trial balance are mistakes in the *double-entry bookkeeping* system which do not alter the debit and credit totals of the *trial balance*. They can be listed under the headings:

- complete reversal of entries – the account that should have had the debit entry has been credited and the account that should have had the credit entry has been debited
- error of commission – entries are debited or credited to the wrong account
- error of omission – no entry is made in any account
- error of original entry – an error is made transferring the amount from the source document to the *book of prime entry*
- error of principle – entries are debited or credited in the wrong class of account
- compensating error – error(s) on the debit side of an account(s) equals error(s) on the credit side of account(s)

Worked example: the following errors have been discovered in the books of Josie Chan:

i) £137 goods sold to Fiona have been debited to sales account and credited to Fiona

ii) Rent paid £700 has been debited to the rates account

iii) £1270 insurance premium paid by cheque has not been entered in the books of account

iv) A purchase invoice from Tashara £963 has been entered in the purchase day book as £936

v) Service charges for the vehicle fleet £6450 have been entered in the vehicles account

vi) Rent received £600 per quarter has been totalled as £2300. The following accounts have been undercast: wages by £34; stationery by £28; drawings by £38.

Required:

The journal entries necessary to correct the errors in Josie's books of account.

Solution:

Journal

Type of error (not part of the answer)		Dr £	Cr £
i) Reversal of entries	Fiona	137	
	Sales		137
ii) Error of commission	Rent	700	
	Rates		700
iii) Error of omission	Insurance	1270	
	Bank		1270
iv) Error in original entry	Purchases	27	
	Tashara		27
v) Error of principle	Motor expenses	6450	
	Vehicles		6450
vi) Compensating errors	Wages	34	
	Stationery	28	
	Drawings	38	
	Rent received		100

Remember the journal is a book of prime entry – the above entries should now be posted to the correct ledger accounts.

estimates are given to a customer who wishes to know what a job will cost. The supplier of the goods (or service) will prepare a costing based on the likely expenditure on labour, materials, other direct costs and overheads.

even production flow ensures that a business can keep its resources employed at the same level throughout the year. With an uneven production flow it may be necessary for a manufacturing business to put its workforce on short time or even dismiss a number of workers. (See *production budget*.)

exceptional items are items that are part of a company's normal trading activities but stand out because of their size. (See *extraordinary items* and *prior year adjustments*.)

exchange of debentures occurs when *debentures* in a *holding company* are given in exchange for the debentures in the *subsidiary company* it has taken over.

expenditure is the value of resources an organisation has used in the *acquisition* of goods or services during an *accounting period*. Expenditure is calculated using the *accruals concept*. It measures actual economic activity. For example, Vanessa rents a small shop for £65 per week. She has not yet paid the rent for this week, yet her expenditure on rent for this week is £65. (See *expenses*.)

expenses are the cash payments made to acquire goods and services during an *accounting period*. The cash paid could relate to previous, present or future accounting periods. For example, Helen rents a small office for £50 per week. She pays this week's rent and the rent she owes for last week. The expense for rent is £100; the *expenditure* is £50 per week.

exposure draft (ED) is a discussion document sent to interested parties prior to the drafting of a *Financial Reporting Standard* (*FRS*). After consultation and receiving comments, an *accounting standard* may be produced.

extended trial balance incorporates into the *trial balance* format all the adjustments that are necessary before the preparation of a business's *final accounts*. The use of the extended trial balance is now common in accountancy firms. It ensures that all adjustments, that take place after the trial balance has been extracted from the business's *ledger*, are incorporated into the final accounts using double entries.

The extended trial balance is a working document on which all post-balance-sheet adjustments are made. It should be emphasised that there is no one specific layout. Users of the extended trial balance can adapt it to suit their own needs. For examination purposes, students are advised to consult past papers to familiarise themselves with the layout favoured by particular examination boards.

Worked example: the following trial balance was extracted from the books of T Trout as at 31 December 19*7:

	Dr £	Cr £
Fixed assets	120 000	
Capital		73 550
Drawings	17 000	
Sales		172 000
Purchases	97 000	
Rent	6 300	
Insurance	1 750	
Other expenses	43 250	
Provision for depreciation of fixed assets		50 000
Provision for doubtful debts		850
Debtors	6 000	
Creditors		7 500
Stock 1 January 19*7	11 200	
Bank	1 200	
Suspense	200	
	303 900	303 900

Since the trial balance was extracted, two errors have been discovered:

i) the rent account has been undercast by £200
ii) a £5000 fixed asset had been debited in error to 'other expenses' account.

Additional information:

iii) stock at 31 December19*7 was valued at £13 400
iv) rent £1500 was owed at 31 December 19*7
v) insurance £250 was paid in advance at 31 December 19*7
vi) fixed assets are to be depreciated at the rate of 10% per annum on cost
vii) provision for doubtful debts is to be increased to £900

Required:

An extended trial balance as at 31 December 19*7 for T Trout.

Solution:

See next page.

---

external sources of finance: cash resources obtained from agencies outside a business. This may be done by:

- selling shares
- selling *debentures*
- borrowing from financial institutions, both long and short term
- *factoring*
- obtaining grants from the government or the European Community

extraordinary items are, according to *SSAP 6*, 'material items which derive from events or transactions that fall outside the ordinary activities of the company and which are therefore expected not to recur frequently or regularly'.

SSAP 6 prescribed different treatment in a company's *final accounts*:

- *exceptional items* should be reported as part of the current year's profits
- extraordinary items, by definition, cannot be shown as part of the *profit and loss account*. Inclusion is likely to mislead the users of the accounts.

The above definition and explanation has been superseded by *FRS 3 reporting financial performance*.

ex works: price does not include delivery costs – the purchaser must bear this cost. This item would appear as *carriage inwards* and should be added to the purchases of raw materials in the purchaser's *manufacturing account* or added to the purchases figure in the *trading account* of a retail outlet.

T Trout Extended Trial Balance

	Trial balance as at 31 Dec 19*7 DR	CR	Adjustments DR	CR	Accruals prepayments DR	CR	Profit and loss account DR	CR	Balance sheet DR	CR
Fixed assets	120 000		5 000						125 000	
Capital		73 550								73 550
Drawings	17 000								17 000	
Sales		172 000						172 000		
Purchases	97 000						97 000			
Rent	6 300		200		1 500		8 000			
Insurance	1 750					250	1 500			
Other expenses	43 250			5 000			38 250			
Prov. for dep. of fixed assets		50 000	12 500	12 500			12 500			62 500
Prov for DD		850	50	50			50			900
Debtors	6 000								6 000	
Creditors		7 500								7 500
Stock 1 Jan 19*7	11 200						11 200			
Bank	1 200								1 200	
Suspense	200			200						
	303 900	303 900								
Stock 31 Dec 19*7			13 400	13 400				13 400	13 400	
Accruals/Prepayments					1 500	250			250	1 500
Net Profit							16 900			16 900
			31 150	31 150	1 500	250	185 400	185 400	162 850	162 850

factoring is a service whereby a debt factor will take over the responsibility for the collection of monies owed to a business. A fee is charged for this service and is deducted from the debts recovered before payment is made to the debtor. This service is designed to improve the *cash flow* of a business. The factor might provide:

- sales accounting – including maintaining the *sales ledger*, invoicing, sending out statements and collecting the debt
- credit management facilities – including assessment of customers' credit-worthiness
- finance against *sales invoices* – the factor will pay a large percentage of the total on issue of the sales invoice, with the balance being paid when the debtor settles the invoice

Factoring avoids valuable cash resources being tied up in allowing credit to customers. It guarantees a regular cash flow, and can save money that would normally have been spent on administration costs.

This service should not be confused with *invoice discounting*.

factory overhead expenses are costs incurred in the manufacturing process. They are also known as *indirect costs* which cannot be identified easily with the product being produced. (See also *overheads*.)

factory profit: see *manufacturing accounts*

favourable variances occur when actual results are better than the results predicted in a budget. If the actual results increase the profit that has been predicted in the budget, the variance is said to be a favourable variance. If, however, the variance reduces the profit that was predicted in the budget, then the variance would be adverse.

Favourable variances arise when:

- actual revenue is greater than budgeted revenue, or
- actual expenditure is less than budgeted expenditure.

(See *variances*.)

fictitious assets are assets that have no resale value, but are entered on the balance sheet. An example would be prepayments.

FIFO: see *methods of stock valuation*

final accounts is the name given to the *trading* and *profit and loss accounts* of a business. *Manufacturing accounts* are included in the term in the case of a business that produces its own goods for resale.

Some people also include the *balance sheet* as part of the final accounts. Technically, this is incorrect since the balance sheet is not an account, it is a compilation of the balances outstanding in the *books of account* at the business financial year end.

Finance Act is an Act of Parliament which confers, on the government of the day, the power to raise taxes. It is based on the Budget proposed each year by the Chancellor of the Exchequer.

financial accounting is the recording and presentation of business transactions in order to supply information to the owners of a business on the performance of their investment.

Financial Reporting Standards (FRS) are gradually replacing *Statements of Standard Accounting Practice (SSAP)*. Initially drafts for discussion (DDs) are circulated and later published as financial reporting exposure drafts (FREDs). (Note: neither FREDs nor DDs are assessed at GCE Advanced level or by AAT.)

Financial Services Act is the Act of Parliament which regulates the financial services industry in its dealings with the general public.

financial year is a twelve-month period for which a business prepares its *trading* and *profit and loss accounts*. The financial year can start at any date during the year.

first-in-first-out method of stock issue (FIFO): see methods of stock valuation

fixed asset register is a record of all the *fixed assets* owned by a business. It lists all the important facts about all the assets of the business. The register shows:

- date of *acquisition*
- description
- cost
- unique registration number of each fixed asset
- location of each fixed asset
- method of *depreciation* to be applied
- *aggregate depreciation* to date
- details of revaluations where necessary
- estimated useful life

and when disposed of:

- date
- proceeds
- authorisation for disposal

The total cost or valuation of all assets listed in the register should agree with the balance in the fixed asset accounts in the *general ledger*. Similarly, the totals of depreciation in the register should agree with the balances on the depreciation accounts in the general ledger.

The register is a detailed analysis of the fixed asset accounts. It is not part of the *double-entry bookkeeping* system; it is a memorandum book.

Physical checks of the assets held by a business should be made against the entries in the register.

fixed asset replacement reserve: a *revenue reserve* set aside out of profits to provide funds for the purchase of replacement assets in the future. It is essential that these funds are available in liquid form. The bookkeeping entries to record this transfer are:

Debit:	Profit and loss appropriation account	**Credit:**	Fixed asset replacement reserve

fixed assets are assets of a business which are held for more than one financial period. They are not purchased primarily to be resold; they are held to help generate profits for the business.

Fixed assets are listed in reverse order of *liquidity*, the most permanent coming first and ending with the fixed assets that can most easily be turned into cash. This is a typical list of fixed assets for a manufacturing business:

- land and buildings
- plant and machinery
- fixtures and fittings
- office equipment
- motor vehicles

Totals of fixed assets are usually shown in the *balance sheets* of *limited companies* under the headings:

- *tangible fixed assets*
- *intangible fixed assets*
- *investments*

The details are shown in the notes to the accounts; these include, for each type of asset:

- cost or valuation at the beginning and end of the year
- movements (purchases and sales)
- *depreciation* charge for the year, accumulated depreciation to date and the effect that any disposals have had on depreciation
- methods of depreciation used and the rates

fixed asset turnover ratio: the ratio of sales to *fixed assets*. If a business has fixed assets with a *net book value* of £100 000 and its annual turnover is £860 000, the fixed asset turnover ratio would be:

$$\text{FORMULA:} \quad \frac{\text{sales}}{\text{book value of fixed assets}} = \frac{860\ 000}{100\ 000}$$

$$= 8.6 \text{ times}$$

$$\text{or £116.3 per £1000 of sales}$$

This ratio measures the utilisation the business is obtaining from its investment in fixed assets. If the ratio is low compared with similar businesses, it would indicate that the managers may not be using their fixed assets to their full potential.

fixed budgets remain unchanged in the short run whatever output is achieved by the organisation.

fixed capital accounts do not change by the introduction of profits from the *partnership profit and loss appropriation account*. They remain fixed from year to year, unless there is a deliberate injection of new capital by a partner, or if a partner has the permission of other partners to withdraw capital.

Fixed capital accounts are almost a necessity if the partnership agreement allows the partners to be credited with interest on capital as part of their profit share.

Interest on fixed capital accounts is an appropriation of profits and should be credited to the partners' current accounts.

ISLE COLLEGE
RESOURCES CENTRE

III

fixed charge on the assets means that the *debentures* have as their security certain named assets of the company. This means that if the company were to go into *liquidation* the proceeds from the sale of the specific asset(s) would first of all be used to pay off the debenture holders. Any surplus remaining would be used to help pay any other creditors of the company.

fixed costs are costs which do not change with levels of a business's activities. They are also called *period costs*, as they are time based. Examples include indirect wages of supervisors, rent and rates. In the long run, fixed costs can change, for example the supervisory staff may get a pay rise, the landlord may put up the rent, the local authority may charge more for business rates.

fixed overheads are also known as *fixed costs*.

fixed production overhead variance shows the difference between the budgeted fixed production overhead and the actual fixed production overhead. Fixed production overheads are *fixed costs* incurred in a factory. These costs are absorbed into the product by using:

- a direct labour hour rate
- a direct labour cost rate, or
- a machine hour rate

(See *absorption*.)

The fixed production overhead variance has two subvariances:

- fixed production overhead expenditure variance, calculated as:

FORMULA: $\dfrac{\text{budgeted fixed}}{\text{production overhead}} - \dfrac{\text{actual fixed}}{\text{production overhead}}$

- fixed production overhead volume variance, calculated as:

FORMULA: $\dfrac{\text{standard}}{\text{absorbed cost}} - \dfrac{\text{budgeted fixed}}{\text{production overhead}}$

flexible budgets recognise that cost patterns may vary according to levels of activity. A *fixed budget* approach to *variable costs* can give very misleading results.

One of the aims of a standard costing system is that it should highlight areas of good practice and areas where problems are occurring. A standard costing system makes comparisons between standard costs and the costs actually incurred. It is always important when making comparisons of any description that like is compared with like. Standard costs need to be flexed in order to make valid comparisons.

Worked example: the manager of a business had budgeted to produce 480 000 pairs of trainers in a year. The standards set were:

square metres of material: 88 000   labour hours to be used: 12 000

The actual number of trainers produced was 420 000 pairs. Actual materials used were 85 000, and actual labour hours worked were 10 100.

Required:

A calculation to determine whether the business has been efficient in the use of materials and labour.

Solution:

Since the business produced only $\frac{7}{8}$ of the trainers set in the standard ($\frac{420\,000}{480\,000}$), one could reasonably expect that only $\frac{7}{8}$ of the materials set in the standard would be used and that only $\frac{7}{8}$ of the labour hours set in the standard would be needed to complete the work.

So $\frac{7}{8} \times 88\,000 = 77\,000$ m² of materials should have been used.

In fact 85 000 m² were used, so 8000 m² of materials have been wasted.

Similarly, $\frac{7}{8}$ of the standard labour hours should have been used. $\frac{7}{8} \times 12\,000 = 10\,500$ hours of labour.

In fact only 10 100 hours were used, so the labour force has been more efficient.

Standards should always be flexible to take into account variations in production levels.

---

floating charge on the assets means that *debentures* have as their security unspecified assets. If a company were to go into *liquidation*, proceeds from the sale of the assets would be used to pay the debenture holders.

fluctuating capital accounts show the amount of capital invested by each partner together with all residual profits and losses accrued to them. The accounts are credited with profits due to each partner, as calculated in the *profit and loss appropriation account.*

Worked example: Yusef and Mandy are in partnership. Their capital account balances on 1 June 19*6 are Yusef £45 000; Mandy £32 000. Their partnership agreement allows Mandy a partnership salary of £2000 per annum; it allows interest on capital of 8% per annum calculated on the balance at the start of the financial year; residual profits are to be shared in the ratio of 2:1 respectively. The profit for the year ended 31 May 19*7 was £52 400.

Partnership drawings for the year were Yusef £19 740; Mandy £ 17 891. The partnership maintains fluctuating capital accounts.

Required:
i) the partnership profit and loss appropriation account for the year ended 31 May 19*7 for Yusef and Mandy
ii) the partnership capital accounts as at 31 May 19*7

Solution:

i) **Yusef and Mandy profit and loss appropriation account for the year ended 31 May 19*7**

			£	
Net profit			52 400	
Less salary	– Mandy		2 000	
			50 400	
Less interest on capital	– Yusef	3 600		
	– Mandy	2 560	6 160	*cont'd*

44 240

	Yusef	Mandy		Yusef	Mandy
Share of residual profits – Yusef | 29 493 | | | |
– Mandy | 14 747 | | | 44 240 |

ii) ——————————————— Capital accounts ———————————————

	Yusef	Mandy		Yusef	Mandy
	£	£		£	£
Drawings	19 470	17 891	Balances b/d	45 000	32 000
			Salary		2 000
			Interest on capital	3 600	2 560
Balance c/d	58 623	33 416	Share of profits	29 493	14 747
	78 093	51 307		78 093	51 307
Balances b/d				58 623	33 416

FOB (free on board) is seen on import and export *invoices* indicating that the quoted price does not include shipping costs. All expenses are paid by the supplier only until the goods are on board.

FOB shipping point appears on import and export *invoices* and means that the supplier pays all costs until the goods are taken off the ship in the country of destination. The customer then pays any further transportation costs.

folio columns are an aid to help find the other account in the *double-entry bookkeeping* system. A ledger account is laid out like this:

Date	Details	Folio	Amount	Date	Details	Folio	Amount
			£				£
3 Jan	Cash	* cb 12	176	21 Dec	Purchases	**gl 31	180
3 Jan	Disc Rec	***gl 9	4				

Other entries	*	credit entry	cash column	cb 12	cash book page 12
	**	debit entry	purchases account	gl 31	general ledger page 31
	***	credit entry	discount received account	gl 9	general ledger page 9

folios are the numbers on the pages of *books of account.*

foreign currency translation SSAP 20 deals with the need to translate the value of assets held or liabilities owed in another country into £s. The standard sets out clear rules for dealing with the problem of which rate of exchange to use. Assets and liabilities should be translated using the exchange rate as it stood when the transaction took place. Monetary assets and liabilities should be translated at the rate prevailing at the *balance sheet date.* Any exchange gains or losses on settled transactions should be reported as part of the profit or loss arising from ordinary activities.

SSAP 20 also makes a distinction between the accounting procedures that should be applied when dealing with an individual company, and those that apply when preparing group accounts.

foreign exchange reserve: a *revenue reserve* set aside out of profits to guard against a loss incurred through the devaluation of a foreign currency. The bookkeeping entries to record this transfer are:

Debit:	Profit and loss appropriation account	Credit:	Foreign exchange reserve

forfeiture of shares takes place when a *shareholder* fails to pay the calls on the shares purchased when they fall due. It is now extremely rare. A shareholder who could not afford to pay the calls would normally sell the partly paid shares and the purchaser would then become liable for the calls.

When shares are forfeit, the shares are cancelled and, provided the company's *Articles of Association* do not prevent it, the company may reissue them. The original shareholder will lose any monies that have been paid. The bookkeeping entries can be followed in the worked example below.

Note: this is no longer assessed by all examination bodies, therefore you should check your syllabus to determine whether your course requires knowledge of this procedure.

Worked example: Lemmon plc is issuing 40 000 ordinary shares of £1 each, payable 10p on application, 20p on allotment, 30p on first call and 40p on final call. Applications are received with the appropriate monies. All allotment monies are received on the due date.

Bert Hinkle, the holder of 400 shares, fails to pay the first and final calls. His shares are forfeit. Later the shares are reissued to Lesley Peacock at 90p per share. She pays in full for the shares.

Required:

The journal entries (including cash transactions) to record the share issue, the forfeiture and the reissue of the shares in the books of Lemmon plc.

Solution:

Journal

	Dr £	Cr £
Cash	4 000	
Application and allotment		4 000
Cash	8 000	
Application and allotment		8 000
Application and allotment	12 000	
Ordinary share capital		12 000
Cash	11 880	
First call		11 880
First call	12 000	
Ordinary share capital		12 000
Forfeit shares	120	
First call		120
Cash	15 840	
Final call		15 840

cont'd

| Final call | 16 000 | |
| Ordinary share capital | | 16 000 |

| Forfeit shares | 160 | |
| Final call | | 160 |

| Ordinary share capital | 400 | |
| Forfeit shares | | 400 |

| Lesley Peacock | 400 | |
| Ordinary share capital | | 400 |

| Cash | 360 | |
| Lesley Peacock | | 360 |

| Forfeit shares | 40 | |
| Lesley Peacock | | 40 |

| Forfeit shares | 80 | |
| Share premium | | 80 |

format 1 and format 2 layouts for the published profit and loss account of a limited company are prescribed in the *Companies Act 1985*. Before the Act became law, companies could produce their own version of *published accounts* provided that disclosure requirements were observed.

There are, in fact, four profit and loss formats allowed. Formats 3 and 4 are horizontal versions of formats 1 and 2 and are rarely seen in practice.

Once the format has been chosen it should be used each year unless the *directors* of the company decide that a change is necessary.

Format 1	Format 2
1 Turnover	1 Turnover
2 Cost of sales	2 Change in stocks of finished goods and work in progress
3 Gross profit	3 Own work capitalised
4 Distribution costs	4 Other operating income
5 Administration expenses	5 (a) Raw materials and consumables
	(b) Other external charges
6 Other operating income	6 Staff costs (a) wages and salaries
	(b) social security costs
	(c) other pension costs
	7 (a) Depreciation and other amounts written off tangible and intangible fixed assets
	(b) Exceptional amounts written off current assets
	8 Other operating charges
7 Income from shares in group companies	9 Income from shares in group companies
8 Income from shares in related companies	10 Income from shares in related companies
9 Income from other fixed asset investments	11 Income from other fixed asset investments

10 Other interest receivable and similar income

11 Amounts written off investments

12 Interest payable and similar charges

13 Tax on profit or loss on ordinary activities

14 Profit or loss on ordinary activities after taxation

15 Extraordinary income

16 Extraordinary charges

17 Extraordinary profit or loss

18 Tax on extraordinary profit or loss

19 Other taxes not shown under the above items

20 Profit or loss for the financial year

12 Other interest receivable and similar income

13 Amounts written off investments

14 Interest payable and similar charges

15 Tax on profit or loss on ordinary activities

16 Profit or loss on ordinary activities after taxation

17 Extraordinary income

18 Extraordinary charges

19 Extraordinary profit or loss

20 Tax on extraordinary profit or loss

21 Other taxes not shown under the above items

22 Profit or loss for the financial year

Format 2 does not show *gross profit* but requires more detail in certain areas.

formation expenses: expenses incurred by a company when it comes into existence. They must be written off in a company's first *accounting period*.

forward buying: the purchase of materials, commodities or currency to be delivered at some date in the future.

founders shares are also known as *deferred shares*.

free on board: see *FOB*

fringe benefits are items given to employees in addition to their salary or wage. The benefits could include a company car, private medical insurance, etc. Sometimes colloquially called 'perks'.

FRS 1: see *cash-flow statements*

FRS 2: see *accounting for subsidiary undertakings*

FRS 3: see *reporting financial performance*

FRS 4: see *capital instruments*

FRS 5: see *reporting the substance of transactions*

FRS 6: see *acquisitions and mergers*

FRS 8: see *related party disclosures*

full-cost pricing allocates all manufacturing costs to products. It also values unsold stocks of finished goods at their total cost of manufacture. This is in line with *stocks and long-term contracts SSAP 9*. Full-cost pricing is also known as *absorption costing*.

fund flow statements identify any movements in assets, liabilities and capital that have taken place during the financial year, and the effects that these changes have had on net liquid funds. They used to be an obligatory part of a company's *annual report*, but have not been required since *cash-flow statements FRS 1* came into operation for reporting periods ending on or after 23 March 1992.

future differential costs: costs which 'belong' to a project and would be avoided if the project were not undertaken. These should be the only costs considered when deciding between two or more alternative strategies.

G

Garner v Murray (1904) rule applies if one or more partners are unable to settle their debt to a *partnership* after dissolution. Any debit balance occurring on a *partnership capital account* after dissolution should be settled by the partner(s) introducing money from private resources outside the business. If the partner(s) is unable to do this because of his/her insolvency, the deficiency is to be shared between the other partners in the ratio of the balances in their capital accounts shown in the last *partnership balance sheet.*

Worked example: George, Harriet and Iris were in partnership sharing profits and losses in the ratios 3:2:1 respectively. The partnership was dissolved. After the realisation of all the partnership assets the following balances remained in the partnership books:

		Dr £	Cr £
Capitals	George		26 432
	Harriet	6 340	
	Iris		14 884
Bank balance		34 976	

Harriet was unable to settle any part of her deficiency on capital account. Before dissolution the capital account balances were:

George	50 000
Harriet	2 000
Iris	30 000

Required:

A calculation showing how the deficiency on Harriet's capital account is cleared.

Solution:

George will have to bear $\dfrac{£50\ 000}{£50\ 000 + 30\ 000} \times £6340 = £3962.50$

Iris will have to bear $\dfrac{£30\ 000}{£50\ 000 + 30\ 000} \times £6340 = £2377.50$

---

gearing is the ratio of fixed interest bearing capital to the company's total capital. It shows the proportions of capital provided by the owners of a business and the proportions provided by others. The calculation is:

FORMULA: $\dfrac{\text{fixed-cost capital}}{\text{total capital}}$

which is:

$$\dfrac{\text{long-term loans} + \text{preference shares}}{\text{issued ordinary share capital} + \text{all reserves} + \text{long-term loans} + \text{preference shares}}$$

More than 50 %	Less than 50%
High geared companies	Low geared companies
High debt	Low debt
High risk	Low risk

Worked example: the following balances have been extracted from the books of account of two separate businesses:

	Gooi plc	Tomkins plc
	£000	£000
Ordinary shares	1000	60
Reserves	980	110
Preference shares	450	
8% debentures	300	50
Long-term bank loan		250

Required:

Calculate the gearing ratio for Gooi plc and Tomkins plc.

Solution:

$$\text{Gooi plc} = \frac{450 + 300}{1000 + 980 + 450 + 300} = \frac{750}{2730} \times 100 = 27.47\%\text{: low geared}$$

$$\text{Tomkins plc} = \frac{50 + 250}{60 + 110 + 50 + 250} = \frac{300}{470} \times 100 = 63.8\%\text{: high geared}$$

A company with a high proportion of fixed interest, long-term capital (high geared) must service the debt whatever its profit level. In times when the company earns good profits, a highly geared company will have few problems servicing the debt, but when profits are low (or negative) the fixed return funding has still to be serviced and this may put the future of the company at risk.

gearing adjustment was required by SSAP 16 (*current cost accounting*). It tried to measure the *shareholders*' gain arising from the fact that when long-term borrowings were to be repaid in the future, the repayment would be in depreciated currency.

gearing ratio: see *gearing*

general ledger contains all impersonal ledger accounts. Entries in *personal accounts* are recorded in the *sales* and *purchase ledgers*. In practice, some accounts that should be in the general ledger are kept separately. For example, the cash account and the bank account might be kept in the *cash book* because they are used so frequently. Also, a business person may keep his/her capital account, loan accounts and drawings accounts in a *private ledger* to which he/she alone has access.

General ledger accounts can be classified into:

- *real accounts* – the accounts where transactions dealing with *tangible fixed assets* are recorded, e.g. land and buildings, vehicles
- *nominal accounts* – where revenues and expenses are recorded, e.g. wages, rent, etc.

The general ledger is called the *nominal ledger* in computer programs.

general reserve: a *revenue reserve* appropriated from profits to strengthen the financial position of a company. The bookkeeping entries to record this transfer are:

| Debit: | Profit and loss appropriation account | Credit: | General reserve |

going-concern concept states that a business is assumed to be continuing in existence for the foreseeable future. *Disclosure of accounting policies (SSAP 2)* identifies this as one of four fundamental *accounting concepts* (the others being *accruals concept, consistency* and *prudence*).

The major consequence of the going-concern concept is that assets are valued at cost, not what they would fetch if sold (as a going concern, a business will need its assets and is therefore not going to sell them).

going-rate pricing means that a business may be a price taker where large numbers of producers are selling a very similar product. No one producer is large enough to dominate the market and be able to set a higher price.

In a market dominated by a price leader, the smaller producer(s) may have to accept a price for the product that is lower than that dictated by the leader.

goods for own use are goods taken from a business for private consumption by a *sole trader* (or partners in a *partnership*). The business resources withdrawn by the owner(s) of a business for private use are *drawings*.

Worked example: David Patel owns a clothing shop. During August he took £163 clothing from the business for his own use. He also made private telephone calls amounting to £16.

Required:

Journal entries to record the above transactions in David Patel's books of account.

Solution:

Journal

	Dr £	Cr £
Drawings	163	
Purchases		163
Drawings	16	
Telephone charges		16

---

goods in transit have been sent to a branch from head office, but have not yet been received at the branch. This means that the branch current account in the head office *books of account* will not replicate the head office current account in the branch's records. The two accounts need to be the same in order to cancel each other out when the business's *final accounts* are prepared.

Goods in transit are entered as a balance on the credit side of the branch current account, and brought down as a debit balance to start the next *accounting period*.

For a worked example, see *branch accounts*.

goods received note: a document recording items that have been received into stores or a warehouse. In reality, it is often a book (goods received book) rather than a document. It provides a full list of all goods received. A copy is sent to the accounts department where it is compared to the supplier's *invoice* when it is received.

goodwill: see *accounting for goodwill SSAP 22*

goodwill, basis of valuation: the accepted factors that can be taken into account when arriving at a value for the *goodwill* of a business. What is acceptable to the parties involved in the transaction will depend on the type of business in question. Methods used to value goodwill include:

- average weekly sales for the previous accounting period × an agreed figure
- gross annual fees × an agreed figure
- average annual net profit × an agreed figure
- *super profits* × an agreed figure

The agreed multiple has to be acceptable to the parties involved in the purchase of the business.

grants are monies given by the European Community, central government or a local authority to a business towards expenditure incurred or to be incurred. The grant may be given for *capital expenditure* purposes or for *revenue expenditure*. (See *accounting for government grants SSAP 4*.)

gross loss occurs when the *cost of sales* is greater than the net sales.

gross profit is calculated by deducting the *cost of sales* from the net sales figure. The calculation takes place in the *trading account* of a business.

gross profit margin: also known as the *margin*.

gross profit mark-up: also known as the *mark-up*.

group accounts are prepared when two or more companies are controlled by a single management team and the businesses act as one. The *holding company* must produce a set of final accounts like any other *limited company*. In addition, to comply with statutory requirements, a set of final accounts must be prepared for the group as a whole entity. (See *consolidated balance sheet* and *consolidated profit and loss account*.)

group undertaking is the term used in the *Companies Act 1985* for a *subsidiary company*.

guaranteed minimum wage ensures by legislation that workers' pay per hour cannot fall below a set level.

Halsey premium bonus scheme is used to reward *direct labour* for saving time in the production process. This method rewards the worker with a payment based on 50 per cent of the time saved.

Worked example: Philip is paid at the rate of £6.00 per hour. The time allowed to complete a task is 20 hours. The actual time taken by Philip to complete the task is 17 hours.

Required:

Calculate the gross pay due to Philip using the Halsey premium bonus scheme after completing the task.

Solution:

$$£$$

Philip's gross pay for the task = 111.00

(17 hours × £6.00 + 1.5 hours bonus × £6.00 (half of the 3 hours saved))

Halsey–Wier premium bonus scheme is a variation on the *Halsey premium bonus scheme,* but instead of a bonus based on 50 per cent of the time saved, the bonus is based on 30 per cent of the time saved.

Worked example: Tim is paid at the rate of £8.00 per hour. The time allowed to complete a task is 26 hours. The actual time taken by Tim to complete the task is 24 hours.

Required:

Calculate the gross pay due to Tim using the Halsey–Wier premium bonus scheme after completing the task.

Solution:

$$£$$

Tim's gross pay for the task = 196.80

(24 hours × £8.00 + 3/5ths hour bonus × £8.00 (30% of the 2 hours saved))

---

hardware is the generic term used to describe the machine parts of a computer. The hardware of a computer system consists of:

- microprocessor – containing the circuits and chips which are capable of storing and manipulating data
- keyboard – enables the operator to input data and to give instructions to the computer
- monitor – the television-like screen which allows the operator to see information stored in the microprocessor

- disk drive – reads the information that is stored on the hard disk and the floppy disks
- printer – produces printouts (hard copy)

head office: the main administrative headquarters of a business. One would normally find the more senior staff based at head office.

head office maintaining branch accounts: see *branch accounts*

high day rates is a time-based method of paying workers. Higher hourly rates of pay are paid to workers than would normally be paid. This method of pay is designed to attract top quality workers. These workers should be able to work more effectively and more efficiently, so the firm should benefit through increased productivity.

high-street banks are the main British banks which accept deposits from customers and allow withdrawals by customers from their bank accounts.

hire purchase allows goods to pass to a 'customer' while the title (ownership) of the goods remains with the seller until the last payment, plus a small purchase fee, has been paid. The purchaser is in fact hiring the goods until the final payment has been made.

The following example shows the bookkeeping entries when an asset is purchased under a hire-purchase agreement.

Worked example: Peters & Co. purchases a machine for a hire-purchase price of £18 090 from Duck plc on 1 January 19*5. The agreement provides that three instalments of £6030 be paid on 31 December 19*5, 19*6 and 19*7. The true rate of interest is 10% and the cash price of the machine is £15 000.

Required:

Show:
i) the supplier's account
ii) the machinery account
iii) the hire purchase interest account.

Solution:

Duck plc

19*5			19*5		
31 Dec Cash	6 030		1 Jan	Machinery	15 000
31 Dec Bal c/d	10 470		31 Dec HP interest		1 500
	16 500				16 500
19*6			19*6		
31 Dec Cash	6 030		1 Jan	Bal b/d	10 470
31 Dec Bal c/d	5 487		31 Dec HP interest		1 047
	11 517				11 517
19*7			19*7		
31 Dec Cash	6 030		1 Jan	Bal b/d	5 487
			31 Dec HP interest		543
	6 030				6 030

This amount has been rounded down

Machinery

19*5	
1 Jan Duck plc 15 000	

Hire purchase interest

19*5	19*5	
31 Dec Duck plc 1 500	31 Dec P & L a/c	1 500
19*6	19*6	
31 Dec Duck plc 1 047	31 Dec P & L a/c	1 047
19*7	19*7	
31 Dec Duck plc 543	31 Dec P & L a/c	543

(See also *accounting for leases and hire-purchase contracts SSAP 21.*)

historic cost accounting is the traditional way of accounting whereby all financial transactions are recorded using the actual cost of purchase. The advantages of using historic cost as a basis for preparing accounts are:

- it is objective
- it is easily understood
- it is easily applied to the double-entry system
- auditors find verification fairly straightforward
- it is recognised by the Inland Revenue

holding company owns more than 50 per cent of the *ordinary shares* in a *subsidiary company*. For example:

Masters Ltd has an issued share capital of 400 000 ordinary shares of £1 each. Driscoll plc acquires 210 000 of the shares in Masters Ltd for £437 700.

Since Driscoll plc owns more than 50% of the issued share capital of Masters Ltd, Driscoll plc is the holding company, Masters Ltd is its subsidiary company.

Extracts from each company's balance sheet would show:

Driscoll plc balance sheet as at 31 December 19*7

	£
Investment in subsidiary at cost	437 700

Masters Ltd balance sheet as at 31 December 19*7

Ordinary share capital	400 000

Note:

It is not obvious from looking at Masters Ltd balance sheet who are the owners of the ordinary shares.

holding costs are the costs of holding stocks of goods. It is composed of storage costs, storekeepers' wages, insurance costs, interest on capital tied up in the stocks being held and any other costs involved in holding stocks.

horizontal financial analysis compares each component in the financial statements of a business over a two-year period. For example:

If sales in 19*6 were £768 000 and in 19*7 they were £812 000, the percentage change is 5.73% $\dfrac{(44\,000)}{(768\,000)}$

If net operating expenses in 19*6 were 134 000 and in 19*7 they rose to £141 000, the percentage change is 5.2% $\dfrac{(7\,000)}{(134\,000)}$

Although the actual calculations are fairly straightforward, the skill in gaining management knowledge relies on the ability to interpret and analyse the changes shown. This enables remedial action to be taken if results indicate that this is necessary. (See also *vertical financial analysis.*)

horizontal presentation of final accounts means that the *trading* and *profit and loss accounts* are shown with a debit side and a credit side. This is how they appear in the *general ledger,* where they are used to close down the *nominal accounts.* Modern practice generally shows the *final accounts* of a business in a vertical format.

The horizontal presentation of a profit and loss account could look like this:

Theresa O' Malley profit and loss account for the year ended 31 March 19*7

		£		£
Wages		43 876	Gross profit	170 419
Rent and rates		9 451	Discounts received	504
Discounts allowed		705	Rent received	1 500
Insurances		2 577		
Advertising		650		
Bad debts		191		
Provision for doubtful debts		48		
Provision for depreciation:				
Machinery	350			
Office equip't	120	470		
Net profit		114 455		
		172 423		172 423

(See also *vertical presentation of final accounts.*)

human resource accounting has attempted to incorporate the value of managers and workers into traditional accounting statements. The difficulty encountered is one of objectivity. What value does one put on a good boss or a good worker? Who does the valuation?

ideal standards are based on the assumption that production can be carried out in perfect conditions. They are also known as potential standards. The *CIMA* definition of an ideal standard is one that 'can be attained under the most favourable conditions, with no allowance for normal losses, waste and machine downtime'.

Many managers consider that the setting of ideal standards can demotivate staff.

idle time: see *time sheet*

impersonal accounts: accounts which do not relate to a person or business. They are found in the *general ledger*. They can be divided into:

- *real accounts* – the accounts where transactions dealing with *tangible fixed assets* are recorded, e.g. plant and machinery, office equipment, etc.
- *nominal accounts* – where revenues and expenses are recorded, e.g. insurances, advertising, etc.

imprest system is the system used to maintain a *petty cash book*. A set amount of money (the float) is given to the petty cashier. The petty cashier pays out small amounts of money as the need arises for postages, travelling expenses, office sundries, etc. When the float gets low the petty cashier receives money from the main cashier to restore the float to the original set amount. (See *petty cash book*.)

incentive bonus: extra pay given to workers to encourage them to work harder.

incentive payment schemes offer extra pay to workers to make them work more efficiently. (See *premium bonus pay schemes, Halsey premium bonus pay scheme, Halsey–Weir premium bonus pay scheme* and *Rowan premium bonus scheme*.)

income and expenditure account: the name given to the *profit and loss account* of a non-trading organisation. The expenditure is shown on the debit side of the account and the incomes are shown on the credit side.

The income and expenditure account can be presented in a vertical format. Incomes are listed and total expenditure is deducted, giving either a surplus (excess of income over expenditure) or a deficit (excess of expenditure over income).

For the preparation of an income and expenditure account, see *club accounts*.

income in advance is shown in the *balance sheet* as a creditor. It represents monies that have been paid by a debtor before the due date.

Worked example: Tom McDonald has a financial year end on 28 February each year. He sublets part of his premises to James Janowski. The rental is £1200 per quarter payable in advance. James' first payment is due on 1 January 19*7; he pays on 6 January 19*7.

Required:

A profit and loss account extract for Tom McDonald for the year ended 28 February 19*7, and an extract from a balance sheet as at that date.

Solution:

Tom McDonald profit and loss account extract for the year ended 28 February 19*7

	£
Gross profit	*****
Add rent receivable	800

Balance sheet extract as at 28 February 19*7:

Current liabilities
Rent receivable paid in advance   400

income outstanding is shown on the *balance sheet* as a debtor. It represents monies that are owed by a debtor at the due date.

Worked example: Ravi Lall has a financial year end on 30 June each year. He sublets part of his premises to Angus Lefevre. The rental is £3000 per quarter payable in advance. The first payment is due on 1 January 19*7; subsequent payments are to be made on 1 April, 1 July and 1 October. Angus paid his rent on 27 January 19*7 and has yet to make another payment.

Required:

An extract from the profit and loss account of Ravi Lall for the year ended 30 June 19*7 and an extract from the balance as at that date.

Solution:

Ravi Lall profit and loss account extract for the year ended 30 June 19*7

	£
Gross profit	*****
Add rent receivable	6000

Balance sheet extract as at 30 June 19*7

Current assets
Rent receivable owing   3000

income tax: an annual tax on a person's income. The annual plan of how taxes are to be raised (together with planned government expenditure) is outlined in the Budget presented to Parliament each year. The proposals are made law through the resultant *Finance Act*.

Income tax is administered by the Board of Inland Revenue, which is also responsible for *corporation tax* and *capital gains tax*. Routine administration throughout the country is carried out in 'districts'. The head of each district is an Inspector of Taxes who quantifies each person's liability. This now follows the process of self-assessment in the case of many taxpayers. When a person's tax liability is agreed, the tax is paid to the Collector of Taxes.

incomplete records: the generic term used to describe organisations that do not keep a full double-entry set of financial records. These organisations tend to be:

- small businesses that do most of their business on a cash basis
- clubs and societies (see *club accounts*)

As with the preparation of the *final accounts* of clubs and societies, there are four key stages used when preparing the accounts of cash-based businesses:

- prepare an opening *statement of affairs* (similar to an opening *balance sheet*)
- prepare a summary of the business bank account (often given in a question) and a cash summary
- prepare adjustment accounts (to take into account the *accruals concept*)
- prepare the final accounts

Worked example: Helmut Schott owns a delicatessen. He does not keep proper books of account. He supplies you with the following information for his financial year ended 31 August 19*7:

Summarised bank account for the year ended 31 August 19*7

	£		£
Balance 1 September 19*6	1 042	Payments to creditors	41 671
Takings banked	93 004	Wages	24 533
		Rent	4 000
		Rates	1 200
		Drawings	12 000
		Other business expenses	9 719
		Balance 31 August 19*7	923
	94 046		94 046

All business takings were paid into the bank with the exception of:

	£
Stationery	670
Drawings	2 693

The following additional information is also available at 31 August:

	19*6	19*7
	£	£
Stock	567	814
Debtors	437	210
Creditors	1 720	2 181
Rent owed	200	300
Rates prepaid	48	112
Fixtures at valuation	10 000	9 000
Vehicle at valuation	6 000	3 000
Cash in hand	181	149

Required:

A trading and profit and loss account for the year ended 31 August 19*7 and a balance sheet as at that date for Helmut Schott.

Solution:

Stage 1 – prepare an opening statement of affairs. (Do this quickly as it is not part of the answer it is part of your working papers – the order in which you list your assets and liabilities is not important.)

		£
Assets –	bank	1 042
	stock	567
	debtors	437
	rates paid in advance	48
	fixtures	10 000
	vehicle	6 000
	cash	181
		18 275
Liabilities –	creditors	(1 720)
rent owed		(200)
Capital – 1 September 19*7		16 355

Stage 2 – prepare a bank account – no need; this is given in the question. Prepare a cash summary.

	£		£
Balance 1 September 19*6	181	Stationery	670
Cash takings (missing figure)	3 331	Drawings	2 693
		Balance 31 August 19*7	149
	3 512		3 512
Balance 1 September 19*7	149		

Stage 3 – prepare adjustment accounts,

Debtors adjustment

Balance b/d	437	Cash	93 004
Trading a/c			
(missing			
figure)	92 777	Balance c/d	210
	93 214		93 214
Balance b/d	210		

Creditors adjustment

Cash	41 671	Balance b/d	1 720
		Trading a/c	
		(missing	
Balance c/d	2 181	figure)	42 132
	43 852		43 852
		Balance b/d	2 181

Rent

Cash	4 000	Balance b/d	200
Balance c/d	300	P&L (missing)	4 100
	4 300		4 300
		Balance b/d	300

Rates

Balance b/d	48	P&L(missing)	1 136
Cash	1 200	Balance c/d	112
	1 248		1 248
Balance b/d	112		

Stage 4 – preparation of final accounts – at last – what the question asked for. Up to now no marks have been scored but all the hard work has been done.

Helmut Schott trading and profit and loss account for the year ended 31 August 19*7

	£	£
Sales (92 777 + 3331)		96 108
Less cost of sales		
Stock 1 September 19*6	567	
Purchases	42 132	
	42 699	
Less stock 31 August 19*7	814	41 885
Gross profit		54 223
Less expenses		
Wages	24 533	
Rent	4 100	
Rates	1 136	
Stationery	670	
Other business expenses	9 719	
Depreciation – fixtures	1 000	
vehicle	3 000	44 158
Net profit		10 065

Balance sheet as at 31 August 19*7

		£	£
Fixed assets –	Fixtures	10 000	
	Less depreciation	1 000	9 000
	Vehicle	6 000	
	Less depreciation	3 000	3 000
			12 000
Current assets			
Stock		814	
Debtors		210	
Bank		923	
Cash		149	
Rates paid in advance		112	
		2 208	
Less current liabilities			
Creditors	2 181		
Rent owed	300	2 481	(273)
			11 727
Capital			16 355
Add profit			10 065
			26 420
Less drawings (12 000 + 2693)			14 693
			11 727

incremental costs are the extra costs incurred when the level of activity increases within a business. Incremental costs are generally *variable costs* but in some cases an increase in activity may need to be supported by additional *fixed costs*, e.g. the rental of another workshop or the purchase of additional machinery.

Incremental costing shows the difference in costs which results from different levels of a business's activities. (See also *marginal costing*.)

incremental salary scales give the employee regular annual salary increases, as in the teaching profession, the police force, etc.

indirect costs: are expenses which cannot be identified directly to the end-product. They are also known as factory overheads. They include *indirect labour costs* and *indirect material costs*.

indirect expenses are any factory expenses that are not directly identifiable with the final product. Examples include factory rent and rates, *depreciation* of factory machinery, etc. They appear as factory overheads in a *manufacturing account*.

indirect labour costs are the costs involved in employing staff whose work cannot be directly identified with the final product. Examples include wages paid to maintenance engineers, the wages of supervisory staff, etc. These costs appear as factory overheads in a *manufacturing account*.

indirect material costs are the costs incurred in acquiring materials which cannot be directly identified with the final product. Examples include factory cleaning materials, machine lubricating oil, etc. These costs appear as factory overheads in a *manufacturing account*.

inflation is a sustained increase in the general level of prices within an economy.

inflation accounting was introduced after the British economy experienced high levels of inflation in the late 1960s and early 1970s. Many people were concerned that the use of *historic cost accounting* was not giving a *true and fair view* of the financial state of businesses. The result of this concern was the issue of SSAP 7 accounting for changes in the purchasing power of money by the *Accounting Standards Committee*.

information technology (IT) is the use of technology to acquire, store, process and distribute information. The technology used includes computers and telecommunications equipment.

input tax is the *VAT* that a business pays to a supplier, based on the total *invoice* price less any cash discount that might be available for prompt payment. The purchaser can claim this tax back.

insolvent: the term applied to a person (or business) who is unable to settle debts when they fall due.

insolvent partner: see *Garner v Murray (1904)*

intangible assets: non-physical assets, i.e. assets which cannot be seen or touched. Examples include *goodwill*, brand names and patents.

integrated accounting system: defined by *CIMA* as 'a set of accounting records which provides financial and cost accounts using a common input of data for all accounting purposes'.

integrated system of branch accounting uses a branch stock adjustment account to calculate the gross profit earned by a branch. (See *branch accounts*.)

interest is the charge made by a lender on a loan. A borrower has to pay for the use of the money borrowed. Interest is calculated as a percentage of the sum. (See *annual percentage rate*, *compound interest* and *simple interest*.)

interest cover measures a business's ability to service its long-term borrowing out of profits. A low interest cover would indicate to *shareholders* that *dividends* might be in jeopardy if profits are not maintained. The calculation is:

FORMULA: $\dfrac{\text{profit before interest and tax}}{\text{interest payable}}$

Worked example: James Hilton Ltd's profits before interest and tax are £160 000. Interest payments are £14 000 per annum.

Required:

Calculate the interest cover for James Hilton Ltd.

Solution:

$$\text{interest cover} = \frac{\text{profit before interest and tax}}{\text{interest payable}} = \frac{£160\,000}{£14\,000} = 11.42 \text{ times}$$

---

interest on partners' capital accounts is an appropriation of the profits of a *partnership*. It skews the profits towards the partner(s) who has more capital invested in the business.

It should be emphasised that this is not interest like that earned on a bank deposit account. Interest on capital is part of the way that partnership profits may be divided. Partners should not be credited with interest on capital as a right – it must be part of the *partnership agreement*.

Interest on capital should be credited to the partners' current accounts. The bookkeeping entries are:

Debit: Profit and loss appropriation account   **Credit:** Partners' current accounts

interest on partners' drawings can be included in a *partnership agreement*. It is an attempt to deter partners from drawing out too much cash in the early part of the financial year. The bookkeeping entries are:

Debit: Partners' current account   **Credit:** Profit and loss appropriation account

interest payments are a revenue expense. They should be shown in the business *profit and loss account*. *Capital repayments* reduce the amount shown as outstanding on the *balance sheet*.

inter-firm comparisons of financial results can be used by managers as a performance indicator, or by potential investors as a means of deciding which business to invest in.

Inter-firm comparisons have value only if:

- the firms are in the same line of business – it would not be sensible to compare the financial results of a furniture manufacturer with the financial results of a motor vehicle manufacturer
- they use the same *accounting bases* – it would not be sensible to compare the financial results of a business whose managers used *straight line methods* of depreciating their *fixed assets*, used *AVCO* to value closing stocks, and *pro-*

vided for bad debts at a rate of 5 per cent on debtors with a business using *reducing balance methods* of depreciation, using *FIFO* as the method for valuing closing stocks, and *providing for doubtful debts* at the rate of 1 per cent on debtors

- the businesses have a similar structure – it would not be sensible to compare the financial results of Jane Dixon's corner shop selling groceries with the results of Tesco

An effort must be made to ensure that, as far as possible, 'like with like' comparisons are made. Even so, it could be argued that this is impossible because each firm has:

- a different set of managers
- a different workforce
- a different set of market circumstances

interlocking accounts are defined by *CIMA* as 'a system in which the cost accounts are distinct from the financial accounts, the two sets of accounts being kept continuously in agreement by the use of *control accounts* or reconciled by other means'.

internal audit: see *audit*

internal auditor is a member of staff who examines in detail the efficiency of a business and how systems are being operated within the business. The results are checked against standards prescribed in the business's *strategic plan* or departmental action plans.

The results of the audit should enable managers to identify areas of weakness, which can be targetted for improvement. It can also highlight areas of good practice which could be adapted to make other parts of the business more efficient.

internal financing means obtaining or conserving cash resources from within a business. This can be done by:

- retaining profits ('ploughing back')
- running stocks down if possible without jeopardising future orders
- better credit control
- selling surplus *fixed assets*

internal rate-of-return method of capital investment appraisal takes the *time value of money* into account when making a *capital investment appraisal*. The internal rate of return represents the true interest rate earned by the investment over the course of its economic life. It is the discount rate that will cause the *net present value* of the investment to be zero.

The internal rate of return can be found by trial and error, by guessing a number of discount factors until the correct guess gives a net present value of zero.

Worked example: the cost of capital for Damansara plc is 14%. The managers are considering a three-year project which will cost £100 000. The net cash flows from the project are expected to be:

	£
Year 1	40 000
Year 2	60 000
Year 3	80 000

**ISLE COLLEGE
RESOURCES CENTRE**

The following are extracts from the present value tables for £1:

	12%	14%	15%	16%	18%
Year 1	0.893	0.877	0.870	0.862	0.847
Year 2	0.797	0.769	0.756	0.743	0.718
Year 3	0.712	0.675	0.658	0.641	0.609

Required:

Calculate the internal rate of return on the new project being considered by Damansara plc.

Solution:

Let us try 12%:

	Cash flows £	Present value factor	Net present value £
Year 0 (now)	(100 000)	1	(100 000)
Year 1	40 000	0.893	35 720
Year 2	45 000	0.797	35 865
Year 3	50 000	0.712	35 600
			7 185

The return is positive, so the internal rate of return is greater than 12%. Let us try 18%:

Year 0	(100 000)	1	(100 000)
Year 1	40 000	0.847	33 880
Year 2	45 000	0.718	32 310
Year 3	50 000	0.609	30 450
			(3 360)

The return is negative, so the internal rate of return is less than 18%. Let us try 16%:

Year 0	(100 000)	1	(100 000)
Year 1	40 000	0.862	34 480
Year 2	45 000	0.743	33 435
Year 3	50 000	0.641	32 050
			(35)

The return is negative, but only just, so the internal rate of return is just below 16%.

The project should be undertaken since the return on the project exceeds Damansara plc's cost of capital.

International Accounting Standards (IAS) are *accounting standards* which have been issued by the *International Accounting Standards Committee* and are applicable internationally. This is to enable the users of accounts to be able to make judgements and comparisons based on the results of businesses from a range of countries.

International Accounting Standards Committee (IASC) is a committee of accountants from many different countries whose brief is to try to harmonise the way that accounts are presented throughout the world.

interpretation of accounts is an attempt to explain what has happened to a business and to predict what might happen to the business in the future. The process must be careful and methodical. Data must be collected, ratios calculated and trends observed. Only then can analysis begin.

It can prove to be a very difficult task, since most users of accounts do not have access to the 'full' picture. They may have to use a set of *published accounts*. In order to interpret the results shown by the ratios and trends, a series of questions need to be answered:

- Has *profitability* increased or decreased?
- Has the sales margin increased or decreased?
- Has the proportion of turnover used to pay expenses increased or decreased?
- Has the *return on capital employed* increased or decreased?
- Are the changes due to increased profitability or to increased injections of capital?
- Has increased capital employed been as a result of internal financing or because of external financing?
- How has the *liquidity* position of the business changed?

These are just some of the questions that will help to interpret the calculations used in *ratio analysis*.

inventory is an American expression for *stocks*.

investment analysts are employed by stockbroking firms to examine, in detail, the performance of businesses in certain sectors of the market.

investment appraisal is the process of determining the future *net cash flows* or *profitability* of a capital project (See *accounting rate of return, payback method of capital investment appraisal, net present value method of capital investment appraisal*, and *internal rate of return.*)

investment ratios: see *dividend cover, dividend yield, earnings per share, gearing, interest cover* and *price/earnings ratio.*

investments are shown on a *balance sheet* as either *fixed* or *current assets*, depending on their nature. If a company intends to keep the investments on a continuing basis they should be treated as fixed assets, while investments to be held for a short time period should be shown as a current asset.

Investments are shown at cost. If the investments are listed on a recognised *stock exchange*, then the aggregate market price must be noted.

investment trust: a company whose business is to buy and sell other companies' shares. The shares of investment trusts can be purchased on the *stockmarket.*

investor: a person who puts money into shares, *bonds*, building societies or on deposit with some other financial institution.

Institutional investors are organisations, such as insurance companies and pension funds, that invest large sums of money in shares and bonds.

invoice: the document that is sent to a credit customer. It is sent by the seller to the customer demanding payment, usually within a stipulated time. (See *VAT invoice.*)

invoice discounting is a method used by a business to obtain early payment of *invoices*. The business sells its sales invoices at a discount to an invoice discounting company which will collect the full amounts due. The debtor is unaware of this arrangement.

invoice factoring: see *factoring*

irr: see *internal rate-of-return method of capital investment appraisal*

irrelevant costs are costs which should be ignored when making decisions between alternative courses of action. They are *past* or *sunk costs*. That is, they are costs undertaken some time ago and any future commitments will not affect them or be affected by them. Future *common costs* can also be ignored when deciding between alternative strategies.

issued share capital: the *nominal share capital* which has been issued to *shareholders*. This figure cannot exceed the *authorised share capital*.

issue of debentures: the bookkeeping entries are similar to those used for the *issue of shares*. The word 'debenture' should be substituted for the words 'share capital'.

issue of shares: the issue of shares is like any other contract – it requires an offer and an acceptance.

The invitation to treat is made by advertising and by the issue of a prospectus. The prospective *shareholders* (applicants) apply for shares and send cash with the application form. The company then allots shares to the applicants (now *allottees*). Any unsuccessful applicants will have their application moneys returned. The allottees send money due on allotment. Calls are made, and shareholders pay the calls when due.

These are the bookkeeping entries necessary to record a share issue:

	Debit	Credit
On application	Bank	Application and allotment account
On allotment	Bank	Application and allotment account
Unsuccessful applicants	Application and allotment account	Bank
When allotment is complete	Application and allotment account	Share capital account
On call	Bank	Call account
When call(s) are complete	Call account	Share capital account

Worked example: Howitt plc was formed with an authorised share capital of 500 000 ordinary shares of £1 each. 200 000 of these shares were offered to the public on the following terms:

50 pence on application
30 pence on allotment
20 pence on first and final call

Note:

There is only one call; the first is also the last call.

Applications were received for 371 000 shares. The directors decided to allot the shares to applicants for 300 000 shares on the basis of two shares for every three shares for which applications had been received. The balance of money received on application was to be applied to the amounts due on allotment. Unsuccessful applicants were repaid. All call money was received on the due date.

Required:

Write up the journal (including cash) to record the above transactions in the books of Howitt plc.

Solution:

Journal

	£	£
Cash	185 500	
Application and allotment		185 500
Monies received on application		
Application and allotment	35 500	
Cash		35 500
Monies returned to unsuccessful applicants		
Cash	10 000	
Application and allotment		10 000
Balance of cash from successful applicants due on allotment		
Application and allotment	160 000	
Ordinary share capital account		160 000
Transfer of successful applicants to ordinary share capital account		
Cash	40 000	
Call		40 000
Monies received on first and final call		
Call	40 000	
Ordinary share capital account		40 000
Transfer of call to ordinary share capital account, shares now fully paid		

IT: see *information technology*

JIT: see *just-in-time (JIT) method of stock purchasing*

job card: see *time sheet*

job costing: the system of costing which allocates and *apportions* elements of cost to a job being undertaken to a client's specific instructions. A printer will use job costing when costing out the printing of invoices, letterheaded stationery and business cards. For example, Tommy Davidson, a local builder, who has been employed to build a kitchen extension for the Graham household, will use job costing to arrive at the price the Grahams will have to pay.

job sheet (or card) records the quantities and values of raw materials, *direct labour*, direct expenses and any overheads used on a job. The job sheet is, in essence, an account for the job. When the job is complete, and the customer has been invoiced, the profit or loss can be calculated. Managers can compare the sheet with the original estimate.

joint costs: see *common costs*

joint products are the main products of a process that have their own high saleable value. In contrast, *by-products* arise as incidentals to the main production process and will not command the same high saleable value as the main product.

journal is a *book of prime entry*. It is also known as the journal proper. It is not part of the *double-entry bookkeeping* system. It is used to record the entries:

- in the *general ledger* when a firm starts in business
- used to close the ledgers down when a business ceases to trade
- when there is a purchase of *fixed assets* on credit
- when fixed assets are sold on credit
- required when making transfers from one ledger account to another
- required when correcting errors in ledger accounts

The use of the journal is necessary because:

- the entries above do not 'fit' into any other book of prime entry
- unusual transactions must be entered in a book of prime entry in the same way as all other transactions
- it reduces the likelihood of only using one entry in the double-entry system
- it reduces the likelihood of a fraud being perpetrated, since the journal is an integral part of the *audit trail.*

just-in-time (JIT) method of stock purchasing is a method of *stock control* that enables a business to reduce its stock holding to very low levels.

The purchaser arranges for materials and components to be delivered when they are required. The purchaser must be confident that the supplier can guarantee delivery and quality just before it is needed for processing. Many customers and suppliers are now linked by computer network, which enables orders to be placed when stocks are required.

JIT purchasing reduces stock-holding costs and, if the computer network is used, it can also reduce administration costs.

K

key factor: see *limiting factor*

L

labour costs: see *direct labour costs* and *indirect labour costs*

labour efficiency variance: see *direct labour efficiency variance*

labour variance: see *direct labour variance*

labour wage rate variance: see *direct labour wage variance*

last-in-first-out method of stock valuation (LIFO): see *methods of stock valuation*

lead time: the time that a supplier takes to deliver goods after receipt of an order.

lease: a written contract for the letting or renting of a building or piece of land. Vehicles and machinery can also be leased.

ledger: the book in which all the financial entries concerning a business are entered. The ledger is usually split into three parts:

- *purchase ledger*
- *sales ledger*
- *general ledger*

(See *division of the ledger.*)

legal entity has a separate existence from that of its members. A *limited company* is regarded as having an existence in its own right. This means that a limited company can sue and be sued separately from its *shareholders.* The shareholders are not liable for the debts of the company beyond the amounts they have agreed to pay on their shares.

lessee: the person to whom a lease has been granted.

lessor: the owner of a good being leased.

liabilities are monies that are owed for goods and services supplied to a business, or for money borrowed by the business. (See *current liabilities* and *long-term liabilities.*)

life membership: permanent membership of a club offered in return for a one-off payment. The club benefits by having large payments which can be used for some extraordinary expenditure, e.g. to purchase the freehold of the grounds of the club or to refurbish a club house. The member benefits by having 'free' membership in subsequent years.

The committee of the club must remember that the annual income received in the future could be lower, and this will affect the future *cash flows* of the club.

The bookkeeping entries on receipt of payments for life membership are:

Debit:	Cash book	Credit:	Life membership account

Each year a proportion of the life membership account is transferred to the *income and expenditure account.* The bookkeeping entries will then be:

Debit:	Life membership account	Credit:	Income and expenditure account

LIFO: see *methods of stock valuation.*

limited company: an organisation that has a separate *legal identity* to that of its owners. The owners' (*shareholders'*) liability is limited to the shares that they hold in the company. Companies are either *private limited companies* (Ltd) or *public limited companies* (plc). Both types of limited company must register with the *Registrar of Companies.* Once registered, a private limited company can start to trade, and a public limited company will issue its *prospectus.* When the minimum capital has been raised, a public limited company can start to trade.

limited liability means that the liability of *shareholders* for the debts of a *limited company,* of which they are members, is limited to the amount they agreed to subscribe.

For example, if a shareholder purchases 500 £1 shares in a limited company, once he/she has paid this amount (plus any premium), he/she is not liable to make any further payments if the company goes into *liquidation.*

limited liability company: see *limited company*

limited partner: must register under the provisions of the Limited Partnership Act 1907, and, like the *shareholders* in a *limited company,* the limited partner's liability is limited to the amount of capital invested by him/her.

limiting factor: defined by *CIMA* as 'anything which limits the activity of an entity'. Also known as key factor.

A limiting factor could be:

- a shortage of materials
- a shortage of skilled labour
- a lack of productive capacity in a factory
- a lack of stock-holding facilities

It is essential that the managers use any limiting factor to obtain maximum advantage for the business.

Worked example: Bobtine plc manufactures four products that use the same type of skilled labour. At the moment there is a shortage of the skilled labour necessary to produce all four products. The following information relates to Bobtine plc:

Product	A	B	C	D
Selling price per unit (£)	160	200	250	300
Maximum demand for the product	4000	6000	5000	3000
Material costs per unit (£)	16	20	24	24
Labour costs per unit (£)	28	21	49	35
Labour hours per unit	4	3	7	5
Other direct costs	10	7	12	9

The available skilled labour hours is restricted to 30 000 hours.

Required:

A calculation showing the level of production for each product which will maximise profits for Bobtine plc.

Solution:

Contribution earned per product:

	A	B	C	D
Selling price per unit (£)	160	200	250	300
Marginal (variable) costs per unit (£)	54	48	85	78
Contribution per unit (£)	106	152	165	222
Contribution per hour of skilled labour used	26.50	50.67	23.57	44.40
	$\left(\dfrac{106}{4}\right)$	$\left(\dfrac{152}{3}\right)$	$\left(\dfrac{165}{7}\right)$	$\left(\dfrac{222}{5}\right)$
Ranking	3rd	1st	4th	2nd

Bobtine plc should produce 6 000 units of product B   total hours used 18 000
and 2 400 units of product D   total hours used 12 000

All labour hours are now used.

This production pattern will maximise Bobtine plc's profits under these circumstances.

However, management may decide it wishes to keep providing a full range of products and so produce some of each product.

---

liquidation: see *bankruptcy*

liquidity: the ability of a business to gain access to sufficient cash or near-cash assets in order to meet everyday commitments. It is important for the day-to-day survival of a business; it is as important as *profitability*. Many businesses that go into *liquidation* do so, not because they are unprofitable, but because of their lack of liquidity.

Liquid assets are cash, bank current account balances, debtors and stock.

liquidity ratio: see *acid test ratio*

liquidity ratios: see *acid test ratio* and *current ratio*

loan: money which has been lent and must be repaid at a date sometime in the future.

loan capital: part of the medium- to long-term capital of a *limited company* provided by either banks or *debenture* holders.

loan interest: the charge made by the provider of a loan for the use of the money. It is calculated as a percentage based on the capital borrowed. Interest on any type of loan is debited to the *profit and loss account*.

lodgements are amounts paid into a business bank account. They are entered on the debit side of the *bank cash book* or in the debit *bank column* in a traditional *cash book*. The source document is a *bank paying-in slip*.

Lodgements are shown in the credit column of the business's bank statement.

long-term contract: see *contract costing*

long-term liabilities are debts that are not due for payment within the next *accounting period*. They include long-term bank loans, mortgages and, in the case of *limited companies, debenture* stock. In the *final accounts* of limited companies, long-term liabilities are shown under the heading of:

Creditors   amounts falling due after one year

loss occurs when the expenses of a business are greater than its incomes. Although it is preferable that a business makes a profit, a loss may be tolerated in the short term, but the situation cannot be sustained in the long run. How long a business can suffer losses without going into *liquidation* depends on the magnitude of its financial resources.

loss leader is a very popular item whose price is cut in order to attract customers. The supplier, generally a retail outlet, relies on the customer purchasing other full-priced products at the same time as the loss leader.

lump sum: an amount of money given as one single payment rather than in a number of instalments. On retirement, some pension schemes give a large one-off payment followed by regular monthly payments from the pension fund.

machine hour rate method of absorbing overheads: see *absorption*

mainstream corporation tax is the balance of a company's *tax liability* remaining after payment of *advance corporation tax (ACT)* during the relevant *accounting period*. It is paid by the company nine months after the end of its accounting period.

make or buy decisions are reached in a manufacturing business by the application of *marginal costing* principles. A business may decide to make its own product because:

- it is not produced by another manufacturer
- it is not produced by another manufacturer to the right specification
- the business does not wish to be reliant on another business
- the marginal costs of production are lower than the price quoted by the other manufacturer

---

Worked example: O'Reilly Ltd produces tregs. The costings to produce tregs are:

	£
Variable costs per unit	28
Fixed costs per unit	13
Total cost	41

The managers of O'Reilly Ltd have been approached by a Spanish manufacturer who will supply tregs at a cost of £35.

Required:

Advise the managers of O'Reilly Ltd whether they should continue to manufacture tregs or purchase them from the Spanish supplier.

Solution:

O'Reilly Ltd should continue to produce tregs.

	Make	Buy
	£	£
Variable costs	28	35
Fixed costs	13	13
Total cost	41	48

---

management accounting uses financial information:

- to make decisions affecting the future of a business
- to evaluate past decisions
- to make decisions about the allocation and use of a business's resources

Managers require information in order to formulate strategies, to plan and to control the business.

management buy out: the purchase of a business by its managers or, in the case of a *limited company*, the purchase of the company by its senior managers and *directors*.

management by exception: according to the *CIMA* definition, this is 'the practice of focusing on activities requiring attention and ignoring those that appear to be running smoothly'. *Variance analysis* facilitates management by exception since it highlights areas of business which deviate from the predetermined standards.

management by objectives seeks to establish personal targets for all levels of an organisation. These objectives are tested to see if the targets have been achieved within in a given time span.

Departmental managers are set clearly identifiable, measurable work targets for all the members of his/her department. The targets are set by consultation with the job holder and his/her immediate superior. This involvement of personnel at all levels of the organisation should ensure that the organisational goals coincide with the managers' personal goals.

management information systems provide a variety of information which will enable the managers to run a business efficiently and effectively. The information is generally stored on a computer which can be accessed by managers and employees of all levels on a 'need to know' basis.

manager's commission: performance-related pay for the manager of a business or branch of a business. It is an incentive payment, usually paid as an addition to the manager's basic salary. The amount can be calculated as a percentage of the profits before *commission* is deducted or as a percentage of the profits after the commission is deducted.

Worked example: Frump Ltd operates two retail branches, one in Dressley the other in Kilton.

Clarry, the manager of the Dressley shop, is paid a basic salary plus 5% commission payable on net profits earned by the branch before deduction of her commission.

Eddie, the manager of the Kilton shop, is paid a basic salary plus 5% commission based on net profits earned by the shop after deduction of his commission.

Both shops earned a profit of £17 500 this year.

Required:

Calculate the commission due to Clarry and Eddie.

Solution:

Clarry's commission $= £17\,500 \times \dfrac{5}{100} = £875$

Eddie's commission $= £17\,500 \times \dfrac{5}{105} = £833.33$

---

managing director (MD): the *director* who is in charge of the day-to-day running of a whole *limited company*. The MD delegates responsibilities to the individual directors on the senior management team with regard to the running of the various sections of the business that they head. The managing director reports to the *chair of the board of directors*. (See *directors*.)

manufacturing accounts are the *final accounts* that are prepared to show all the factory costs involved in the production of a final product. The manufacturing account is divided into two sections. These correspond to the nature of the costs involved in the production process:

1 *prime cost* – all the *direct costs* associated with the product(s), e.g. raw materials, *direct labour*, royalties
2 *factory overheads* – all other costs associated with the manufacturing process

The two sections added together give the total production cost, which is transferred to the *trading account* so that the cost of goods sold figure can be ascertained.

Before transferring the total production cost to the trading account, a stock adjustment needs to be made for work in progress.

In a manufacturing business, there are three types of stock:

- raw materials – an adjustment to the purchases of raw materials is necessary to determine the value of raw materials actually consumed in the production process
- partly finished goods (*work in progress*) – this adjustment is necessary in order to remove the prime costs and overheads that are included in the value of this type of unsold stock
- finished goods – the adjustment is necessary to calculate the value of goods sold at cost price

---

Worked example: the following balances have been extracted from the books of Tinkle plc, a manufacturing company:

		£000
Stocks at 1 September 19*6		
Raw materials		120
Work in progress		37
Finished goods		174
Purchases	raw materials	1 356
	indirect materials	37
Factory wages	direct	512
	indirect	106
Office salaries		234
Rent and rates	factory	31
	offices	11
Carriage	inward	4
	outward	7
Power		67
Royalties		9
Heating and lighting costs	factory	34
	offices	12
Other indirect factory expenses		60
Sales		2 693
Machinery		950
Office equipment		384

Additional information:

Stocks at 31 August 19*7

Raw materials	135
Work in progress	32
Finished goods	180

Depreciation machinery 10% per annum
                   office 12.5% per annum

Required:

A manufacturing account for the year ended 31 August 19*7 for Tinkle plc.

Solution:

Tinkle plc manufacturing account for the year ended 31 August 19*7

	£000	£000
Stocks of raw materials 1 September 19*6		120
Purchases of raw materials	1356	
Carriage inward	4	1360
		1480
Less stocks of raw materials 31 August 19*7		135
Raw materials consumed		1345
Direct wages		512
Royalties		9
Prime cost		1866
Factory overheads		
Indirect materials	37	
Indirect labour	106	
Factory rent and rates	31	
Power	67	
Factory heat and light	34	
Factory expenses	60	
Depreciation of machinery	95	430
		2296
Work in progress 1 September 19*6		37
		2333
Less work in progress 31 August 19*7		32
Production cost of completed goods		2301

Some manufacturing businesses transfer their goods from the factory at cost plus a certain percentage, or at what the goods might have cost if purchased from another manufacturer. This process will not increase the overall profits of the business, it will merely distinguish the profits earned by two separate *cost centres*.

SSAP 9 stocks and long-term contracts requires that stocks be shown in the *balance sheet* at cost of production prices. If a manufacturer uses a system of production cost plus a percentage *mark-up*, the stocks of finished goods include an element of factory profit. This contravenes:

- the concept of *prudence*
- the *realisation concept*

so this profit needs to be eliminated in the *profit and loss account* since the *net profit* will be overstated by the amount of the *unrealised profit*. The profit element included in the closing stock must also be eliminated from the *closing stock* included on the balance sheet as a *current asset*, since stocks should be valued at cost (or net realisable value if this is lower than cost), not cost plus a mark-up!

Worked example: the balances shown in the previous example have been extracted from the books of Tinkle plc at 31 August 19*7. It is company policy to transfer manufactured goods to the company trading account at cost + 20%.

Required:

Prepare the following for the year ended 31 August 19*7 for Tinkle plc:
a) provision for unrealised profit
b) an extract from the profit and loss account for the year ended 31 August 19*7 showing the entry relating to the factory profit
c) an extract from the balance sheet as at 31 August 19*7 showing the treatment of the provision for unrealised profit.

Solution:

a) Provision for unrealised profit

	Bal. b/d	29 000	£174 000 = 120% of cost of stock, so
Bal. c/d 30 000	P&L a/c	1 000	£29 000 is the profit loading on £174 000
30 000		30 000	
	Bal. b/d	30 000	£180 000 = 120% of cost of stock, so
			£30 000 is the profit loading on £180 000

b) **Tinkle plc profit and loss account (extract) for the year ended 31 August 19*7**

£

Expenses:
    Provision for unrealised profit   1000

c) **Tinkle plc balance sheet (extract) as at 31 August 19*7**

Current assets	£000	£000	£000
Stocks			
Raw materials		135	
Work in progress		32	
Finished goods	180		
Less provision for unrealised profit	30	150	317

---

manufacturing overheads: all expenses incurred in running a factory other than those that are included in the *manufacturing account* under the *prime cost* heading. Manufacturing overheads include:

- *indirect material costs* – those materials which cannot be directly identified with the product(s), e.g. cleaning materials used in the factory
- *indirect labour costs* – wages which cannot be directly identified with the product(s), e.g. supervisory wages

- *indirect expenses* – other expenses which cannot be directly identified with the product(s), e.g. factory rent and rates, factory insurances, etc.

(See *manufacturing accounts*.)

manufacturing profit: see *manufacturing accounts*

margin: this term generally refers to the gross margin, and shows a business's gross profit as a percentage of the net sales. The margin can be improved by either purchasing (or manufacturing) cheaper goods or by increasing the selling price to customers. It shows how many pence gross profit is earned out of every £ of sales. The calculation is:

FORMULA: $\dfrac{\text{gross profit}}{\text{sales}} \times 100$

Worked example: the following data refers to Wert & Co:

	£
Sales	134 091
Cost of sales	56 859
Gross profit	77 232

Required:

Calculate the gross margin earned by Wert & Co.

Solution:

$$\text{gross margin} = \frac{\text{gross profit}}{\text{sales}} \times 100 = \frac{77\ 232}{134\ 091} \times 100 = 57.6\%$$

No comment can be made as to whether this is a good margin or not. Trends should be observed or comparisons made with other similar businesses.

---

marginal costing: a costing method based on the extra costs incurred and extra revenues generated by the production and sale of an additional item(s). It requires a clear distinction between *variable costs* and *fixed costs*. No attempt is made to allocate fixed costs to *cost centres* or *cost units*.

Marginal costing is used when:

- costing special one-off contracts or jobs (see *special-order pricing*)
- considering whether to make or buy a product (see *make or buy decisions*)
- choosing between competing alternative courses of action (see *competing courses of action*)
- when a business has a *limiting factor*
- calculating the *break-even point* for a product

(See *contribution pricing*.)

marginal costs: the extra costs involved in producing one additional unit of production. For example, Tocle & Son produce 1540 units of a product at a total cost of £34 723. When Tocle & Son produce 1 541 units the total cost rises to £34 947. The marginal cost of the marginal product is £224.

marginal revenue: the extra revenue generated by the sale of one additional unit of production.

margin of safety: the difference between the actual sales achieved, or forecast as achievable, and the break-even level of sales. The margin of safety indicates to management how far sales can fall before the business will move out of profit and into a loss-making situation. Clearly, the greater the margin of safety, the better for the business.

The margin of safety is generally expressed in units, but can be expressed in sales value or as a percentage of sales.

Worked example:
> break-even level of sales = £414 000
> expected level of sales = £1 380 000

Required:

The margin of safety expressed as a percentage of expected total turnover.

Solution:

Expected level of sales can drop by 70% before the break- even point is reached.

$$\text{margin of safety in percentage terms} = \frac{1\,380\,000 - 414\,000}{1\,380\,000} \times 100$$

$$= \frac{966\,000}{1\,380\,000} \times 100 = 70\%$$

For a worked example using graphical means, see *break-even point*.

market analyst makes a detailed examination and analysis of a market and then reports on his/her findings.

marketing is defined by the Chartered Institute of Marketing as 'the management process responsible for identifying, anticipating and satisfying customer requirements profitably'.

market penetration pricing: see *penetration pricing*

market skimming pricing occurs when a new product is launched. The manufacturer can charge a high price before competition reduces the market price. Manufacturers often justify this type of price setting as an attempt to recoup *research and development costs,* before competition reduces their margins.

market value: the price placed on a good by the forces of demand and supply prevailing in the market.

mark-up shows a business's *gross profit* as a percentage of the *cost of sales*. The mark-up of a business can be improved by either purchasing (or manufacturing) cheaper goods or by increasing the selling price to customers.

It shows how many pence of gross profit has been added to each £ of the cost of the sales. The calculation is:

$$\text{FORMULA: } \frac{\text{gross profit}}{\text{cost of sales}} \times 100$$

Worked example: the following data refers to Wert & Co:

	£
Sales	134 091
Cost of sales	56 859
Gross profit	77 232

Required:

Calculate the mark-up earned by Wert & Co.

Solution:

$$\text{mark-up} = \frac{\text{gross profit}}{\text{cost of sales}} \times 100 = \frac{77\ 232}{56\ 859} \times 100 = 135.83\%$$

master budget: a *profit and loss account* and a *balance sheet* prepared from all the operational budgets. Examination questions will often ask for the preparation of a budgeted (or forecast) profit and loss account and budgeted (forecast) balance sheet.

The preparation of the budgeted *final accounts* is no different from the preparation of a 'normal' set of final accounts, but remember that some budgets are prepared on a cash basis (*cash budget*) whilst the master budget is prepared using the *accruals concept*.

matching concept: see *accruals concept*

material costs: see *direct material costs and indirect material costs*

materiality: if the inclusion or exclusion of information would mislead the users of a financial statement, then that information is material. For example, a business supplies the office junior with a ruler, costing 87 pence. The ruler will be used for, say, ten years. Theoretically, the ruler is a fixed asset and as such it should be depreciated over its useful economic life. Clearly, to do this would not be cost effective. The purchase is therefore treated as revenue expenditure and debited to office sundries. Doing this would not mislead a prospective investor, so it is not a material transaction.

On the other hand, if a computer system costing £180 000 was debited to office expenses, this would significantly change profits and would mislead the users of the accounts. This is therefore a material transaction.

material price variance: see *direct material price variance*

material usage variance: see *direct material usage variance*

maximum number of partners is generally 20. There are, however, a number of exceptions, e.g. solicitors and accountants.

maximum number of shareholders in a *public limited company* is determined by the number of shares issued.

MD: see *managing director*

measured daywork grades the efficiency of workers and pays them accordingly. A standard level of performance is agreed at 100%, and performance is then categorised into efficiency bands. If 100% were paid £7.50 per hour:

- efficiency band 90%–100% might be paid £6.00 per hour
- efficiency band 100%–120% might be paid £9.00 per hour

medium-sized companies are those that satisfy two of the following conditions:

- less than £11.2 million turnover
- total assets of less than £5.6 million
- average number of employees does not exceed 250

They are allowed certain 'filing exemptions' in the accounts that they submit to the *Registrar of Companies*. This is to protect them from rival businesses acquiring sensitive information.

Analyses of turnover and profit are not required, but the *balance sheet* must be prepared in full, and a *directors' report* must be filed with the accounts. (See *reporting requirements for medium-sized companies*.)

members' equity: the total of issued ordinary shares plus all the *reserves*.

memorandum accounts: these are kept to give additional information about entries in the double-entry system. They are not, in themselves, part of the double entry system. For example, when *control accounts* are integrated into the double-entry system, *personal accounts* in the *purchase* and *sales ledger* will be kept as memorandum accounts only. If the personal accounts are part of the double-entry system, then the control account is used only as part of the control system.

Worked example: Johnson purchases £176 goods from McTavish on credit.

Required:

The journal entries in Johnson's books to record the purchase if:
a) control accounts are integrated into the system
b) control accounts are not integrated.

Solution:

Journal

	Dr £	Cr £
a) Purchases	176	
Purchase ledger control		176
b) Purchases	176	
McTavish		176

Memorandum of Association: a document filed with the *Registrar of Companies* before a *limited company* can become incorporated. It defines the external relationship of the company to the outside world. The details filed include:

- the company's name, address and registered office
- share capital
- the company's objectives

merchant bank offers banking services to industry and businesses, and deals internationally.

merger takes place when a company issues its shares in exchange for the shares in another company. Sometimes a new company is formed and issues its shares to the *shareholders* in two or more 'old' companies. In neither of these circumstances has any cash changed hands. In both cases there is usually mutual agreement to the *takeover*.

methods of stock valuation are used to value the *closing stocks* of a business in order to prepare the *final accounts*.

Some businesses keep very detailed records of stock receipts and stock issues, making entries in the stores *ledger* after every transaction. This is known as a perpetual method and would be used by a business that needs to cost out its work very carefully. Most businesses using this method would have the system computerised.

Other businesses will take stock only once, at the year end. This is known as a periodic method. The local mini-market or newsagents would probably use this method.

The overriding principle with regard to stock valuation is that stocks should be valued at the lower of cost or net realisable value. The following are the most frequently used methods of valuing the issues of stock from stores:

- first in first out (FIFO) – assumes that the first goods purchased will be the first ones to be delivered to the requisitioning department
- last in first out (LIFO) – assumes that the goods received most recently will be the first ones issued for use
- weighted average cost (AVCO) recalculates the average cost of goods held in stock each time a new delivery of stock is received. Issues are then made at the weighted average cost

Important note: all the methods described above are only methods of calculating the value of closing stocks, they are not necessarily methods of issuing stock to requisitioning departments.

Worked example: Kitson Ltd purchases Vf/7 components to use in its manufacturing process. The following were the receipts and issues of the component during the month of January:

	Receipts		Issues
7 January	6 @ £6	10 January	5
12 January	10 @ £7	19 January	7
21 January	8 @ £8	28 January	7

Required:

Calculate the value of closing stocks of component Vf/7 using:
i)   FIFO method of issuing stock from stores
ii) LIFO method of issuing stock from stores
iii) AVCO method of issuing stock from stores.

Solution:

i) FIFO

	Receipts	Issues	Balance
7 January	6 @ £6		£36.00
10 January		5	6.00
12 January	10 @ £7		76.00
19 January		7	28.00
21 January	8 @ £8		92.00
28 January		7	40.00

ii) LIFO

7 January	6 @ £6		36.00
10 January		5	6.00
12 January	10 @ £7		76.00
19 January		7	27.00
21 January	8 @ £8		91.00
28 January		7	35.00

iii) AVCO

7 January	6 @ £6		36.00
10 January		5	6.00
12 January	10 @ £7		76.00 (£6.91 ave cost)
19 January		7	27.64 (£6.91 × 4)
21 January	8 @ £8		91.64 (£7.64 ave cost)
28 January		7	38.20 (£7.64 × 5)

Since each of the above methods gives a different closing stock figure it should be obvious that gross profits will differ according to which method is used.

The advantages and disadvantages of each of the methods of stock valuation are:

FIFO:

advantages –
- it is probably the method that the lay person would intuitively use
- issue prices are based on the prices that have actually been paid for the stock
- closing stock values are based on the most recent prices paid
- it is an acceptable method from the point of view of the *Companies Act 1985, SSAP 9* and for Inland Revenue purposes

disadvantages –
- issues from stock are not at the most recent prices and this could influence the costing of work
- in times of rising prices, FIFO shows higher profit figures earlier – goes against the concept of prudence

LIFO:

advantages –
- value of closing stock is based on the prices actually paid for the stock
- issues are valued at the most recent prices

disadvantages –

- it is less realistic than FIFO since it assumes that most recent purchases will be issued before the older stock
- most recent prices are not used for stock valuation
- it is unacceptable for taxation purposes and under SSAP 9

AVCO:

advantages –

- prices are averaged so it recognises that issues from stock have equal value to the business
- variations in issue prices are minimised, marked changes are ironed out
- it allows comparison of profit figures to be made on a more realistic basis
- closing stock valuations are fairly close to the latest prices paid (the method is weighted towards the most recent purchases)
- it is an acceptable basis for the purposes of SSAP 9 and the Companies Act 1985

disadvantages –

- it requires a new calculation each time new stock is purchased
- the price charged for issues will not agree with the price paid to purchase the stock

minimum disclosure requirements for a *limited company* are stipulated by law. The main statutory requirements required by the *Companies Act 1985* are:

- a *profit and loss account*
- a *balance sheet*
- a *directors' report*
- an *auditors' report*

minimum shareholders in a *public limited company* is two.

minority interests: if a *holding company* owns less than 100 per cent of the issued ordinary shares in its *subsidiary*, the shares that it does not hold are held by minority interests.

minority shareholders are *shareholders* who own less than half of the shares in a *limited company*.

MIS: see *management information systems*

MMC: see *Monopolies and Mergers Commission*

money measurement concept states that only transactions that can be measured in monetary terms should be included in the business *books of account*. Because of their subjectivity it is extremely difficult to put a value on:

- managerial efficiency
- skill and efficiency of the workforce
- good customer relations

None of these can be included in the final accounts.

monetary working capital adjustment (MWCA) was required by SSAP 16 (*current cost accounting*). It took the difference between trade debtors and trade creditors and tried to calculate the loss and gain accruing to a business in times of

ISLE COLLEGE
RESOURCES CENTRE

inflation (borrowers gain, lenders lose). Both opening and closing net monetary working capital were indexed to represent an average value for the year.

Monopolies and Mergers Commission (MMC) investigates potential monopoly situations which might operate against the interests of the consumer. The Director General of Fair Trading or the Secretary of State for Trade and Industry can refer monopolies for investigation to the Commission. (A business which has at least 25 per cent of the market share is regarded as a monopoly.) A report of the investigation is submitted to the Secretary of State who decides whether or not any action is needed.

mortgage: a legal agreement whereby money is loaned to purchase property. The title deeds to the property are held by the *mortgagor*.

mortgage debenture: see *debentures*

mortgagor: the person or financial institution who is the lender of money to a mortgagee (the borrower) to purchase property.

name: a person who provides security for insurance arranged by a syndicate at Lloyds of London.

narratives are required when entries are made in a *journal*. This indicates to a reader why the entries are being made in the two *ledger* accounts. An entry in a journal to transfer an incorrect entry might read like this:

	Dr	Cr
T Phelps	46	
T Philips		46

Correction of error: Sales £46 to T Phelps incorrectly entered in T Philips account.

National Insurance: state insurance which pays for medical care, hospitals and social security payments.

National Insurance contributions: monies paid into the National Insurance scheme by both employers and employees.

National Insurance number: the number given to an individual as an identification for social security reasons.

nationalised industries: industries which are owned by the state. They are in the *public sector.*

net asset value (NAV): the total value of an organisation. It is calculated by deducting all external liabilities from all assets owned by the organisation.

Worked example: the business assets and liabilities of John Fallon are as follows: Premises at book value £120 000; machinery at book value £30 000; vehicle at book value £18 000; stock at cost £6000; debtors £1800; creditors £1300; bank balance £1200; mortgage £40 000.

Required:

Calculate the net asset value of John Fallon's business.

Solution:

		£
Premises		120 000
Machinery		30 000
Vehicle		18 000
Stock		6 000
Debtors		1 800
Bank balance		1 200
		177 000
Mortgage	40 000	
Creditors	1 300	41 300
Net asset value		135 700

The net asset value is equal to the capital structure of the organisation. Also known as net worth.

---

net asset value per share: the *net asset value* of a *limited company* divided by the number of ordinary shares issued.

Worked example: Ousby plc has an issued share capital of 800 000 ordinary shares of 25 pence each. The company has a net asset value of £184 000.

Required:

Calculate the net asset value per share for Ousby plc.

Solution:

net asset value per share $\dfrac{£184\ 000}{800\ 000}$ = 23 pence per share

---

net book value: the value of an asset as shown in an organisation's *books of account*. It is calculated by deducting the *aggregate depreciation* charged on the asset to date from the balance standing in the asset account.

Worked example: the ledger of Westby Industries Ltd shows the following accounts as at 31 December 1997:

Land & buildings at valuation	Provision for depreciation of land & buildings
Balance b/d 500 000	Balance b/d 40 000
Vehicles at cost	**Provision for depreciation of vehicles**
Balance b/d 127 000	Balance b/d 67 000
Machinery at cost	**Provision for depreciation of machinery**
Balance b/d 430 000	Balance b/d 120 000

Required:

Calculate the net book value of land and buildings, vehicles and machinery for Westby Industries Ltd.

Solution:

Net book values: Land and buildings £460 000 (£500 000 – £40 000)
Vehicles £60 000 (£127 000 – £67 000)
Machinery £310 000 (£430 000 – £120 000)

Remember: the net book value does not represent how much the assets would fetch if they were sold.

net borrowings: the borrowings of a business less any cash the business is holding in its bank accounts.

net cash flow: the difference between the cash received by an organisation and the cash being spent by the organisation.

net current assets: the excess of *current assets* over *current liabilities*, also known as working capital. If a business's current liabilities exceeds its current assets, then this would be known as net current liabilities.

net dividend per share: the dividend per share after the deduction of any personal income tax.

net loss: the balance shown on the *profit and loss account* when expenses incurred by a business exceed the *gross profit* earned by the business.

net margin shows a business's *net profit* as a percentage of net sales. It reveals how much the business earns out of every £1 of net sales, after all expenses have been met.

Net margin shows how efficiently the business's expenses are being controlled. To improve the ratio, the business must reduce the proportion of expenses paid out of every £1 of turnover. The calculation is:

FORMULA: $\dfrac{\text{net profit}}{\text{sales}} \times 100$

Worked example: the following is the summarised trading and profit and loss account for Gray & Co:

	£
Sales	129 056
Cost of sales	57 330
Gross profit	71 726
Less expenses	49 702
Net profit	22 024

Required:

Calculate the net margin for Gray & Co.

Solution:

net margin $= \dfrac{\text{net profit}}{\text{sales}} \times 100 = \dfrac{22\,024}{129\,056} \times 100 = 17.07\%$

---

net present value method of capital investment appraisal uses the present value of *net cash flows* (cash inflows minus cash outflows using today's price levels), less the initial investment. If the net present value of the investment is positive then the investment is acceptable; if the net present value is negative then the investment should be rejected on financial grounds. (Note: the business may still undertake the investment for non-financial reasons, e.g. to avoid redundancies in the workforce. See *social accounting*.)

When comparing mutually exclusive projects, a business should accept the investment(s) which gives the greatest net present value, and the investments giving the lower returns should be rejected.

Worked example: Michelle Vogt is considering whether to purchase a new machine costing £20 000. She estimates that the future cash flows generated by the machine will be:

	Revenue receipts	Operating payments
	£	£
Year 1	8 000	7 000
Year 2	12 000	9 000
Year 3	17 000	12 000
Year 4	20 000	13 000
Year 5	26 000	16 000

Her cost of capital is 10%. All costs are paid and all revenues are received on the last day of each year. The following is an extract from the present value tables of £1 at 10%:

	10%
Year 1	0.909
Year 2	0.826
Year 3	0.751
Year 4	0.683
Year 5	0.621

Required:

Advise Michelle whether, on financial grounds, she ought to invest in the new machine.

Solution:

Year	Cash flows £	Present value factor	Net present value £
0 (now)	(20 000)	1	(20 000)
1	1 000	0.909	909
2	3 000	0.826	2 478
3	5 000	0.751	3 755
4	7 000	0.683	4 781
5	10 000	0.621	6 210
			(1 867)

Michelle should not buy the new machine since it would yield a negative net present value.

---

net profit: the excess of *gross profit* over expenditure. It is calculated on the *profit and loss account* by deducting all business expenditure from the gross profit.

net profit margin: see *net margin*

net profit-to-sales ratio: see *net margin*

net realisable value: see *methods of stock valuation*

net salary: a person's income after tax, *National Insurance* and other voluntary deductions have been deducted from their gross salary. It is also known as take-home pay.

net worth: see *net asset value*

new issues: previously unissued shares issued from the *authorised share capital* of a company. The issue can be to:

- the general public (for bookkeeping entries see *issue of shares*)
- existing *shareholders* as a bonus (scrip) issue (for bookkeeping entries see *bonus shares*, or
- existing shareholders as a *rights issue*

next in first out (NIFO): a method of valuing finished goods at the end of the *accounting period* which uses the replacement cost of the goods not their historical cost.

NIFO: see *next in first out*

nominal accounts are *general ledger* accounts that record incomes and expenses such as purchases, sales, wages, rent, business rates, etc.

nominal ledger: the name given to the *general ledger* in computer programs.

nominal share capital: see *authorised share capital*

nominal value of ordinary shares: the face value or par value of shares. Once shares have been issued their market price can rise or fall. After a number of years it is unlikely that the *market value* will bear any resemblence to the nominal value. Any *rights issue* or issues to the general public are unlikely to be at the nominal value; the price will be fixed by the *directors* after reference to the current market price when the decision to raise more capital is taken.

non-adjusting events: according to SSAP 17, these 'are events which arise after the *balance sheet date* and concern conditions that did not exist at that time. Consequently they do not result in changes in amounts in the financial statements. They may, however, be of such *materiality* that their disclosure is required by way of notes to ensure that financial statements are not misleading'.

non-controllable costs: see *controllable costs*

normal losses are losses of materials in the normal production process which cannot be avoided. In certain processes liquids will evaporate, when producing timber-based products off-cuts of wood will be lost, etc. No matter how efficient or effective a production process, there will still be these kinds of uncontrollable waste.

notice of coding is sent to a taxpayer and his/her employer at the beginning of each tax year. The notice indicates the tax code to be used in calculating the tax to be deducted from the employee's gross pay. The tax code is based on the total of the *personal allowances*.

notional expenses are sometimes included in costings to ensure that expenses which should be included are charged to the job. For example, a manufacturing business might own its factory. A notional rent figure could be included in the costings to arrive at the total costs to be charged to a job.

notional profit: the value of certified work to date on a *contract*, less the costs involved on the contract to date, less some provision in anticipation of any unforeseen circumstances. The concept of notional profit is applied when a contract has already incurred large costs and the contract is still some way off completion.

npv: see *net present value*

objectivity avoids bias when making asset valuations. Assets are therefore valued at cost for *balance sheet* purposes. *Limited companies* do, from time to time, revalue certain assets to reflect current market price. (See *asset revaluation*.)

omissions are bookkeeping errors which will not be revealed by extracting a *trial balance*. They should be corrected by using the *journal*.

Worked example: a purchase invoice for £57 received from Grant King has been destroyed. It has not been entered in the purchase day book.

Required:

Journal entries to rectify the error of omission.

Solution:

Journal

	Dr £	Cr £
Purchases	57	
Grant King		57

---

on-cost: an alternative name used for *fixed costs*.

open cheque: see *cheque*

opening entries in a business's books are recorded in the *journal*.

Worked example: Tom has just purchased an existing business from Sarah. He has paid a purchase consideration of £85 000. He has used £45 000 of his own savings and he has borrowed £40 000 from his bank. The assets (at book value) taken over from Sarah are:

Premises £42 000; fixtures and fittings £17 500; vehicle £4200 and stock £2600.

Required:

The journal entries required to open the ledger accounts in Tom's books of account.

Solution:

Journal

	Dr £	Cr £
Premises	42 000	
Fixtures and fittings	17 500	
Vehicle	4 200	
Stock	2 600	
Goodwill	18 700	
Capital		45 000
Bank loan		40 000
	85 000	85 000

opening stock: the *closing stock* from the previous financial period.

Worked example: refer back to the worked example for *closing stock*. Mary McDougal is now in her second year of trading. Her year end is 30 November 19*8. The entries on the debit side of her purchases account total £35 600. The entries on the credit side of her sales account total £58 000. Mary values her stock on 30 November 19*8 at £6200.

Required:

Prepare the trading account and the stock account as they would appear in the general ledger of Mary McDougal at the end of her second year of trading.

Solution:

At the end of Mary's second year of trading the stock account would look like this:

Stock	
£	
Yr1 Trading a/c 4 500	

If Mary extracted a trial balance, the balance on the stock account would have to be shown since it is a balance in her general ledger. In a trial balance the opening stock is always shown.

Mary's general ledger would show the following two accounts at 30 November 19*8:

Trading account for the year ended 30 November 19*8

	£		£
Stock	4 500		

Stock

	£		£
Yr1 Trading a/c	4 500	Yr2 Trading a/c	4 500

Mary's stock at the end of her second year of trading should now be entered in her stock account in the general ledger.

Trading account for the year ended 30 November 19*8

	£		£
Stock	4 500	Sales	58 000
Purchases	35 600	Stock	6 200
Gross profit c/d	24 100		
	64 200		64 200

Stock

	£		£
Yr1 Trading a/c	4 500	Yr2 Trading a/c	4 500
Yr2 Trading a/c	6 200		

open-market purchase: purchase of shares in a recognised *stockmarket*.

operational costing: the costing of the production processes involved in the manufacture of mass-produced products. The products are made to be held in stock until an order is received. They are not made to a customer's specific requirements.

For example, costing might be made for the production of 10 000 boxes of matches. The total production costs are divided by 10 000 to arrive at the cost of producing one box of matches. Clearly, this is more sensible than trying to calculate the cost of producing one box.

operational gearing: a situation in which a business has high *fixed costs* which are financed by borrowings.

operating statements are used to summarise the *variances* that have been calculated using standard costing techniques. The statement reconciles the budgeted profit with the actual profit achieved:

- the statement starts with the budgeted profit
- the *favourable variances* are added
- the adverse variances are deducted
- the result is the actual profit

For the calculation of the variances see under the appropriate headings.

A standard cost operating statement could look like this:

Sean Drew Ltd standard cost operating statement for the year ended 30 June 19*7

			£	£	£
Budgeted profit					16 700
Sales volume variance					(600)
					16 100
Sales price variance					400
					16 500
Cost variances			Adverse	Favourable	
Direct materials:	price		600		
	usage		100		
Direct labour:	wage rate			200	
	efficiency		50		
Variable production overhead:	expenditure	400			
	efficiency			250	
Fixed production overhead:	expenditure			800	
	efficiency	125			
		1 275		1 250	(25)
Operating profit					16 450
Less: actual administrative overhead				2 350	
actual selling and distribution overhead				4 560	6 910
Actual profit					9 540

opportunity cost: the cost of making a decision in terms of the benefit lost by not using the resources in the next best alternative. (If resources are used, they are not available for use in another situation.) Opportunity cost is not necessarily a monetary cost, it is simply an opportunity forgone. For example, the cost of an evening visit to a relative could be an episode of 'Eastenders' missed on television.

ordinary share capital: the total of all the issued shares held by the *ordinary share-holders*. It must be shown under the headings:

- *authorised share capital*
- *issued share capital*

The number of shares authorised and issued must be shown in the *balance sheet* or by way of a note to the accounts The *nominal value* must also be stated. Ordinary share capital is also known as equity capital.

ordinary shareholders are the owners of a *limited company*. The ordinary share-holders have:

- full voting rights at *shareholders'* meetings
- an interest in the net assets of the company
- an interest in the profits of the company (see *dividends*)

One company may own shares in another company. If a company owns more than 50 per cent of the ordinary shares in another company it can control that company. It can outvote any shareholder or group of shareholders at any shareholders' meeting. (See *holding company* and *subsidiary company*.)

ordinary shares represent part ownership in a *limited company*. They are the most common type of share issued by a limited company. Every limited company has ordinary shares. They are often referred to as equity capital since they take an equal share of any *distributable profits* of a company.

organisation chart shows as a diagram the structure of a business (see diagram on following page). Each job title is shown and formal lines of authority and responsibility are mapped. Very large businesses should have a chart for the business as a whole, as well as departmental or functional organisation charts.

Chains of command should be clear and each person should be answerable to only one other person. The chart should show:

- the different functions and departments
- main responsibilities (in the case of departmental charts)
- who reports to whom
- spans of control
- communication channels

output-related pay schemes: see *piece work*

over-absorption of overheads occurs when more units are produced than predicted in the budget. This means that more overheads are recovered than was intended.

Worked example: in August, Brownlee Industries Ltd budgeted for overhead expenditure of £360 000 for department J on a budgeted output of 120 000 units. The budgeted overhead expenditure for department Q was £128 000 based on a budgeted output of 64 000 units.

Required:

a) Calculate the overhead absorption rate for departments J and Q based on the unit-produced method.

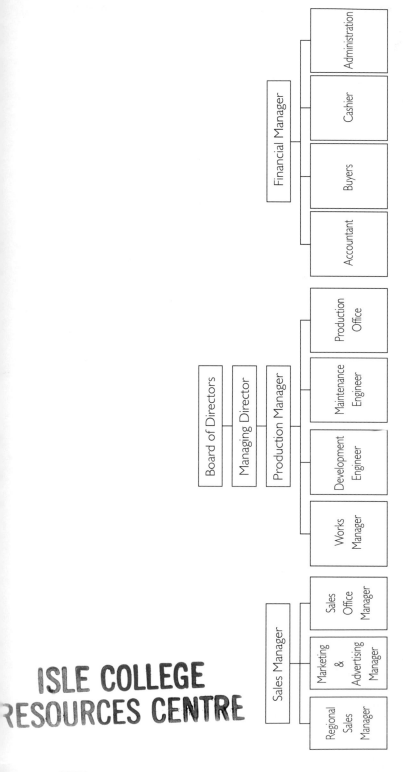

ISLE COLLEGE
RESOURCES CENTRE

b) Calculate for each department the over- or under-recovery of overheads. Department J's actual output was 124 000 units. Department Q's actual expenditure was £129 000.

Solution:

a) overhead absorption rate for department J $= \dfrac{\text{overhead expenditure}}{\text{units produced}}$

$= \dfrac{£360\ 000}{120\ 000} = £3$

overhead absorption rate for department Q $= \dfrac{\text{overhead expenditure}}{\text{units produced}}$

$= \dfrac{£128\ 000}{64\ 000} = £2$

b) department J over-recovery $= £12\ 000$
(124 000 units × £3 recovery rate $= £372\ 000$ – budgeted overheads £360 000)
department Q under-recovery $= £1000$
(actual overheads $= £129\ 000$ – budgeted overheads £128 000)

These figures will be posted to an overhead adjustment account. At the financial year end a credit balance will be posted to the credit of the profit and loss account. A debit balance on the overhead adjustment account will be posted to the debit of the profit and loss account.

If the £12 000 over-recovery and the £1000 under-recovery were the only entries in the overhead adjustment account, at the financial year end the account would show the following entries:

Overhead adjustment account

	£		£
Under-recovery of overheads	1 000	Over-recovery of overheads	12 000
Profit and loss account	11 000		
	12 000		12 000

overall recovery rate can be used where a manufacturing business has a number of production departments. Rather than calculating an overhead recovery rate for each department, a recovery rate for the factory as a whole is calculated. It is also known as the blanket recovery rate. The calculation is:

FORMULA: overall recovery rate $= \dfrac{\text{total factory overheads}}{\text{chosen absorption method}}$

Worked example: Menny plc is a manufacturing company. The total overheads for the whole factory are estimated to be £67 165. The total labour hours worked in the factory for the month of February are estimated to be 28 340 hours.

Required:

Calculate the overall recovery rate for February for Menny plc based on a direct labour hour rate method.

Solution:

$$\text{overall recovery rate} = \frac{\text{total factory overheads}}{\text{chosen absorption method}} = \frac{£67\ 165}{28\ 340} = £2.37$$

overdraft exists when, by arrangement with the bank manager, a business pays more from its current account than it has deposited. A bank overdraft will be a credit balance in the *bank columns* of the *cash book*, and a debit balance on the business's bank statement.

The balance according to the cash book will appear as a credit entry in the *trial balance* and as a *current liability* on the *balance sheet*.

overhead absorption costing: see *absorption costing*

overhead efficiency variance will be favourable if a business has saved money. The *variance* will be adverse if the overheads have cost more than was budgeted for. For a worked example, see *overhead variance*.

overhead expenditure variance will be favourable if a business has saved money. The variance will be adverse if the overheads have cost more than was budgeted for. For a worked example, see *overhead variance*.

overheads are described by *CIMA* as 'expenditure on labour, materials or services which cannot be economically identified with a specific saleable cost'. (See also *factory overhead expenses*.)

overhead variance is the difference between the standard overhead and the actual overheads incurred. The *variances* can be calculated for:

- *fixed overheads*
- variable overheads

The total *fixed production overhead variance* can be calculated by deducting the actual fixed production overheads from the flexed standard fixed production overheads. The calculation is:

FORMULA: standard fixed production overhead charged to production − actual fixed production overhead

---

Worked example: the budgeted and actual fixed overheads expenditure involved in the production of 'noddles' is:

	Budgeted £	Actual £
Fixed overheads	175 000	164 000
Direct labour hours of input	35 000	32 000
Direct labour hours of output (standard hours produced)	35 000	31 000

Required:

Total fixed production overhead variance for the production of 'noddles'.

Solution:

	£
Standard fixed production overhead charged to production	155 000
Actual fixed production overhead	164 000
Adverse total fixed production overhead variance	9 000

Fixed production overhead variance can be divided into;

1 Fixed production overhead expenditure variance – this identifies the portion of the total fixed overhead variance which is due to the actual fixed overhead expenditure differing from the budgeted fixed overhead expenditure. The calculation is:

FORMULA: budgeted fixed overhead – actual fixed overhead

Worked example: using the information given above for the production of 'noddles':

Required:

Calculate the fixed overhead expenditure variance.

Solution:

	£	
Standard fixed overhead expenditure	175 000	
Actual fixed overhead expenditure	164 000	
Favourable expenditure variance (over-recovery)	11 000	favourable

2 Fixed production overhead volume variance – this identifies the portion of the total fixed overhead variance that is due to actual production being different from the budgeted production. The calculation is:

$$\text{FORMULA:} \left(\begin{array}{c} \text{actual} \\ \text{production} \end{array} - \begin{array}{c} \text{budgeted} \\ \text{production} \end{array} \right) \times \begin{array}{c} \text{standard fixed} \\ \text{overhead rate} \end{array}$$

Worked example: using the information given above for the production of 'noddles':

Required:

The fixed production overhead volume variance.

Solution:

The standard fixed overhead rate of £5 per hour is calculated on the basis of 35 000 direct labour hours. If exactly 35 000 hours are produced, then the total fixed overheads will be recovered. Actual labour hours are in fact only 31 000 hours so that actual production is 1000 standard hours less than budget. This means that £20 000 of fixed overheads will not be recovered.

(actual production – budgeted production) × standard fixed overhead rate

31 000 – 35 000 × £5

= £20 000 adverse

3 fixed production overhead volume variance – arises because the actual volume of output differs from the budgeted volume. The fixed overhead volume variance can be subdivided into:

- fixed overhead volume efficiency variance – this identifies the part of the overhead variance that might have been caused by the labour force having been more or less efficient than was anticipated when the budget was drawn up. The calculation is:

FORMULA: $\left(\begin{array}{c}\text{standard hours}\\\text{of output}\end{array} - \begin{array}{c}\text{actual hours}\\\text{of input}\end{array}\right) \times \begin{array}{c}\text{standard fixed}\\\text{overhead rate}\end{array}$

Worked example: using the information given above for the production of 'noddles':

Required:

The fixed overhead volume efficiency variance.

Solution:

The actual number of input hours was 32 000 and so one could reasonably expect an output of 32 000 hours. In reality, only 31 000 hours were produced, so the output was 1000 hours less than it should have been. The business has actually lost 1000 hours at £5 per hour. This is £5000 that should have been absorbed.

(standard hours of output − actual hours of input) × standard fixed overhead rate
      32 000   −   31 000   ×   £5

= £5000 adverse

- fixed overhead volume capacity variance – this also indicates a reason why actual and budgeted production might be different. The variance could be caused by labour disputes, material shortages, machine breakdowns, lower demand for the product. The calculation is:

FORMULA: $\left(\begin{array}{c}\text{actual hours}\\\text{of input}\end{array} - \begin{array}{c}\text{budgeted hours}\\\text{of input}\end{array}\right) \times \begin{array}{c}\text{standard fixed}\\\text{overhead rate}\end{array}$

Worked example: using the information given above for the production of 'noddles':

Required:

The fixed overhead volume capacity variance.

Solution:

The budget was drawn up under the assumption that direct labour hours of input would be 35 000 hours, whereas the actual hours of input was 32 000 hours. The difference of 3000 hours represents the under-utilisation of production capacity. The business has failed to absorb £15 000 of fixed overhead budgeted for because of the shortfall in direct labour hours of input.

(actual hours of input − budgeted hours of input) × standard fixed overhead rate
      32 000   −   35 000   ×   £5

= £15 000 adverse

The above variances can be seen more clearly in the following diagram:

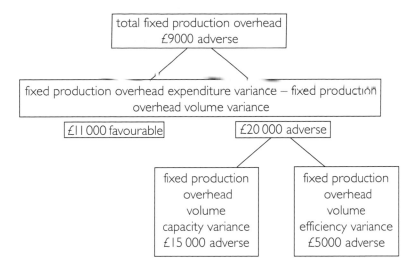

Variable production overhead variance can be divided into:

1 Variable production overhead expenditure variance – when actual cost differs from budgeted cost. It shows the difference between the flexed budgeted variable overhead and the actual variable total overhead incurred. The calculation is:

   FORMULA: flexed budgeted variable overhead – actual variable overhead

2 variable production overhead efficiency variance – arises through the efficiency of labour. It shows the difference between the standard hours of output and the actual hours of input. The calculation is:

   FORMULA: $\left(\begin{array}{c}\text{standard hours} \\ \text{of output}\end{array} - \begin{array}{c}\text{actual hours} \\ \text{of input}\end{array}\right) \times \begin{array}{c}\text{standard variable} \\ \text{overhead rate}\end{array}$

Worked example: the following information applies to the variable overheads for producing 'remcors'.

Budgeted production of remcors was 80 000 units.

Actual production of remcors was 60 000 units.

	£	Hours
Budgeted variable overheads		
(20 000 hours at £5 per labour hour)	100 000	
Actual variable overheads	72 000	
Standard labour hours		20 000
Actual labour hours		18 000

Required:

i) the total variable production overhead variance

ii) the variable production overhead expenditure variance

iii) the variable production overhead efficiency variance

Solution:

i) £

Standard cost of production for variable overheads
   is 60 000 units at £1.25 per unit   75 000
Actual cost of production for variable overheads   72 000
Total variable production overhead variance   3 000 favourable

ii) To make a comparison between the actual variable production overhead and the budgeted variable production overhead, it is necessary to flex the budgeted figure. The actual variable production overhead was £72 000 from 18 000 hours of labour input, but for that level of activity nine-tenths (18 000/20 000) of £100 000 should have been spent.

£

Budgeted flexed variable production overhead   90 000
Actual variable production overhead   72 000
Variable production overhead expenditure variance   18 000 favourable

iii) The variable production overhead efficiency variance arises because 18 000 direct labour hours of input were required to produce 15 000 standard hours (three quarters or 60 000/80 000 of 20 000). So 3000 hours longer were taken at £5 per labour hour, resulting in a £15 000 adverse variance.

(standard hours − actual hours)× standard variable production overhead rate
   15 000   −   18 000   ×   £5

= £15 000 adverse

---

overtime: time worked in excess of the contractually agreed hours.

overtime premium may be paid to workers who work *overtime*. The premium is usually expressed as 'time and a half' or 'double time' etc. 'Time and a half' means that the basic hourly rate is paid plus a premium of 50 per cent. 'Double time' means that the basic hourly rate is doubled. Overtime premiums might be paid for night work or week-end working.

overtrading occurs when a business attempts to finance expansion without securing the necessary *long*-term finance. This means large investment in stocks and debtors has to be financed by short-term credit from suppliers and from the bank in the form of *overdraft* facilities. The danger is that the trade creditors and the bank may reach a point where they are no longer prepared to support the business. This may result in the business being forced into *liquidation*.

Overtrading is often evident in new businesses in high-growth sectors of the economy run by inexperienced management. It is also a problem experienced by businesses when the economy is moving out of a *recession*.

Negative *working capital* is a symptom of overtrading.

owner's capital: business finance provided by the owner(s).

owner's equity: the total of the issued ordinary share capital and all a company's *reserves*.

Pacioli was an Italian mathematician who wrote the first known book on *double-entry bookkeeping* in 1494. The underlying principles are the same as they were then, but many adaptations have been made to the basic model to suit the needs of today.

paid-up share capital: the part of the *called-up capital* for which a company has received money.

parent undertaking: the accounting term used to indicate that a business has the 'right to exercise a dominant influence' over a *subsidiary undertaking*. The influence may arise by having:

- a right to appoint *directors*
- a control contract
- rights laid out in the *Memorandum* and *Articles of Association*

pareto distribution theory: also known as the 80/20 rule. The application of the rule states that about 80 per cent of the value of a business's stocks will be accounted for by approximately 20 per cent of the total quantity. Around 20 per cent of total customers will account for about 80 per cent of total turnover, etc.

The value of this theory to the managers of a business is that efforts are best concentrated on the key 20 per cent rather than the whole 100 per cent.

partnership exists when two or more persons join together in business with a view to profit.

partnership accounts are prepared in the same way as the accounts of any other business. The *final accounts* could include:

- a *manufacturing account*
- a *trading account*
- a *profit and loss account*

These are all exactly the same as the final accounts of a *sole trader* or *limited company*. Because there is more than one owner, a partnership also needs an *appropriation account* to show how the profits have been shared.

Partnership Act 1890: provisions come into force if a *partnership* does not have a *partnership agreement*. Section 24 of the Act states that in the absence of either an express or implied agreement:

- no partner is entitled to a partnership salary
- no partner is entitled to interest on capital
- no partner is to be charged interest on drawings
- profits are to be shared equally
- any loan made to the business by a partner will earn interest at the rate of 5 per cent per annum

partnership advances or loans made by a partner to a business should be kept separate from any injections of capital. They are treated *at arm's length*. The interest on the loan is debited to the *profit and loss account* like any loan interest payable. The bookkeeping entries are:

Debit: Profit and loss account   Credit: Partner's current account

partnership agreements could be verbal or even implied by the conduct of the partner, but should be in writing to reduce the possibility of disputes or misunderstandings in the future.

A partnership agreement will generally cover the following accounting arrangements:

- the capital to be subscribed by each of the partners
- the rate of interest to be paid on any loans to the partnership by a partner
- the amounts of any salaries to be paid to partners
- the rate of interest, if any, to be given on partners' capital account balances
- the rate of interest, if any, to be charged on partners' drawings
- the ratio in which residual profits or losses are to be shared

partnership appropriation accounts show how a business's profits have been distributed amongst the partners.

Worked example: Trevor and Eunice are in partnership. They have capital account balances of £20 000 and £25 000 respectively. Their drawings for the year were: Trevor £26 439; Eunice £16 771. Their partnership agreement provides that:
Trevor be paid a partnership salary of £2000 per annum
Interest on capital be paid at 8% per annum
Interest on drawings be charged: Trevor £160
                                 Eunice £281
Residual profits or losses are to be shared in the ratios 2:1 respectively.
The net profit for the year ended 31 October 19*7 was £41 762.

Required:

The partnership profit and loss appropriation account for the year ended 31 October 19*7.

Solution:

Trevor and Eunice profit and loss appropriation account for the year ended 31 October 19*7

		£	£
Net profit for the year			41 762
Add interest on drawings – Trevor		160	
Eunice		281	441
			42 203
Less salary –	Trevor		2 000
			40 203
Less interest on capital –	Trevor	1 600	
	Eunice	2 000	3 600
			36 603
Share of profit –	Trevor	24 402	
	Eunice	12 201	36 603

partnership balance sheet is similar, in most respects, to that of any other business. It shows the assets and liabilities of the *partnership*. The difference between the *balance sheet* of a partnership and that of a *sole trader* or *limited company* is in the capital section; there will be a capital account for each of the partners. The capital accounts may be *fixed* or *fluctuating*.

Worked example: using the information above regarding Trevor and Eunice.

Required:

A balance sheet extract showing the capital account details for both partners as at 31 October 19*7. The partnership maintains fluctuating capital accounts.

Solution:

Trevor and Eunice balance sheet extract as at 31 October 19*7

	£	£	£
Capital accounts			
Trevor balance as at 1 November 19*6			20 000
Add salary		2 000	
interest on capital		1 600	
share of profits		24 402	28 002
			48 002
Less drawings		26 439	
interest on drawings		160	26 599
			21 403
Eunice balance as at 1 November 19*6		25 000	
Add interest on capital	2 000		
share of profits	12 201	14 201	
		39 201	
Less drawings	16 771		
interest on drawings	281	17 052	22 149

The partners may have *fixed capital accounts*, in which case all appropriations of profit will be credited to partnership current accounts. (See *partnership current accounts* for an example.)

With current accounts and fixed capital accounts, a balance sheet extract might show:

		£	£
Capital accounts	Rodney		40 000
	Stephanie		45 000
	Theresa		30 000
Current accounts	Rodney	1 286	
	Stephanie	(603)	
	Theresa	941	1 624

partnership capital accounts: see *capital accounts, fluctuating capital accounts, fixed capital accounts.* For a worked example, see *partnership balance sheet.*

partnership current accounts are credited with all appropriations of the partnership profits. The partners' *drawings* and any interest charged on those drawings are debited to the partners' current accounts.

Worked example: Toni, Arnold and Beth are in partnership. The balances standing on their current accounts at 31 October 19*7 were:

	£
Toni	452 Cr
Arnold	34 Dr
Beth	1673 Cr

Their drawings for the year were:

Toni	16 742
Arnold	19 850
Beth	15 788

The partnership profit and loss appropriation account is shown as:

Partnership profit and loss appropriation account for the year ended 31 October 19*7

	£	£
Net profit		53 200
Add interest on drawings – Toni	163	
Arnold	410	
Beth	87	660
		53 860
Salary – Arnold		5 000
		48 860
Interest on capital – Toni	3 400	
Arnold	800	
Beth	2 450	6 650
		42 210
Share of profits – Toni	14 070	
Arnold	14 070	
Beth	14 070	42 210

Required:

The partnership current accounts as they would appear at 31 October 19*7.

Solution:

Partnership current accounts

	Toni	Arnold	Beth		Toni	Arnold	Beth
	£	£	£		£	£	£
Balance b/d		34		Balances b/d	452		1 673
Drawings	16 742	19 850	15 788	Salary		5 000	
Int. on drawings	163	410	87	Int. on cap'l	3 400	800	2 450
				Sh. of profit	14 070	14 070	14 070
Balances c/d	1 017		2 318	Balance c/d		424	
	17 922	20 294	18 193		17 922	20 294	18 193
Balance b/d		424		Balances b/d	1 017		2 318

partnership dissolution might occur when:

- a partner dies
- a partner retires
- a partner is bankrupt (see *bankruptcy*)
- the partners agree that the *partnership* should be terminated

On dissolution the partnership assets will be disposed of and the liabilities settled. The settlement should be in the following order:

1 creditors
2 partners' loans
3 partners' *capital accounts*

Unless an examination question indicates anything to the contrary, assume that the partnership will collect any monies due from debtors and will pay the partnership creditors. Any loans to the partnership should be paid off, including loans made by any partner. Partners' loans should not be transferred into their capital accounts. Loans of any description are liabilities and must be settled before capital account balances.

All assets to be disposed of are debited to the *realisation account*. This means that the only accounts remaining in the partnership *books of account* will be the business bank account, the partners' current accounts, the partners' capital accounts and the realisation account.

Any current account balances should be transferred to the partners' capital accounts. The profit (loss) on dissolution is calculated and transferred to the partners' capital accounts. The bank balance should not be shared out in any prescribed way – the bank account should be used to balance off the partners' capital accounts.

Worked example: David, Laura and Susan are in partnership sharing profits and losses 2:2:1. They agree to dissolve their partnership on 30 November 19*7. Their balance sheet on that date was as follows:

Fixed assets	£	Capital accounts		£
Premises	140 000	David	80 000	
Machinery	60 000	Laura	70 000	
Vehicles (3 cars)	14 000	Susan	50 000	200 000
	214 000			
Current assets		Current accounts		
Stock	16 000	David	3 000	
Debtors	7 000	Laura	1 000	
Bank	3 000	Susan	2 000	6 000
	26 000			
		Loan – Susan		25 000
		Creditors		9 000
	240 000			240 000

The stock was sold for £14 700 cash.

The premises and machinery were taken over by Lime Ltd. The purchase consideration was £240 000 being made up of 90 000 £1 ordinary shares. The partners have agreed that shares in Lime Ltd be distributed in the ratio of their last agreed capital account balances.

The vehicles were taken over by the partners at the following agreed valuations:
Car 1 by David valued at £3500
Car 2 by Laura valued at £6500
Car 3 by Susan valued at £1000
The debtors paid £6800 in settlement.
The creditors accepted £8100 in settlement.
Costs of dissolution were £3950.

Required:

The realisation account, cash account and the partners' capital accounts to close the partnership books of account.

Solution:

Realisation account

Discount allowed to debtors	200	Discount received from creditors			900
Premises	140 000	Bank (stock)			14 700
Machinery	60 000	Lime Ltd			240 000
Vehicles	14 000	Capitals (cars)	David		3 500
Stock	16 000		Laura		6 500
Costs	3 950		Susan		1 000
Profit on dissolution					
David	12 980				
Laura	12 980				
Susan	6 490				
	266 600				266 600

Capital accounts

	David	Laura	Susan		David	Laura	Susan
Realisation (cars)	3 500	6 500	1 000	Balances b/d	80 000	70 000	50 000
Lime Ltd – Shares	96 000	84 000	60 000	Curr. accounts	3 000	1 000	2 000
				Realis. profit	12 980	12 980	6 490
				Cash	3 520	6 520	2 510
	99 500	90 500	61 000		99 500	90 500	61 000

Bank

Balance b/d	3 000	Loan – Susan	25 000
Debtors	6 800	Creditors	8 100
Realisation – stock	14 700	Costs	3 950
Capital accounts David	3 520		
Laura	6 520		
Susan	2 510		
	37 050		37 050

Note:

Even though there are only 90 000 shares in Lime Ltd they have a value of £240 000. The partners will receive 36 000 shares, 31 500 shares and 22 500 shares respectively valued at £96 000, £84 000 and £60 000.

When a partner has a debit balance on his/her capital account after dissolution and he/she is insolvent, the ruling in *Garner v Murray (1904)* should be applied.

partnership profit and loss account is no different to any other *profit and loss account*. Note: if a partner has made a loan, any interest on the loan should be debited to the partnership profit and loss account, and be credited to the partner's current account.

partnership retirement means that the partnership ceases to exist on the retirement date (see also *retiring partner*). The following day the partnership recommences, with one less partner, as a new business. By way of example, Zack, Jack and Jill are in partnership. Jack retires on 30 June 19*7. Up to midnight on 30 June 19*7 the business has three owners – Zack, Jack and Jill. One microsecond after midnight the business has two owners – Zack and Jill.

When a partner retires (or dies) it is necessary to prepare a *profit and loss account* and an *appropriation account* up to the date of the retirement. It is also necessary to prepare another profit and loss account and appropriation account for the period immediately after the retirement up to the 'normal' financial year end. (In examination questions partners will retire or die at convenient times during the year!)

When a partner leaves a business it is necessary to have the business valued. It is no longer a going concern.

Worked example: Zack, Jack and Jill are in partnership sharing profits 3:2:1. On 30 June 19*7 Jack retires from the partnership. The partnership balance sheet as at that date is shown below.

Zack, Jack and Jill Balance sheet as at 30 June 19*7

	£			£
Premises	150 000	Capital	Zack	90 000
Machinery	16 000		Jack	63 000
Vehicles	31 000		Jill	56 000
Stock	4 350			
Debtors	9 150	Current liabilities		8 500
Bank	7 000			
	217 500			217 500

The following valuations have been agreed on 30 June 19*7 by the partners:

	£
Premises	210 000
Machinery	8 000
Vehicles	19 000
Goodwill	26 000

Other assets and liabilities are valued at book value.

Zack and Jill have agreed to share profits and losses in their new partnership in the ratio 3:1.

Required:

The partnership balance sheet immediately after Jack's retirement. The partnership have negotiated a bank loan in order to clear Jack's capital account balance.

Solution:

Revaluation account

	£			£
Machinery	8 000	Premises		60 000
Vehicles	12 000	Goodwill		26 000
Capitals Zack	33 000			
Jack	22 000			
Jill	11 000			
	86 000			86 000

Capital accounts

	Zack	Jack	Jill		Zack	Jack	Jill
	£	£	£		£	£	£
Cash		85 000		Balances b/d	90 000	63 000	56 000
Balances c/d	123 000		67 000	Revaluation	33 000	22 000	11 000
	123 000	85 000	67 000		123 000	85 000	67 000
				Bal's b/d	123 000		67 000

Zack and Jill balance sheet as at 30 June (after Jack's retirement):

	£			£
Premises	210 000	Capital Zack		123 000
Machinery	8 000	Jill		67 000
Vehicles	19 000			
Goodwill	26 000	Loan		85 000
Stock	4 350			
Debtors	9 150	Current liabilities		8 500
Bank	7 000			
	283 500			283 500

Goodwill should be written off (SSAP 22), so:

Goodwill

	£			£
Realisation	26 000	Capital Zack		19 500
		Jill		6 500
	26 000			26 000

Goodwill is written off in the partners' profit sharing ratios. There are now only two partners in the business sharing profits and losses 3:1, so:

Zack and Jill balance sheet as at 30 June (after Jack's retirement)

	£			£
Premises at valuation	210 000	Capital	Zack	103 500
Machinery at valuation	8 000		Jill	60 500
Vehicles at valuation	19 000			
Stock	4 350	Loan		85 000
Debtors	9 150	Current liabilities		8 500
Bank	7 000			
	257 500			257 500

partnership salaries are paid to partners who have a particular responsibility, skill or extra workload. Even though this benefit is called a salary it should be remembered that it is in fact part of the profits; it is not a salary like you or I may earn from our workplace.

The bookkeeping entries to record the salary payment is:

Debit: Profit and loss appropriation account   **Credit:** Partner's current account

par value: the face value or nominal value of a share. For example, £1 *ordinary shares* have a par value of £1. Ten pence shares have a par value of 10 pence.

past costs: see *irrelevant costs*

payback method of capital investment appraisal: one of the simplest and most frequently used methods of *capital investment appraisal*. It measures the length of time that is required for a stream of cash proceeds from an investment to recover the original cash outlay that was necessary to acquire that investment.

Worked example: Jackie Curran is considering the purchase of a machine for her business. There are currently two models that will suit her needs:

	Machine CA 6	Machine NJ 4
	Cost £55 000	Cost £65 000
	Estimated net cash flows	Estimated net cash flows
	£	£
Year 1	20 000	25 000
Year 2	22 000	28 000
Year 3	25 000	32 000
Year 4	28 000	35 000

Required:

Calculate the payback period for each machine.

Solution:

Machine CA 6 payback 2 years 6.24 months.
Machine NJ 4 payback 2 years 4.5 months.

The major criticism of the payback method of capital investment appraisal is that it does not take into account the *time value of money*. In order to overcome this criticism, many businesses use the method and discount the estimated *cash flows* by using the appropriate *cost of capital* for the business.

Worked example: Jackie's cost of capital is currently 11%. The following is an extract from the present value table of £1 at 11%:

	11%
Year 1	0.901
Year 2	0.812
Year 3	0.731
Year 4	0.659

Required:

Calculate the discounted payback for the two machines considered previously.

Solution:

Machine CA 6

	Cash flows	Present value factor	Net present value
	£		£
Year 0	(55 000)	1	(55 000)
Year 1	20 000	0.901	18 020
Year 2	22 000	0.812	17 864
Year 3	25 000	0.731	18 275
Year 4	28 000	0.659	18 452

The discounted payback for machine CA 6 is 3 years 0.55 months.

Machine NJ 4

Year 0	(65 000)	1	(65 000)
Year 1	25 000	0.901	22 525
Year 2	28 000	0.812	22 736
Year 3	32 000	0.731	23 392
Year 4	35 000	0.659	23 065

The discounted payback for machine NJ 4 is 2 years 10.1 months.

The discounted payback is the most commonly used method of capital investment appraisal in the UK. It is especially useful when a business is faced with *liquidity* constraints and requires a fast repayment from the investment. It is also used in conjunction with the *net present value* or the *internal rate-of-return* methods in order to determine which investments may require closer scrutiny.

PAYE (pay as you earn): a method of collecting income tax. Income tax is deducted from the employee's wage by the employer. PAYE deductions are paid to the Inland Revenue each month by the employer.

At the beginning of each tax year the Inland Revenue allocates a code number to each taxpayer. The code number is based on the allowances claimed by the taxpayer (an allowance gives relief from paying tax).

payee: see *cheque*

payment by results: pay scheme that rewards workers for the actual numbers of units produced. (See *piece work*.)

payroll analysis: a summary of the payroll. It shows the totals of:

- gross pay
- employer's contribution to National Insurance
- employer's contribution to any pension funds

It also summarises the payroll costs to the business. It shows the total amounts payable to:

- the Inland Revenue – for both employer's and employees' contributions for National Insurance and PAYE
- the pension fund – again both employer's and employees' contributions
- employees' net pay

payroll on-costs are the costs that a business has to bear because it is an employer. They are employer's *National Insurance contribution* and any *pension* costs borne by the employer.

penetration pricing: a strategy of employing low prices in order to gain a foothold in a new market. The same techniques may be used to force a competitor out of business. In this case it is known as destroyer pricing.

A *marginal costing* approach is adopted.

Worked example: a British manufacturer enjoys a great deal of success with a product in the home market. The product sells for £36.00. The costs involved in the production of the good are:

Variable costs per unit £14.00
Fixed costs per unit   £10.00

The manufacturer believes that there is a good potential market for the product in China.

Required:

Calculate the lowest price the manufacturer could charge in the Chinese market without lowering total business profits.

Solution:

The lowest price that could be charged is £14.00. This price would cover the manufacturer's marginal costs. The fixed costs are covered by British customers – they do not need to be recovered again. This could help to penetrate the new market. It could mean that other products bearing the same brand name may have an advantage. It might also mean that once consumer loyalty for the product is established in China the price can be increased.

A large manufacturer with ample resources can use the same tactic to force a competitor out of business.

---

pension: money paid to a person who no longer works. The payment is made on a regular basis by the state or by a privately run pension fund.

PEP (personal equity plan): a government-backed scheme to encourage share ownership and investment in UK incorporated companies. Individual taxpayers can each invest a certain amount of money in shares each year. Reinvested *dividends* are free of income tax and reinvested capital gains are free of capital gains tax.

period costs are costs which do not change when production levels change. They are time related. Examples include rent, rates and insurances.

periodic inventory: the term applied when stock is valued at the end of a financial period. The method is probably used by your local newsagent or take-away. The person taking stock makes a list of all stock held and then values each item or group of items. The list is then totalled to arrive at the stock figure on that day.

Since stock is only taken at the year end (a stocktake may take place at other times if interim accounts are prepared), there is little control over stock movements. A major weakness of this method is that any theft or damage may lie undiscovered until the year end.

periodicity requires that regular reports are made to some users of the business accounts. The concept is now established in law:

- The *Companies Act* requires *annual reports* to be sent to the *shareholders*.
- Income tax legislation requires accounts to be submitted to the Inspector of Taxes each year.

perpetual inventory revalues the value of stocks held each time there is a new purchase. Detailed records of stock receipts and issues are recorded in the store's *ledger* or on a *stock record card*.

A perpetual inventory is used in modern supermarkets. Each time goods are scanned at the checkout the computerised stock record card is amended.

The worked examples shown for *methods of stock valuation* are using perpetual methods.

personal accounts are in the names of people or other businesses. Personal accounts will be found in the *purchase ledger* if the people are suppliers of goods and services on credit. They will be found in the *sales ledger* if the people are credit customers.

personal allowances are reliefs from income tax. The allowances are presented to Parliament by the Chancellor of the Exchequer in the Budget. They become law in the subsequent Finance Act.

personnel department: the department in a business responsible for implementing manpower planning policies. It deals with:

- Recruitment – the department is responsible for hiring staff; making sure that staffing levels are sufficient to enable the business to achieve its objectives.
- Training – the department will generally have a budget allocation for this purpose. Close liaison with other departments is essential in this area to ensure that money is spent appropriately.
- Welfare – the department looks after the general well-being of the staff.
- Disciplining of staff.

petty cash book: used to record payments for small day-to-day expenses. It is kept using the *imprest system*. It is an extension of the main *cash book*, taking away many trivial cash transactions which would otherwise cause the main cash book to become overfull.

The petty cash book is written up using the *petty cash vouchers* as source documents. The following is an example of how a petty cash book might be written up:

Dr £	Date	Details	Voucher	Total	Postage	Trav. Exp.	Stat- ionery	Sundry Exp.	Ledger	Folio Cr
75.00	1 May	Cash	cb 72							
	1 May	Post	1	14.00	14.00					
	6 May	Pins	2	0.73			0.73			
	9 May	Rail tkt	3	27.00		27.00				
	15 May	Post and Envelopes	4	15.61	14.00		1.61			
	23 May	Tea & sugar	5	1.04				1.04		
	28 May	J Brett	6	7.88					7.88	cl 82
				66.26	28.00	27.00	2.34	1.04	7.88	
	31 May	Bal c/d		8.74	gl 18	gl 21	gl 25	gl 26		
75.00				75.00						
8.74	1 June	Bal b/d								
66.26	1 June	Cash	cb86							

There will be debit entries of £75.00 and £66.26 on pages 72 and 86 of the main cash book.

In the general ledger there will be credit entries in the postages account (on page 18), travelling expenses account (page 21), stationery account (Page 25) and sundry expenses account (page 26).

There will also be a credit entry in J Brett's account on page 82 of the creditors' ledger.

petty cash vouchers should be filled in each time money is given out of the petty cash float. The voucher should be signed by the person receiving the cash. If a receipt is obtained from outside the business, e.g. post office receipt for postage, bus or train tickets, etc., this can be stapled to the voucher. The petty cash vouchers are used to write up the *petty cash book*.

piece rate: the wage rate paid to workers for the production of one unit (or a batch of units).

piece work: workers are paid according to the number of units manufactured. The calculation of a worker's gross pay is:

FORMULA: number of units made × the piece rate per unit

This method does not pay *overtime* rates. Differential piece work sets different pay levels when set production targets are met.

Worked example: Hughes & Co. uses differential piece work pay rates based on the following:

Workers are paid 40 pence per unit until 300 units are produced.

Production of 301 – 400 units will attract a piece rate of 45 pence per unit.

Production of 401 – 500 units will attract a piece rate of 50 pence per unit. This week Helen has produced 417 units and Douglas has produced 312 units.

Required:

Calculate Helen and Douglas's gross pay for the week.

Solution:

Helen's gross pay		Douglas's gross pay	
	£		£
300 × 40 pence =	120.00	300 × 40 pence =	120.00
100 × 45 pence =	45.00	12 × 45 pence =	5.40
17 × 50 pence =	8.50		
	173.50		125.40

The advantages of piece work are:

- pay is proportionate to work completed
- pay is calculated easily
- time wasting is discouraged
- work is completed quickly
- can lead to greater efficiency

The disadvantages are:

- not suitable for all types of work
- workers' earnings are reduced when production ceases, even in the event of a machine breakdown
- can lead to rushed, substandard products being produced
- more supervision and quality control procedures needed
- may be problems in agreeing the levels of piece rates

planning: involves formulating the paths to be taken so that *business objectives* can be met. The business objectives can be either short or long term. Short-term or operational planning will manifest itself in various budgets. It will provide the foundations for the achievement of the strategic or corporate plan. Long-term planning is also known as *strategic* (or corporate) *planning.*

point of separation: see *common costs*

post-acquisition profits: see *pre-acquisition profits*

post-balance-sheet events: see *accounting for post-balance-sheet events SSAP 17*

posting means entering financial transactions into ledger accounts from one of the *books of prime entry.* For example, the debit entry in Terry Yardley's account in the *sales ledger* has been posted from the *sales day book.* The totals of the sales day book are posted to the credit of the *sales account* in the *general ledger.*

potential standards: see *ideal standards*

pre-acquisition profits and post-acquisition profits together form the annual profits of a *subsidiary company* in the year of *acquisition.* Post-acquisition profits belong to the parent company while pre-acquisition profits do not.

There are two methods of *apportioning* the total profits of the subsidiary into pre- and post-acquisition profits for inclusion into the *consolidated profit and loss account*:

- The whole-year method includes the whole of the subsidiary's turnover, *cost of sales, gross profit* and all expenses in the consolidated profit and loss account. The profit earned prior to acquisition is then deducted.
- The part-year method splits the subsidiary's *profit and loss account* into pre- and post-acquisition periods. Only the post-acquisition profits are then included in the consolidated profit and loss account.

The part-year method is the most commonly used.

preference shares usually carry a fixed rate of *dividend*, and are entitled to repayment of capital in the event of the company being wound up. They do not normally have full voting rights. Voting is usually restricted to times when their dividends are in arrears. Preference shareholders are given preferential rights to dividends but these will be paid only if profits are sufficiently large. They can be:

- cumulative – if the dividend on these shares is not paid in one year, then it accumulates and will be paid in the future when profits are sufficiently large; preference shares are cumulative unless otherwise stated
- non-cumulative – if the profits are insufficient to pay a dividend there is no provision for the arrears to be made up in future years

Dividends are calculated as a set percentage on the nominal value of the shares (see *nominal value of ordinary shares*), generally half being paid as an interim dividend and the other half being paid at the year end as a final dividend. The capital on redeemable preference shares will be repaid at some future date indicated in the title.

Preference shares represent a safer form of investment than *ordinary shares* because of their prior claim to dividends and *capital repayment.*

preferential creditors must be paid before other creditors if a company goes into *liquidation.*

preliminary expenses are the expenses incurred by a *limited company* on incorporation. They should not be capitalised but should be written off to the *profit and loss account* when they are incurred. Also known as formation expenses.

premium bonus pay schemes reward time-efficient work. If a piece of work is expected to take eight hours to complete and a worker is able to complete it in six hours a saving of two hours has been made. A bonus based on the hours saved will be paid to the worker as an addition to his/her basic gross pay.

The three best known versions of premium bonus schemes are:

- *Halsey premium bonus method*
- *Halsey–Wier premium bonus method*
- *Rowan premium bonus scheme*

prepayments of expenses are payments made in advance of the *accounting period* to which they relate. Businesses pay insurance premiums in advance of the time covered by the insurance. *Business rates* are paid in advance. Unused stocks of stationery, packing materials and postage stamps are other examples of prepayments. Prepayments are shown as *current assets* on the *balance sheet.*

Worked example: Derek started in business on 1 January 19*7.

 The following payments were made by Derek in his first year of trading:

 10 January 19*7 Eden District Council £340 for the rating year to 31 March 19*7

 23 January 19*7 Pendle Insurance Brokers £1394 insurance for the year to 31 December 19*7

 17 April 19*7 Eden District Council £458 half year's payment for the rating year to 31 March 19*8

 4 October 19*7 Eden District Council £458 second half year's payment for the rating year to 31 March 19*8

 23 December 19*7 Pendle Insurance Brokers £1453 insurance for the year to 31 December 19*8

Required:

The rates account and the insurance account as they would appear in Derek's books of account at 31 December 19*7.

Solution:

Rates					Insurance			
19*7			19*7		19*7			19*7
10 Jan Bank	340		31 Dec P&L a/c	1027	23 Jan Bank	1394		31 Dec P&L a/c 1394
17 Apl Bank	458				23 Dec Bank	1453		31 Dec Bal. c/d 1453
4 Oct Bank	458		31 Dec Bal. c/d	229		2847		2847
	1256			1256	19*8			
19*8					1 Jan Bal. b/d 1453			
1 Jan Bal. b/d	229							

 The profit and loss account for the year ended 31 December19*7 would show:

Expenses	£
Rates	1027
Insurance	1394

 The balance sheet as at 31 December 19*7 would show:

Current assets	
Prepayments	1682

prepayment of income occurs when income is paid in advance by the payer. A prepayment of income is shown as a creditor under *current liabilities* in the *balance sheet*.

Worked example: Josie sublets part of her premises at a rental of £720 per quarter, payable in advance. Her tenant takes up residence on 1 August 19*7, paying £720. He pays a further £720 on 4 November 19*7. Josie's financial year end is 31 December 19*7.

Required:

Write up Josie's rent receivable account for the year ended 31 December 19*7.

Solution:

<u>Rent receivable</u>

19*7				19*7			
31 December	Profit and loss account	1200		1 August	Bank	720	
31 December	Balance c/d	240		4 November	Bank	720	
		1440				1440	
				19*8			
				1 January Balance b/d 240			

The profit and loss account for the year ended 31 December 19*7 would show:

	£
Gross profit	****
Rent receivable (added)	1200

The balance sheet as at 31 December 19*7 would show:

Current liabilities	
Rent receivable	240

present value places a value for today on earnings or money to be received and expenses to be incurred at some future date. (See *net present value*.)

price/earnings ratio (P/E) makes a comparison between the earnings per share and the current market price of the share. It shows the number of years' earnings that a person is prepared to pay to buy the share.

The higher the ratio, the greater the confidence investors have regarding the prospects of the company, and the higher the market expectations of future profits and *dividends*. A high or low ratio can be judged only in relation to other businesses in the same sector of the market. The calculation is:

FORMULA: $\dfrac{\text{current market price}}{\text{earnings per share}}$

Worked example: the current market price of ordinary shares in Crampies plc is £4.67. The earnings per share is 28 pence.

Required:

Calculate the price earnings ratio for Crampies plc.

Solution:

P/E ratio $= \dfrac{\text{current market price}}{\text{earnings per share}} = \dfrac{467 \text{ pence}}{28 \text{ pence}} = 16.68$ times

price elasticity of demand measures by how much the quantity demanded of a product will change when the producer or the retailer changes the price.

price elasticity of supply measures by how much the quantity of a product supplied by producers will change if the market price changes.

primary ratio: also known as *return on capital employed (ROCE)*.

prime cost: the total of all *direct costs* incurred in producing the product(s) in a manufacturing business. (See *manufacturing accounts.*)

prior year adjustments: see *extraordinary items*

private limited company: a company whose *shareholders* are protected by *limited liability* but whose shares are not available for sale to the general public. If a private limited company needs more capital, the *directors* must find other people willing to invest in that company. As a result, many private companies are family businesses with members of the family or close friends owning all the shares.

private sector comprises all businesses owned by private individuals and not by the state. Marks and Spencer plc is in the private sector, and so is your local take-away. State-owned businesses are said to be in the *public sector.*

private ledger: part of the *general ledger* in which accounts of a confidential nature can be kept. The accounts might include *capital accounts,* and partners' current accounts in the case of a *partnership, drawings accounts,* loan accounts, *profit and loss accounts,* etc.

process costing is applied to the costing of mass-produced products. It would be extremely difficult to cost the price of a rubber washer for use in a tap. Thousands of washers will have been produced from the same pieces of synthetic rubber, and all the washers will have gone through the same processing and machining, so it would be extremely difficult and time consuming to allocate costs to a single washer. It would be even more difficult to *apportion* other overhead costs. (If 2 800 000 washers were produced in a week, and rent for the week £932, rent apportioned = 0.00033 pence!)

Process costing solves this problem. *CIMA* defines process costing as 'the costing method applicable where goods or services result from a sequence of continuous or repetitive operations or processes. Costs are averaged over the units produced during the period'.

The cost of one washer can be ascertained by the formula:

$$\text{FORMULA: } \frac{\text{total costs incurred in washer production for the period}}{\text{number of saleable washers produced in the period}}$$

This method of costing is used when:

- one product is unable to be clearly distinguished from another during the process of manufacture, e.g. pencil erasers
- the product becomes a material or component in the next stage of production
- different products are produced during the same process
- *by-products* are produced during the main process of production

product cost: the total cost incurred in the manufacturing of a product. *CIMA* defines a product cost as 'the cost of a finished article built up from its cost elements'.

production budget is prepared to determine whether the required future levels of production to satisfy the anticipated level of predicted sales are attainable, to anticipate any problems that may arise and to enable management to take remedial action.

A production budget might look like this:

	May	June	July	August
Opening stock of finished goods (units)	100	30	90	50
Units produced	200	240	160	190
	300	270	250	240
Sales	270	180	200	230
Closing stock	30	90	50	10

It can be seen that production varies between 160 units per month and 240 units per month. An even production flow to accomodate the required sales levels would look like this:

	May	June	July	August
Opening stock of finished goods (units)	100	50	90	110
Units produced	220	220	220	220
	320	270	310	330
Sales	270	180	200	230
Closing stock	50	90	110	100

production overheads: also known as factory overheads. These are expenses incurred in the production of a final product which are not *direct costs*. It would be very difficult, if not impossible in the case of certain *indirect costs*, to identify these overheads with the goods being produced. Production overheads include supervisory wages, maintenance engineers' wages, *indirect material costs* and the *depreciation* of plant and machinery.

productivity: the measurement of the rate of output generated by each worker or each machine in a factory. The most common measure used is labour productivity. The greater the productivity rate, the lower the *unit costs* per hour. For example, if a worker on average produces 50 units per week and the pay rate is £300 per week, then the labour cost per unit is £6. If productivity rises and the worker now produces 55 units per week, then labour costs per unit fall to £5.45.

productivity bonus: extra pay given to workers when there has been an increase in productivity.

productivity ratios measure the amount of profit or sales that each employee generates. *Productivity* has always been regarded as a key indicator of the efficiency of an organisation. Often workers' pay deals are linked to increases in productivity.

FORMULA: sales per employee ratio $= \dfrac{\text{sales}}{\text{number of employees}}$

FORMULA: profit per employee $= \dfrac{\text{net profit}}{\text{number of of employees}}$

Worked example: Snodgrass & Co. made a net profit of £76 945 on a net turnover of £864 967. It had an average of 532 employees during the year.

Required:

Calculate the sales and profit per employee ratios for Snodgrass & Co.

Solution:

$$\text{sales per employee} = \frac{\text{sales}}{\text{number of employees}} = \frac{864\,967}{532}$$

$$= £1625.88 \text{ per annum}$$

$$\text{profit per employee} = \frac{\text{net profit}}{\text{number of of employees}} = \frac{76\,945}{532}$$

$$= £144.63 \text{ per annum}$$

It is not possible to say whether these figures are acceptable or not; this would depend on trends and managers' expectations of their workforce.

profit: the excess of income over expenditure. This is not the same as the difference between cash received and cash paid out during a period. Profit is generally calculated by the managers of a business by preparing a *profit and loss account* for a specified time period.

profitability: the ability of a business to make profits. Profits are necessary for the long-term survival of a business, but day-to-day survival depends on the business's *liquidity*.

profitability ratios allow comparisons to be made between businesses of differing sizes when undertaking *ratio analysis*. Ratios ignore absolute figures; figures are converted into percentages when undertaking profitability ratio analysis. The profitability ratios are:

- *mark-up* or gross profit/cost of sales
- *margin* or gross profit/turnover
- *net margin* or net profit/sales
- *return on capital employed*

profit and loss account (1) calculates a business's profit or loss for an *accounting period*. The profit and loss account shows the *gross profit* on the sales, plus any other incomes such as *discounts received*, rents received, *commission* received, profit on disposal of assets. All expenditure incurred during the same time period is then deducted. If incomes exceed expenditures then the business has made a profit. If, however, expenditures exceed incomes the business has incurred a loss.

At the end of each accounting period all revenue expense accounts are closed off by transferring the annual charge to the profit and loss account. This means that the account is ready for entries in the new financial year.

For example: at the end of the year the rent account and the advertising account would be closed by transfer to the profit and loss account. This example does not include any adjustments for accruals or prepayments.

Rent				Advertising			
Cash	1100	P&L account	4400	Cash	179	P&L account	1369
Cash	1100			Cash	548		
Cash	1100			Cash	126		
Cash	1100			Cash	516		
	4400		4400		1369		1369

Profit and loss account extract for the year ended ******

Rent	4400	Gross profit	****
Advertising	1369		

Profit and loss accounts are prepared on an accruals basis, not a cash basis. See *accruals concept* for examples of bookkeeping treatment of accrued income and accrued expenses. See also *prepayments of expenses* and *prepayments of income* for further examples.

Generally, the profit and loss account is combined with the *trading account*, as in the example below. The profit and loss account can be prepared using either a *horizontal presentation* or a *vertical presentation*. The vertical presentation is the more usual layout used today. For example:

Trading and profit and loss account for the year ended 31 August 19*7
(a vertical presentation has been used)

	£	£	£
Sales			87 912
Less cost of sales			
Stock 1 September 19*6		4 203	
Purchases	38 415		
Carriage inward	234	38 649	
		42 852	
Less stock 31 August 19*7		4 371	38 481
Profit and loss account starts here:			
Gross profit			49 431
Add discount received			649
rent received			1 000
			51 080
Less expenses			
Wages	28 566		
Carriage outwards	139		
Rent	4 400		
Rates and insurance	3 561		
Advertising	1 369		
Bad debts	879		
Depreciation: fixtures	1 200		
van	2 500		42 614
Net profit			8 466

profit and loss account (2): the name given to the *revenue reserve* to which a *limited company's retained profit* for the year is credited. This is a major regular source of long-term finance for a successful limited company. It is also known as retained profits and retained earnings. (See *appropriation account*.)

profit and loss appropriation account: see *appropriation account*

profit maximisation is often regarded as the prime motive for the existence of businesses. In reality, this may not be the case. Many *sole traders* and *partnerships* satisfice, that is, they find a level of income which suits their individual needs with regard to, say, leisure time, and merely work towards that, rather than trying to make the maximum amount of profit that the business is capable of.

profit-related pay links workers' pay to the profits earned by a business. This is designed to increase *productivity* in the workforce since bigger profits will mean greater *take-home pay* for the individual.

Worked example: the 1600 workers of Gibbins plc have a profit-related pay scheme based on their pay plus an equal share of 0.04% of the annual company profits, which this year have reached £40 000 000.

Required:

Calculate the annual gross pay for Norman, who has a basic wage of £9500 and Greta, whose annual gross pay is £13 500.

Solution:

Norman will earn £10 500 and Greta will earn £14 500.
(0.04% of £40 000 000 = £1 600 000 to be shared between the 1600 workforce   = £1000 each)

---

profit sharing ratio in a *partnership* is equal unless there is a *partnership agreement* which states how profits are to be shared. This is laid down in the *Partnership Act 1890*. When a partnership agreement exists, the partners have decided how profits are to be shared.

The profit sharing ratio is calculated after partnership salaries and interest on capital have been taken into account, where applicable.

Change in profit sharing ratios of partners affects the structure of a partnership. When partners decide to alter their profit sharing ratios, one partnership ceases to exist and another 'new' partnership takes its place. This means that a revaluation of the partnership assets must take place so that the 'old' partners are credited with what are their dues, before the 'new' partnership takes over.

Worked example: Wilson, Kepple and Betty are in partnership sharing profits and losses in the ratios 2:2:1 respectively. Their balance sheet as at 31 March 19*7 was as
follows:

	£			£
Premises at cost	20 000	Capital	Wilson	30 000
Machinery at cost	18 000		Kepple	20 000
Vehicle at cost	15 000		Betty	15 000
Stock	8 000			
Debtors	4 000	Creditors		3 000
Bank	3 000			
	68 000			68 000

With effect from 31 March 19*7 the partners have agreed that profits should be shared equally. They further agree that goodwill should be valued at £36 000 on that date. Other assets are to be revalued as follows:

Premises at	£80 000
Machinery at	£4 000
Vehicle at	£5 000

Required:

The accounts in the partnership books of account to record the change in the profit sharing ratios, and the balance sheet as it would appear immediately after the change.

Solution:

Revaluation account

Machinery		14 000	Premises		60 000
Vehicle		10 000	Goodwill		36 000
Capitals	Wilson	28 800			
	Kepple	28 800			
	Betty	14 400			
		96 000			96 000

Capital

	Wilson	Kepple	Betty		Wilson	Kepple	Betty
Goodwill	12 000	12 000	12 000	Balance b/d	30 000	20 000	15 000
Balance c/d	46 800	36 800	17 400	Revaluation	28 800	28 800	14 400
	58 800	48 800	29 400		58 800	48 800	29 400
				Balance b/d	46 800	36 800	17 400

Wilson, Kepple and Betty balance sheet as at 31 March 19*7
(after the change in profit sharing ratios)

Premises at valuation	80 000	Capital	Wilson	46 800
Machinery at valuation	4 000		Kepple	36 800
Vehicle at valuation	5 000		Betty	17 400
Stock	8 000			
Debtors	4 000	Creditors		3 000
Bank	3 000			
	104 000			104 000

Note that goodwill has been written off in accordance with SSAP 22.

profit sharing schemes reward employees with a bonus based on the profits of a business. This type of bonus is designed to provide an incentive to the workforce, which should improve the results of the business.

profit/volume chart is prepared by some businesses to show the relationship between profits and levels of output. The conventional *break-even chart* does not show this clearly.

Worked example: the following figures relate to Trems:

Sales of Trems in units	1 000	2 000	3 000	4 000	5 000
	£	£	£	£	£
Sales	8 000	16 000	24 000	32 000	40 000
Variable costs	4 000	8 000	12 000	16 000	20 000
Fixed costs	9 000	9 000	9 000	9 000	9 000

Required:

A profit/volume chart for Trems showing clearly the break-even point for the product.

Solution:

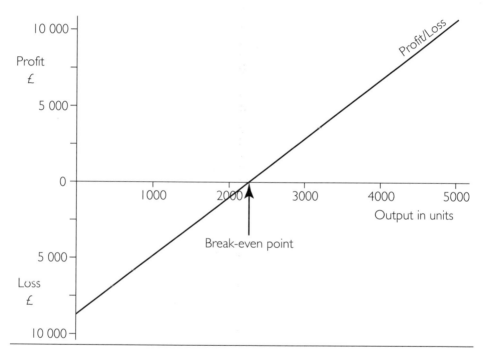

profit/volume method of calculating break-even point: see *profit/volume chart*

profit/volume ratio (P/V): see *contribution/sales ratio*

progress payments are payments made on account by a customer as a *long-term contract* progresses. (See *certification of work done.*)

prospectus details the plans and anticipated profits of a *public limited company* and is issued to prospective *shareholders* in order to encourage them to purchase shares in a company. It is issued once the company has received its Certificate of Incorporation.

provision: an amount set aside out of profits for a known expense, the amount of which cannot be calculated with substantial accuracy. (See *provision for bad debts, provision for depreciation.*)

All provision accounts look the same; only the name and the calculations are different.

Provision for ******

		Balance b/d at beginning of year	1000
Balance c/d at end of year	1700	Profit and loss account	700
	1700		1700
		Balance b/d	1700

You could insert the words 'depreciation of machinery', 'bad debts', 'discounts' or 'unrealised profit' in place of ******, the layout of the account would not change.

The *profit and loss account* for the year would show as an expense:

Provision for { depreciation / bad debts / discounts / unrealised profits } 700

The *balance sheet* would show one of the following:

Fixed asset at cost	*****	Debtors	*******
less depreciation	700	less provision for bad debts	700
Debtors	*****	Stocks of finished goods	*****
less provision for discounts	700	less provision for unrealised profit	700

provision for bad debts: an amount set aside out of profits to cover any outstanding debts, the recovery of which is in doubt. There are two main ways of calculating the amount of the provision. They are:

- by estimation based on past experience gained through knowledge of the particular business, its customers and the general economic business climate
- by drawing up an *ageing schedule of debtors*

The bookkeeping entries to record the provision are:

Debit: Profit and loss account   **Credit:** Provision for bad debts

---

Worked example: at the end of the first year of trading, Ann makes provision for bad debts at the rate of 5% on her debtors. Her outstanding debtors amount to £17 000. At the end of the second year of trading she increases the amount of the provision to 6% on outstanding debts of £23 000. At the end of her third year of trading she reduces the amount of the provision to 4% on outstanding debts of £14 000.

Required:

a) The provision for bad debts account as it would appear in Ann's general ledger.
b) Extracts from the profit and loss accounts showing the amounts transferred at the end of each year from the provision for bad debts account.

Solution:

Provision for bad debts account

Year end 1	Balance c/d	850	Year end 1	P&L account	850
			Start year 2	Balance b/d	850
Year end 2	Balance c/d	1 380	Year end 2	P&L account	530
		1 380			1 380
Year end 3	P&L account	820	Start year 3	Balance b/d	1 380
Year end 3	Balance c/d	560			
		1 380			1 380
			Start year 4	Balance b/d	560

Profit and loss account for the year ended year 1 (extract):

Provision for bad debts   850

Profit and loss account for the year ended year 2 (extract):

Provision for bad debt   530

Profit and loss account for the year ended year 3 (extract):

Overprovision for bad debts   820

---

provision for depreciation: an amount set aside out of profits in each *accounting period* to reflect the cost of using the *fixed asset* in the generation of those profits. This is applying the *accruals* (or matching) *concept*. The bookkeeping entries are similar to those used to record *provision for bad debts*:

Debit: Profit and loss account   **Credit:** Provision for depreciation of fixed asset

Often, the provision for depreciation is merely called 'depreciation" in the *general ledger* and the *final accounts.*

A different provision account should be used for each type of asset.

provision for discounts on debtors: some businesses create a provision for discounts that they may allow credit customers on amounts owed at the end of the financial year. This is to take into account, in the period when the sales have taken place, the reduction in the value of the debtors caused by any discount that may be allowed for settlement within the agreed credit period.

The bookkeeping entries are similar to those used to record *provision for bad debts*:

Debit: Profit and loss account   **Credit:**   Provision for discount on debtors

provision for doubtful debts: another name used for *provision for bad debts.*

provision for unrealised profit: see *manufacturing accounts* for a worked example. The bookkeeping entries are similar to those used to record *provision for bad debts.*

prudence states that, as accountants, we provide for losses as soon as they are anticipated, but we do not recognise profits until they are realised. In other words, it is much safer to understate rather than overstate profits.

The concept arises because certain items are, of necessity, estimates made when preparing periodic accounts, e.g. accrued expenses, prepaid expenses.

If managers or owners were over-optimistic it is possible that profits might be over-stated, and this could result in the resources of the business being depleted by excessive *drawings* or excessive *dividends* being paid. Prudence is sometimes known as conservatism.

public limited companies are owned by their *shareholders*, who usually pay an amount when they apply for the shares, and the balance when the shares have been allotted to them (see *issue of shares*). If the company encounters financial difficulties the shareholders cannot be required to contribute more than an agreed amount of capital. This could result in creditors not being paid what they are owed. To warn potential creditors, the company has to be more open about its affairs than the other forms of business ownership.

The shareholders put the day-to-day running of the company into the hands of *directors*.

public sector comprises organisations that are owned or funded by the state (e.g. the National Health Service) or local authorities (e.g. local libraries).

published accounts are distributed to the *shareholders* at the end of each financial year. They are also filed with the *Registrar of Companies*. All *limited companies* must distribute a set of accounts to the shareholders. However, *small* and *medium-sized companies* can file modified accounts with the Registrar of Companies.

A company draws up detailed *final accounts* for use by the managers of the business. If these were distributed to the shareholders a copy could be used by competitors to undermine the business. A less detailed version of the accounts is therefore published, which affords the company some degree of protection.

The published final accounts must comply with the provisions of the *Companies Act 1985*, schedule 4. This states the information that must be shown and how it should be shown. The statutorily acceptable layouts can be seen under *format 1 and format 2 layouts for the published profit and loss account of a limited company.*

purchase day book is a list of credit purchases. It is written up from the purchase *invoices* received from the suppliers of goods. When it is convenient, the purchase day book is used to post the individual purchases to the credit of the appropriate *personal accounts* in the *purchase ledger*, and the total purchases to the debit of the purchases account in the *general ledger*.

The purchase day book is not part of the *double-entry bookkeeping* system.

Worked example: Debbie Crabbe has made the following purchases on credit. She has received purchase invoices from:
Smiley £170; from Hunt £35; from Priestley £216.

Required:

Write up Debbie's purchase day book and show the relevant postings to the ledger accounts.

**ISLE COLLEGE
RESOURCES CENTRE**

Solution:

Purchase ledger Smiley			Purchase day book		General ledger Purchases		
£	£			£		£	£
	PDB	170	Smiley	170			
			Hunt	35	PDB	421	
			Priestley	216			

Hunt	
£	£
	PDB 35

Priestley	
£	£
	PDB 216

Purchase day book totals: Smiley 170, Hunt 35, Priestley 216, total 421.

General ledger Purchases: PDB 421.

purchase journal: see *purchase day book*

purchase ledger contains the accounts of all the credit suppliers of a business. The accounts are written up from the *purchase day book.*

purchase ledger control account: see *control accounts*

purchase order: the business document used to place an order with a supplier. The responsibility for raising such a document lies with the purchasing department within the business. Usually the top copy of the order is sent to the supplier, a copy is kept by the purchasing department, another is sent to the accounts department and the bottom copy is sent to the goods inward department (or warehouse).

purchase requisition: a document raised by a department which wishes to make a purchase. It will be prepared and given to a manager for approval and signing. The requisition instructs the buying department to go ahead with the purchase.

purchase returns book: sec *purchase returns day book*

purchase returns day book: a *book of prime entry* in which goods returned to suppliers are entered. It is written up from the credit notes received from the supplier.

The book is used to post entries to:

- the debit side of the individual suppliers' accounts in the *purchase ledger*
- the credit side of the purchase returns (returns outward) account in the *general ledger*

Worked example: Waqar Hasami has received the following credit notes:
J Bull £28; R Keane £51; T Klute £8 for goods he has returned to the supplier.

Required:

Enter the credit notes in the purchase returns day book and post to the appropriate ledger accounts.

Solution:

Purchase ledger			Purchase returns day book		General ledger	
J Bull				£	**Purchase returns**	
	£	£	J Bull	28	£	£
PRDB	28		R Keane	51	PRDB	87
			T Klute	8		
R Keane				87		
	£	£				
PRDB	51					
T Klute						
	£	£				
PRDB	8					

purchase returns journal: see *purchase returns day book*

purchases are goods bought by a business for resale in the normal course of business. For Mr Choppe the butcher, sides of beef, pork and sausage skins are purchases. For W H Smith, books, pens and magazines are purchases.

purchases account in the *general ledger* is debited with goods bought by a business for resale in the normal course of business. Entries are posted to the debit of the account from:

- the *purchase day book* in the case of credit purchases; the credit entries will be found in the *personal accounts* of individual suppliers in the *purchase ledger*
- the *cash book* in the case of cash purchases (credit in *cash* or *bank columns*)

purchases book: see *purchase day book*

quick ratio: also known as the *acid test ratio* and the liquidity ratio.

quotation: a response made to a customer's enquiry. It is an offer to sell goods (or services) at the prices, terms and conditions stated in the quotation.

R

ranking of projects prioritises competing *capital expenditure* projects according to their financial desirability. Managers, with a limited capital expenditure budget, are often faced with a number of alternative projects. There is a need to list the projects in order, showing those that are likely to yield the best financial results. Managers may then make a decision as to where money should be best spent.

There may be a *limiting factor* that could affect the decision. This might be *direct materials* or *direct labour.*

rate of return measures the return that will accrue from a particular investment decision. A business might require a decision regarding investment in a capital project, or an individual might require a decision whether to invest in a savings account in a building society or a bank.

A business would calculate the rate of return using one of the following methods of *capital investment appraisal:*

- *accounting rate-of-return*
- *internal rate-of-return*
- *net present value*
- *payback*

An individual would make an investment decision referring to the amount of interest or *dividend* which would come from the investment.

The rate of return is generally expressed as a percentage of the amount invested.

rate of stockturn: see *rate of stock turnover*

rate of stock turnover shows how many times on average that a 'bundle' of stock was sold during the last *accounting period.* The speed of stockturn is an important efficiency ratio. In every 'bundle' of stock held by a business, a large amount of cash and profit is tied up. A rapid turnover of stock will release this cash and profit quickly; the more often the business can sell its stock the more benefit the business will get.

It might seem that the best rate of stockturn might be 365 per year. However, if stock levels fall too low, it might result in lost customers if stock were not available when demanded. In some industries the need to hold large amounts of stock for long periods has been almost totally eradicated with the use of *just-in-time (JIT) method of stock purchasing.* The calculation is:

FORMULA: rate of stockturn $= \dfrac{\text{sales (at cost)}}{\text{stock*}}$

*Stock is obviously at cost, but which stock figure? We use an average!

Worked example: the trading account of Melanie Murphy is shown below:

	£	£
Sales		217 000
Less cost of sales		
Opening stock	13 000	
Purchases	106 000	
	119 000	
Closing stock	11 000	108 000
Gross profit		109 000

Required:

Calculate Melanie's rate of stockturn.

Solution:

$$\text{rate of stockturn} = \frac{\text{cost of sales}}{\text{average stock}} = \frac{108\ 000}{12\ 000} = 9 \text{ times or 40 days (365/9)}$$

Whether this is a good or bad rate of stockturn will depend on the type of product and previous years' rates, or comparison with similar businesses or with the rates prevailing in the industry as a whole.

ratio analysis: a method of analysing the financial results of a business in order to measure its performance. The *final accounts* contain much financial information which can give an insight into the performance of the business. The ratios calculated from the accounts are used by:

- owners
- employees and trade unions
- bank managers
- competitors
- researchers
- press
- Inland Revenue and Customs and Excise
- debtors and creditors
- pressure groups

The figures given are absolutes and as such do not give an indication of the efficiency or effectiveness of the organisation. The relationships between the figures give a better indication. We can then comment on whether the figures are better or worse than:

- trends in the results of the business over a number of years
- results of the business compared with the results of another business in the same business sector
- results of the business compared with the average results of all the businesses in the sector

ratios: the term applied to calculations used to compare the results of businesses using *ratio analysis*. The generic term 'ratio' is applied to results expressed in:

- ratios, e.g. current ratio might be 2.7:1
- percentages, e.g. the mark-up might be 37 per cent

- time, e.g. debtors settle their debts in 34 days on average; stock is turned over 14 times per year

See under the appropriate heading for particular ratios and their calculation. In an examination, always state the model or formula on which your calculations are based.

real accounts are *general ledger* accounts in which the purchase and sale of *fixed assets*, and cash and bank transactions are recorded. (In reality, for convenience the cash and bank accounts are kept separate from the general ledger.)

Real accounts include land and premises, machinery, vehicles, cash and bank.

realisation account: this is used to close the *books of account* and to record the sales of the assets of a *partnership* on dissolution. For a worked example showing the use of a realisation account, see *partnership dissolution*.

realisation concept states that revenue should only be recorded in the business *books of account* when the goods sold have been replaced by a debtor or by cash. Goods sent to a potential customer remain the property of the sender until the customer indicates that he/she has purchased the goods.

realised profits are recognised when a sale takes place and cash is received, or a debtor acknowledges the debt. *Unrealised profits* are not recognised until a contract of sale has been negotiated.

receipts and payments account: essentially a summary of all the cash receipts and cash payments made by a club or society during a financial year. It is the main source of information used in the preparation of *club accounts*.

recession: a time of high unemployment, of shortage of investment by businesses, and a general lack of confidence in the economy. It is officially defined as 'two successive quarterly periods of declining gross domestic product'.

reciprocal services are often provided by servicing departments for other departments within a business. For example, the maintenance engineers might service the catering machinery; the catering department might provide refreshments for the engineers. Similarly, the power-generating section might provide heating services for all departments; the personnel and wages departments might provide services for the power-generating department.

For accounting treatment, see *apportionment of reciprocal service overheads*.

redeemable shares: shares that will be bought back by a company if the fact was stipulated when the shares were first issued. A company can issue redeemable shares of any class, if allowed in the *Articles of Association*. The redemption date may be:

- specified, as in the case of, say, 8 per cent redeemable preference shares 2016 (these will be redeemed in the year 2016)
- at the discretion of the *shareholders* or of the company

redemption of shares and debentures: see *capital redemption reserve* for the bookkeeping entries.

reducing balance method of calculating depreciation calculates the annual *depreciation* charge on the *net book value* of the asset at the previous *balance sheet date*.

Worked example: Akbar Smith purchased a new delivery vehicle on 1 January 19*6 for £18 000. It is his policy to charge depreciation on vehicles at 40% per annum using the reducing balance method of providing for depreciation.

Required:

i) the provision for depreciation of delivery vehicle account
ii) balance sheet extracts as at 31 December 19*6 and 19*7

Solution:

Provision for depreciation of delivery vehicle

19*6			19*6		
31 Dec bal c/d	7 200		31 Dec P&L a/c	7 200	
19*7			19*7		
			1 Jan bal b/d	7 200	
31 Dec bal c/d	11 520		31 Dec P&L a/c	4 320	
	11 520			11 520	
			1 Jan bal b/d	11 520	

Balance sheet extract as at 31 December 19*6

Fixed asset

Delivery vehicle at cost	£18 000
Less depreciation	7 200
	10 800

Balance sheet extract as at 31 December 19*7

Fixed asset

Delivery vehicle at cost	£18 000
Less depreciation	11 520
	6 480

refer to drawer is written on a *cheque* when there are insufficient funds in the account to enable the bank to honour the cheque. The cheque is returned to the person on whose account it is drawn.

Registrar of Companies receives two documents when a business registers as a *limited company*. These documents are:

- *Memorandum of Association*
- *Articles of Association*

When the Registrar approves registration, the business becomes a limited company and is issued with its Certificate of Incorporation. This gives the company the status of a *legal entity* which is separate from the *shareholders*.

Once the minimum capital is raised, the Registrar issues the company with its Certificate of Trading. On receipt of this, a plc can trade.

It is also a requirement of the *Companies Acts* that copies of accounts and *annual reports* for incorporated businesses are lodged with the Registrar of Companies.

related party disclosure FRS 8 is concerned with disclosure of:

- information on related party transactions
- the name of the party exercising control over the reporting entity

The standard states that 'in the absence of information to the contrary, it is assumed that a reporting entity has independent discretionary power over its resources and transactions and pursues its activities independently … Transactions are presumed to have been undertaken on an *arm's length* basis … These assumptions may not be justified when related parties exist …'.

Two or more parties are related when:

- one party has direct or indirect control over the other party
- parties are subject to control from the same source
- one party inhibits another party to the extent that it does not follow its own separate interest
- one party to a transaction subordinates its own separate interest

relevant costs: when making choices between two or more alternative policies, only *future differential costs* need to be considered; *sunk costs* should be disregarded. For example, Ruth is trying to decide whether she should travel by rail or use her own car in order to attend a meeting in Manchester. When she costs out the two methods she should ignore *depreciation*, insurance and road fund tax on her car since these have already been incurred. They are sunk costs and they should have no bearing on her decision.

remittance advice: the document that a customer sends to a supplier, listing all the *invoices*, less any credit notes, that are being paid at that time. The remittance advice is often attached to the statements sent out by the supplier. It can be torn off and sent back to the supplier with the appropriate payment.

reorder levels: see *stock reorder level*

reporting financial performance FRS 3 requires 'reporting entities … to highlight a range of important components of financial performance to aid users in understanding the performance achieved … and to assist them in forming a basis for their assessment of future results and *cash flows*'.

The standard superseded SSAP 6 when issued in October 1992. It modifies the format for the *profit and loss account* as given in the *Companies Act 1985*. It requires that a layered format be used in the presentation of the profit and loss account. This will show clearly:

- the results of continuing operations (including the results of acquisitions)
- the results of discontinued operations
- profits or losses on the sale or termination of an operation
- the costs of a fundamental reorganisation or restructuring
- profits or losses on the disposal of *fixed assets*
- *extraordinary items*
- *exceptional items* (these should be included under the statutory heading to which they relate)

Prior to the issue of the standard it was possible for the earnings per share figure to be increased by excluding certain elements of expenditure, e.g. redundancy costs and costs of reorganisation.

reporting requirements for medium-sized companies are less onerous than those for large companies. To be classified as a *medium-sized company*, two of the following criteria must be satisfied:

- a turnover not exceeding £11 200 000
- a *balance sheet* total not exceeding £5 600 000
- average number of employees not exceeding 250

The following concessions are allowed in the accounts to be filed with the *Registrar of Companies*:

- the *profit and loss account* may show as its first item *gross profit* or *loss* – this is a combination of turnover, *cost of sales* and other operating income shown in *format 1 layout for the published profit and loss account of a limited company*
- analyses of turnover and profit are not required

But

- the balance sheet must be reported in full
- the *directors' report* must be filed with the accounts

reporting requirements for small companies are less onerous than those for large companies. To be classified as a small company, two of the following criteria must be satisfied:

- a turnover not exceeding £2 800 000
- *balance sheet* total not exceeding £1 400 000
- average number of employees not exceeding 50

The following concessions are allowed in the accounts to be filed with the *Registrar of Companies*:

- *profit and loss account* need not be filed
- a modified *balance sheet* may be filed

The minimum disclosures in the balance sheet are:

- *intangible assets*
- *tangible fixed assets*
- *investments (fixed assets)*
- *stocks*
- *debtors*
- investments (*current assets*)
- *called-up capital*
- *share premium account*
- *revaluation reserve*
- other *reserves*
- profit and loss account

reporting the substance of transactions FRS 5 requires companies to ensure that financial statements observe the commercial substance of transactions rather than just their legal form. In the vast majority of cases, the commercial substance of the transactions is likely to be the same as their legal form. The main applications of the standard will be in cases where:

- an asset is being acquired using a *hire-purchase* contract
- a transaction is only part of a series of transactions, and that single transaction can only be fully understood as part of the whole series
- a transaction includes options and it is very likely that the company will exercise one of the options

research and development: exploring new scientific methods of manufacturing and, generally, using the results to produce an end-product.

Research and development can be:

- pure research – no end-result was envisaged when the research was under-taken in the first place; its aim is to increase knowledge
- applied research – is directed towards a practical application, e.g. a cure for asthma
- development – is the application of knowledge gained in research to pro-duce or improve a product or a process before it is marketed commercially

research and development costs are normally written off in the financial period in which they occur; they are treated as *period costs*. The costs might be carried forward and *amortised* over the useful life of the process, if they can be clearly identified with future commercial viability. (See *accounting for research and development SSAP 13*.)

reserves: the *Companies Acts* do not give a formal definition of a reserve. However, it is generally accepted that reserves do not include:

- *provisions for depreciation*
- provisions for known *liabilities*
- *provisions for taxation charges*

So, reserves are amounts set aside out of profits that are not provisions.

retail price index: a measure of the average level of prices of goods and services bought by final consumers. Each item in the index is given a weighting according to its relative importance in the total of consumers' expenditure. A base year is select-ed and the index is given a value of 100 at that time. Over time, price changes in the economy are measured and expressed as changes in the value of the index.

For example, if the index stood at 100 in 1985 and at 211 today, this would indicate that, on average, prices had risen by 111 per cent between 1985 and today.

retained profits: also known as retained earnings and *profit and loss account (2)*.

retainer: see *retention money*

retention money: money held back by a client after a *long-term contract* has been completed. This allows the client time to determine whether the contract has been completed satisfactorily. If it has not been completed to the satisfaction of the client, the money will be held until the work is complete. Retention money can also be held in case the contract is not completed by the date stipulated in the contract.

retiring partner means that a structural change has occurred in the ownership of a *partnership*. Before the partner's retirement date one business was in existence, after the retirement date 'new' partners emerge to start a 'new' business.

For example, Carrie, James and Maurice are in partnership. James retires on 30 April 19*7. Carrie, James and Maurice are the proprietors of the business until midnight on 30 April. One microsecond after midnight the proprietors of the business are Carrie and Maurice.

When a partner retires, the business is valued so that the departing partner can take his/her dues. This can sometimes cause a problem if the retiring partner has large capital and current account balances standing to his/her credit. To allow the partner to withdraw his/her balances as cash could cause severe liquidity problems for the business. To overcome this problem the new partnership might:

- borrow sufficient funds to pay the retiring partner
- transfer the balances to a loan account and repay the capital over a number of years
- take in a new partner and use his/her capital injection to pay the retiring partner

---

Worked example: Yolande, Zena and Albert are in partnership sharing profits and losses 3:3:2. Yolande retired on 31 May 19*7. At that date the partnership balance sheet showed:

	£	£
Fixed assets:		
Premises		80 000
Fittings		12 000
Vehicles		26 000
		118 000
Current assets:		
Stock	9 000	
Debtors	13 000	
Bank balance	1 750	
	23 750	
Less current liabilities:		
Creditors	6 750	17 000
		135 000
Capital accounts:		
Yolande		50 000
Zena		40 000
Albert		40 000
		130 000
Current accounts:		
Yolande	1 500	
Zena	2 150	
Albert	1 350	5 000
		135 000

The partners have agreed the following asset values at close of business on 31 May 19*7:

	£
Premises to be revalued at	150 000
Fixtures to be revalued at	7 000

Yolande will retain the business car she has been using at an agreed value of £7500 (it has a book value of £9000).

The two remaining cars to be revalued at	14 000
Debtors are valued at	12 500
Goodwill to be valued at	80 000

The partners have agreed that any balance remaining in Yolande's capital account be transferred to a loan account initially. No goodwill account is to remain in the partnership books of account. Profits and losses will be shared equally in the new partnership.

Required:

i) Yolande's capital account showing the amount transferred to her loan account.

ii) The partnership balance sheet as it would appear on I June 19*7 after Yolande's retirement.

Solution:

i)

Capital account – Yolande

Vehicle	7 500	Balance b/d	50 000
Loan a/c	96 500	Current a/c	I 500
		Revaluation a/c	52 500
	104 000		104 000

ii) **Zena and Albert balance sheet as at 31 May 19*7**
(after Yolande's retirement):

	£	£
Fixed assets:		
Premises at valuation		150 000
Fixtures at valuation		7 000
Vehicles at valuation		14 000
		171 000
Current assets:		
Stock	9 000	
Debtors	12 500	
Bank	1 750	
	23 250	
Less current liabilities:		
Creditors	6 750	16 500
		187 500
Capital accounts:		
Zena		52 500
Albert		35 000
		87 500
Current accounts:		
Zena	2 150	
Albert	1 350	3 500
Loan account – Yolande		96 500
		187 500

return on capital employed (ROCE) shows the percentage return on the capital invested in a business. There are a number of different measures for ROCE, so it is important in an examination to indicate to the examiner which measure you are using (if you have been given a choice). Write down the model that you are using.

ROCE is an important ratio (it is often called the primary ratio). Many of the other ratios are elements of the ROCE. The calculation is:

ISLE COLLEGE
RESOURCES CENTRE

FORMULA: $\dfrac{\text{profit before interest and tax}}{\text{capital employed}} \times 100$

Capital employed is:

- all share capital – *ordinary share capital* and preference share capital (see *preference shares*)
- all *reserves*
- any long-term *loans*
- *debentures* (in the case of a *limited company*)

Some users of accounts use the opening capital employed, some use the closing capital employed, and some use an average figure. For examination purposes, unless given precise instructions in the question, use the formula that you feel most comfortable with.

Worked example: Shuvelle and Bruce plc has a profit before interest and tax of £871 056 and capital employed of £4 000 000.

Required:

Calculate the return on capital employed for Shuvell and Bruce plc.

Solution:

$\text{ROCE} = \dfrac{\text{profit before interest and tax}}{\text{capital employed}} = \dfrac{871\ 056}{4\ 000\ 000} \times 100 = 21.78\%$

It is impossible to comment on whether or not this is a good ROCE. Clearly it should be as large as possible, but we really need previous years' figures or figures relating to the industry as a whole in order to make a judgement.

ROCE indicates how much profit has been earned by each £100 of long-term capital invested in a business. When comparing ROCE for different businesses, it is important to make sure that they are:

- in the same line of business
- using the same production techniques
- using the same accounting policies

The ratio can be used:

- by investors, when considering an investment opportunity
- by managers, when considering a capital investment decision – the project may be inappropriate if the cost of capital is greater than the ROCE
- when considering the purchase of a *subsidiary*
- in different departments of a business to assess their viability

Other versions of this ratio are:

- $\dfrac{\text{net profit before tax}}{\text{shareholders' funds}} \times 100$

- $\dfrac{\text{net profit after tax}}{\text{shareholders' funds}} \times 100$

- $$\frac{\text{net profit after tax and preference dividend}}{\text{shareholders' funds excluding preference shares}} \times 100$$

A major weakness of using ROCE and the *return on owners' equity* is that both ratios are based on the historic cost of the business's assets. If asset values are inaccurate then the capital employed figure must also be inaccurate.

return on owners' equity: a refinement of the *return on capital employed (ROCE)* calculation, measuring the return on the funds invested by the ordinary *shareholders.* The calculation is:

FORMULA:
$$\frac{\text{net profit before interest and tax but deducting preference dividends}}{\text{issued ordinary share capital} + \text{all reserves}} \times 100$$

The net profit after deducting preference dividend is the profit available for the ordinary shareholders before the deduction of interest and taxation.

returns are goods that have been sent back to the supplier because they are unsuitable in some way. The supplier will, generally, issue a credit note which the customer can set off against future purchases.

The bookkeeping entries can be seen under *purchase returns day book* and *sales returns day book.*

returns inward: see *sales returns*

returns inward book: see *sales returns day book*

returns inwards day book: see *sales returns day book*

returns inward journal: see *sales returns day book*

returns outward: see *purchase returns*

returns outward book: see *purchase returns day book*

returns outward day book: see *purchase returns day book*

returns outward journal: see *purchase returns day book*

revaluation of assets takes place when:

- there is a structural change in the ownership of a partnership, or
- the *directors* of a *limited company* believe that the *balance sheet* values of some *fixed assets* are not representative of their *market value.*

revaluation reserve is created by the *directors* of a *limited company* when *fixed assets* are revalued upwards. It is a *capital reserve,* so it is not available for distribution as cash dividends. It can be used for the issue of *bonus shares. Sole traders* and *partnerships* do not create revaluation reserves. (See *going-concern concept.*)

Worked example: R Preston plc balance sheet extract as at 30 November 19*7:

	£	£
Fixed assets		
Premises at cost	170 000	
Less depreciation	12 000	158 000

The directors have recently had the premises valued by Maybins, a firm of professional valuers, at £210 000.

Required:

Journal entries to record the revaluation in the books of R Preston plc.

Solution:

Journal:

	Dr £	Cr £
Premises	40 000	
Provision for depreciation of premises	12 000	
Revaluation reserve		52 000

revenue expenditure: expenditure on everyday running costs of a business.

revenue receipts: receipts received in the normal course of business, e.g. receipts from cash sales. Rent received, *commission* received, etc. are also revenue receipts. They are credited to an appropriate revenue account in the *general ledger*, i.e. rent receivable is entered on the credit side of the rent receivable account, not the credit of the rent payable account.

At the financial year end the accounts are closed by a transfer to the *profit and loss account*:

Debit: The revenue received account **Credit:** Profit and loss account

revenue reserves are retained earnings that have been withheld from *dividend* distribution in order to strengthen the financial position of a company. Revenue reserves are a very important source of finance for *limited companies*.

The amount to be transferred to the reserve is debited to the *profit and loss appropriation account* and credited to the appropriate *reserve* account. This reduces the amount of profits available for cash dividends. Revenue reserves are created at the discretion of the *directors*.

Revenue reserves are available for distribution to the *shareholders* in the form of cash dividends by debiting the reserve account and crediting the profit and loss appropriation account. Revenue reserves can also be used for the issue of *bonus shares*.

Examples of revenue reserves are:

- *fixed asset replacement reserve*
- *foreign exchange reserve*
- *general reserve*
- *profit and loss account*

reversal of entries: see *errors not affecting the balancing of the trial balance*

reverse order of liquidity: see *fixed assets* and *current assets*

rights issue of shares is offered to existing *shareholders*. The right is to purchase a set number of new shares at a stated price. The number of shares that can be purchased by any one individual is based on their present holding. The rights issue might be one new share for every three already held, one for seven, etc. The right can be sold or given to another person if the shareholder does not wish to exercise his/her right.

The price of the shares is usually a little cheaper than the market price since the company does not have the same administrative expenses to pay on the issue.

The bookkeeping entries are exactly the same as the entries for an *issue of shares* to the public at large.

Rowan premium bonus scheme is used to reward *direct labour* for saving time during the production process. This method rewards the worker with a proportion of the time saved.

$$\text{FORMULA: proportion of time saved} = \frac{\text{time taken}}{\text{time allowed}} \times \text{time saved}$$

Worked example: Alexandra is paid £7.00 per hour. The time allowed to complete a task is 10 hours. The actual time taken by Alexandra to complete the task is 7 hours.

Required:

Calculate the gross pay due to Alexandra after completing the task.

Solution:

$$\text{Alexandra's gross pay} = (7 \text{ hrs} \times £7.00) + \left(\frac{\text{time taken}}{\text{time allowed}} \times \text{time saved} \right)$$

$$= (7 \text{ hrs} \times £7.00) + (70\% \times 3 \text{ hrs} \times £7.00)$$

$$= £63.70$$

---

running balance accounts: *ledger* accounts where the balance is adjusted each time a transaction takes place. They are widely used, and rather than showing a traditional debit/credit layout, a three-column approach is used. You will probably have encountered this layout on your bank statement, if you have a bank account.

A traditional *sales ledger* account would be laid out like this:

G Drood

		£			£
1 May	Balance b/d	416	15 May	Cash	410
23 May	Sales	1307		Discount allowed	6
27 May	Sales	198	25 May	Returns	23
			31 May	Balance c/d	1482
		1921			1921
1 June	Balance b/d	1482			

The running balance version of the same account is:

G Drood

		Debit £	Credit £	Balance £
1 May	Balance			416 Dr
15 May	Cash		410	6 Dr
	Discount allowed		6	000
23 May	Sales	1307		1307 Dr
25 May	Returns		23	1284 Dr
27 May	Sales	198		1482 Dr

S

safety stock: the amount of stock held in excess of the normal expected usage. It is held to provide a buffer in case some unforeseen circumstance occurs, e.g. an urgent rush order or temporary difficulty in obtaining stocks from suppliers.

salaries are payments, usually monthly, made to administrative employees with a contract of employment.

sales account records the value of goods sold to customers during a financial year. The sales account is a *nominal account* and is found in the *general ledger.*

Sales may be:

- cash sales – these occur when a customer exchanges cash or a cheque, immediately, for the goods sold. The bookkeeping entries are:

Debit: Cash   **Credit:**   Sales account in the general ledger

- credit sales – payment for the goods sold takes place at some future time. The bookkeeping entries are:

Debit: Customers' account in sales ledger   **Credit:**   Sales account in general ledger

When large numbers of credit sales take place, the credit sales are entered in a *sales day book* prior to entry in the double-entry system.

The sales that are recorded in the sales account are those that form the normal trading activities of the business.

Sales of *fixed assets* are recorded in an *asset disposal account.*

For example, J Last owns a shoe shop. The sales account is credited with sales of shoes, trainers, shoe polish, etc. The asset disposal account is credited with the sale of an old display unit.

sales analysis book: a breakdown of sales by product. It is often used in businesses that sell a number of different products. It enables management to see the level of sales for each particular product line. The analysis facilitates the compilation of departmental *final accounts.* (See *columnar day books* and *departmental accounts.*)

sales book: see *sales day book*

sales budget shows predicted sales and the revenues that they are expected to generate for the budget period. It is generally the first budget to be prepared, since most businesses are sales led. Once the sales budget has been prepared, the other budgets can be prepared taking into account what is shown by the sales budget.

A sales budget can be subdivided into analysis columns which show information that is important to that particular business. Analysis can be into:

- products
- national or international regions
- departments
- sales representatives and sales office
- customers (in the case of a business with a few large customers)

sales day book: a list of *credit sales*. It is written up from copy *sales invoices* sent to customers when a sale is completed. When it is convenient, the sales day book is used to post debit entries in the *personal accounts* in the *sales ledger* and a credit entry in the *sales account* in the *general ledger*. The sales day book is not part of the double-entry system.

Worked example: Frank Lumley has sold goods on credit to P Kew £51, R Hess £89, J Kay £410.

Required:

Write up Frank's sales day book and show the relevant postings to the ledger accounts.

Solution:

Sales ledger			Sales day book		General ledger	
Kew				£	**Sales**	
	£	£	Kew	51	£	£
SDB	51		Hess	89		SDB 550
			Kay	410		
Hess				550		
	£	£				
SDB	89					
Kay						
	£	£				
SDB	410					

sales forecasts: estimates of anticipated sales for the next time period based on the information available. They are used as the main basis for the preparation of the *sales budget*. Amongst other things, a sales forecast draws on:

- market research
- representatives' field reports
- trade sources for specific business intelligence
- general economic forecasts

to determine the budgeted demand for sales of the product(s).

Once the volume of sales has been forecast, total sales revenue can be forecast by taking into account the business's pricing policy.

sales invoice: the formal demand sent to a credit customer asking for payment for goods sold. The *invoice* will generally show:

- seller's name and address
- purchaser's name and address
- seller's *VAT* number (if VAT registered)
- date of invoice/tax point
- description of items sold
- the quantity and price of individual items sold

- details of trade discount if applicable
- invoice total plus VAT (the rate should be indicated)
- the amount payable
- details of cash discounts available
- date when amount is due

sales journal: see *sales day book*

sales ledger: contains the accounts of all the business's credit customers. Cash sales do not appear in this ledger. The entries in the sales ledger are posted from the *sales day book.*

The sales ledger is also known as the debtors' ledger since any balances outstanding on any of the accounts are amounts owed by debtors.

sales ledger control account checks the arithmetic accuracy of all entries posted to the *sales ledger.* (See *control accounts.*)

sales margin variance is the difference between the budgeted profit from sales and the actual profit from sales. It is used to analyse the performance of the sales department.

The total sales margin variance calculation is:

FORMULA: actual profit based on standard unit costs − budgeted profit based on standard unit costs

This can be subdivided into:

- sales margin price variance:

FORMULA: (actual margin based on standard unit costs − standard margin based on standard unit costs) × actual sales volume

- sales margin volume variance:

FORMULA: (actual sales volume − budgeted volume) × standard profit margin

---

Worked example: Brittas plc produces and sells a single product the 'inkle'. The standard costs of producing an inkle total £48. The standard selling price of an inkle is £65. The budget based on standard cost for an output of 100 000 inkles is shown below:

	£
Sales	6 500 000
Total standard cost	4 800 000
Budgeted profit	1 700 000

The actual results show:

Sales 95 000 units at £66 each	6 270 000

Required:

i)   total sales margin variance for inkles
ii) sales margin price variance for inkles
iii) sales margin volume variance for inkles

Solution:

i)

	£
Actual sales revenue	6 270 000
Standard cost of sales (95 000 × £48)	4 560 000
Actual profit margin	1 710 000

	£
Actual profit margin	1 710 000
Budgeted profit margin	1 700 000
Total sales margin variance	10 000 favourable

ii) The change in the selling price of inkles has led to an increase in the profit margin of £1 per unit (the change in price has increased profit from £17 per unit to £18 per unit). Actual sales volume of 95 000 gives a favourable sales margin price variance of £95 000.

(actual margin − standard margin)× actual sales volume
     £18   −   £17   ×   95 000
= £95 000 favourable

iii) A comparison of budgeted sales volume with actual sales volume shows by how much sales have deviated from budget. When multiplied by the standard profit margin, the result will show how much the change in volume of sales has impacted on profits. Budgeted sales were 100 000 units, but actual sales were only 95 000 units. The reduction in sales of 5000 units has reduced profit by £17 per unit = £85 000.

(actual sales volume − budgeted sales volume)× standard profit margin
     95 000   −   100 000   ×   £17
= £85 000 adverse

---

sales variance: the difference between standard sales revenue and actual sales revenue. The variance is made up of:

- *selling price variance*
- sales volume/profit variance

Worked example: the budgeted sales for 'shrids' was 17 000 units at a selling price of £900 each. The actual sales volume was 16 875 at a selling price of £895 each. The standard cost per unit was £500.

Required:

Calculate:
a) the selling price variance
b) the sales volume profit variance
c) the total sales variance.

Solution:

We need to use a modified grid, as shown in *direct labour cost variance*.

standard quantity × standard profit
                                          } = sales volume profit variance
actual quantity × standard profit

actual quantity × standard price

actual quantity × actual price

$\left.\begin{array}{c}\\\\\end{array}\right\}$ = selling price variance

So:

sq × sp   17 000 × 400   =   £6 800 000

aq × sp   16 875 × 400   =   £6 750 000

= £50 000   adverse sales volume profit variance

aq × sp   16 875 × 900   =   £15 187 500

aq × ap   16 875 × 895   =   £15 103 125

= £84 375   adverse selling price variance

total sales variance   £134 375

---

sales volume/profit variance: see *sales variance*

sales returns book: see *sales returns day book*

sales returns day book: a record of goods that have been returned by customers. It is written up from copy credit notes that have been sent to customers. When it is convenient, the returns are posted from this day book to the credit of the *personal accounts* in the *sales ledger* and the debit of the sales returns (*returns inward*) account in the *general ledger*.

Worked example: Pam Deli has had some sales returned as unsatisfactory. She has issued the following credit notes to her customers: Tomkins £18, Cubby £139, Sapper £46.

Required:

Write up Pam's sales returns day book and show the relevant postings to the ledger accounts.

Solution:

Sales ledger Cubby			Sales returns day book		General ledger Sales returns		
£	£			£		£	£
	SRDB	139	Tomkins	18		£	£
			Cubby	139	SRDB	203	
			Sapper	46			
Sapper				203			
£	£						
	SRDB	46					
Tomkins							
£	£						
	SRDB	18					

---

sales returns journal see *sales returns day book*

Saloman v Saloman and Company Ltd 1897 confirmed the distinction between a company and its *shareholders*. A *limited company* has a legal status separate from that of its owners, and as such, from that date, limited companies became separate *legal entities*.

savings banks accept deposits, and customers receive interest on those deposits.

scrip issue: see *bonus shares*

secured loan: a loan which has an asset pledged as security for the loan. Some *debenture* stock is secured, with the assets of the company pledged as security. If the company were to go into *liquidation*, the assets would be sold and used to repay the debenture holders. If there was a surplus after paying the debenture holders, the remaining cash would go towards paying off the preference *shareholders* and finally the ordinary shareholders.

segmental reporting SSAP 25 is designed to help the users of accounts to assess the contribution made to the overall *profitability* of a company (or group) by different classes of business or by operations in different geographical areas.

A 'separate class of business' is a separate product or service, or a group of related products or services. If a business produces more than one product it is helpful for an investor to know how profitable each product is. Similarly, if a business has significant sales in the Far East and in the USA, it might be helpful to know how much of the company's profits derive from each area. (Overseas trading carries the risk of exchange rate fluctuations, imposition of import controls, etc.)

The standard builds on the *Companies Act 1985* and requires, for each segment, disclosure of:

- turnover analysed between inter-group, inter-segment and customers' sales
- profit or loss before tax, minority interests and *extraordinary items*
- *net assets* (allowing *return on capital employed* to be calculated)

sellers' market occurs when there is a limited supply of particular goods and a large demand. This means that sellers can demand high prices for their goods.

selling price variance: see *sales variance*

semi-variable costs: costs which cannot be classified as either *fixed costs* or *variable costs* because they contain an element of both. An example of a semi-variable cost is the charge for electricity consumption. The standing charge is the fixed cost element – it must be paid even when no electricity is used. The variable element is the charge based on the number of units of electricity used.

separate valuation principle is a fifth fundamental *accounting concept* identified in the *Companies Act 1985*. It states that when valuing an asset or liability for *balance sheet* purposes, each component item of the asset or liability must be valued separately and then aggregated.

service cost centres are non-productive departments which provide a service to production departments. Examples include maintenance, personnel, canteen.

service costing can be applied to:

- the provision of support functions in a manufacturing business
- the costing involved in a business in the service sector of the economy, e.g. transport

ISLE COLLEGE RESOURCES CENTRE

The costing techniques are similar to those applied to any other department in a business; costs are allocated and apportioned using the usual methods. The costs allocated and apportioned to a service department will be absorbed by the departments that use the service (see *apportionment of service cost centre overheads*).

For the techniques used for apportioning the costs of departments providing reciprocal services, see *apportionment of reciprocal service costs*.

In the case of a business in a service sector of the economy, overheads will be recovered in the same way as they are recovered in a manufacturing business by the use of an appropriate method of absorption.

service departments support the activities of other departments, e.g. personnel, finance, technical support, maintainance, etc.

shareholders: the owners of a *limited company* by virtue of owning shares in that company. A company's share capital is, generally, divided into:

- *ordinary shares*
- *preference shares*

shareholders' funds are made up of:

- the share capital of the company, plus
- all *reserves*

Note that this is different from equity capital. Equity capital is that capital which is owned by the ordinary shareholders. Preference shares are not part of the equity capital of a company. If a company is wound up, all the equity capital remaining is distributed to the ordinary shareholders.

share premium account arises when shares are issued by a *limited company* at a price greater than par. The extra amounts received are credited to a share premium account.

Worked example: a limited company issues 100 000 shares with a nominal value of £1 at a price of £4.50.

Required:

The entries in the company's general ledger.

Solution:

Cash				Ordinary share capital	
	£		£	£	£
Ordinary share cap'l	100 000			Cash	100 000
Share premium acc.	350 000				
				Share premium account	
					£
				Cash	350 000

The share premium account is a *capital reserve*. It cannot be transferred to the company's *appropriation account* and used for cash dividend purposes. It can be used to:

- issue *bonus shares*
- write off *preliminary expenses*

- provide any premium payable on the *redemption of shares* (but only if the share premium account was created by the issue of those shares originally)

shift premium: see *shift work*

shift work: if a business operates its production process 24 hours per day, the day will generally be split into three shifts. A different group of workers will work each shift, ensuring that 24-hour production is maintained.

The workers who are required to work on the evening and night shifts will generally be paid a shift premium to compensate them for working unsocial hours.

short-term planning identifies the building blocks or the components of any *long-term planning* that an organisation may undertake.

simple interest is calculated on the capital sum borrowed when a loan is agreed. No further calculations of interest are made.

Worked example: Percy borrows £700 from Shark & Co. The simple interest charge is 12%. The loan has to be repaid in 24 equal instalments.

Percy will pay $\dfrac{£700 \times 112\%}{24} = £32.67$

This is in fact greater than 12% since after the first month Percy should only be charged interest on £667.33.

(See *annual percentage rate (APR)* and *compound interest.*)

simplified method of apportioning overheads of reciprocal service departments: also known as the *elimination method of apportioning overhead costs of reciprocal services.*

simultaneous equation method of apportioning of reciprocal service departments' costs: see *apportionment of reciprocal service overhead costs*

single-entry bookkeeping: a method of recording financial transactions that relies on the use of the *cash book* as the main source of information for preparing the *final accounts.* It is mainly used in the preparation of final accounts for:

- small cash-based businesses
- clubs and societies

In the cash book, debit entries are made for receipts of cash and cheques, credit entries are made for cash and cheque payments. The 'opposite' double entries are not made in a *ledger.* (See *incomplete records.*)

sinking fund is built up by investing regular amounts of money in order to provide a set amount to meet a future need like the purchase of a new machine, or the repayment of a loan.

small companies: by definition, small companies must fulfil two of the following criteria:

- a turnover not exceeding £2 800 000
- *balance sheet* total not exceeding £1 400 000
- average number of employees not exceeding 50

They are allowed 'filing exemptions' in the accounts that they file with the *Registrar of Companies*. This is to protect their interests from rival businesses. (See *reporting requirements for small businesses*.)

social accounting takes note of the fact that not all accounting decisions are taken on purely financial grounds. The *money measurement concept* states that only transactions that can be recorded in cash terms are entered in the business *books of account*. This means that many things that have a direct bearing on the conduct and results of the business are missing from the financial statements.

Profitability is of vital importance to all businesses, but there has been a move in recent years to consider the impact that business has on society at large. We are all consumers, perhaps employees, and we all live in an environment which is influenced in many ways by the business world. Social accounting recognises that a business which fails to consider the social implications of its policies may well find that some of those policies are counterproductive, and that *profitability* might be affected. An unhappy workforce could cause a fall in *productivity*. Similarly, a business which pollutes a locality may find that turnover falls through bad publicity. In 1995, for example, many consumers throughout Europe refused to purchase Shell products because of the company's proposal to dispose of the Brent Spar oil platform in the North Sea.

software is used to instruct computer *hardware* how to perform. Programs are contained in magnetic form on floppy disks. When a disk is inserted into the disk drive, the instructions on it are read by the computer and used by the operator. Programs can be transferred from the software onto hard disk so that they are ready for use at any time.

Software packages for accounting include:

- *spreadsheets*
- *sales* and *purchase ledger accounts*
- *nominal* (general) *ledger accounts*
- payroll
- stock records
- *final accounts*

sole trader: a type of business ownership where the business is owned and controlled by one person.

solvency: the ability to pay all outstanding debts when they fall due.

sources of finance: the various ways in which funds can be raised for business use. These are important, since a business cannot function in either the short run or the long run without adequate finance.

Short-term finance depends to a large extent on a business's ability to manage its working capital well. Good management of working capital will ensure sufficient cash resources to pay everyday running expenses. A good rate of *stock turnover* will release cash tied up in the stock on a regular basis.

A short *debtors' payment period* will also bring cash quickly into the business on a regular basis. Credit sales now form a large proportion of many businesses' turnover.

Outstanding balances in the *sales ledger* represent cash tied up in debtors. This cash is actually providing finance for the business's customers.

If there is a lack of short-term finance, a business may have to resort to:

- disposal of surplus stocks
- *factoring*
- negotiating *overdrafts*

Long-term financing can take the form of:

- issuing new shares for cash
- issuing *debentures*
- grants from local and central government and from the EC

Cash may be conserved for use in other areas of the business by using:

- credit terms for the purchase of assets
- *hire-purchase* agreements
- leasing arrangements
- sale and lease back

special-order pricing uses *marginal costing* techniques to arrive at a decision whether to accept a special 'one-off' order or not. If the order gives a positive contribution and the following conditions hold, then it should be accepted:

- the order should not displace other business
- there must be spare capacity in the production department
- regular customers must not be aware of the customers receiving the special price
- special prices should not set a precedent for future pricing
- the special-price customer should not be in a position that will allow them to sell to others at below regular price

A negative contribution might be acceptable:

- to keep skilled workers
- to keep machinery working
- in order to stimulate full-price orders in the future

Worked example: Clough Engineering manufactures one product, the 'yut'. The following information relates to the production of yuts:

		£
Selling price per yut		200
Costs per unit:	direct materials	45
	direct labour	63
	fixed costs	18

There is spare capacity in the factory.

A German retailer has indicated that he is willing to purchase 1000 yuts, but he is only prepared to pay £120 per unit.

Required:

Advise the managers of Clough Engineering whether or not they should accept the order.

Solution:

The order ought to be accepted. It makes a positive contribution of £12 per unit.

contribution = selling price per unit – variable costs per unit
$$= £120 – £108 (45 + 63)$$
$$= £12$$

---

speculator: a person who buys and sells securities or commodities in the expectation that a change in the price will earn him/her a profit. (See *bear and bull.*)

split-off point: see *common costs*

spreadsheet: a computer program into which numerical data can be inputted. It can be used to build statistical and financial models. A template composed of rows and columns is set up as memory cells and, by the use of formulae entered into these cells, calculations and changes to models can be made. The spreadsheet can be observed on screen or it can be printed out as a hard copy.

Spreadsheets are used in businesses to:

- budget
- appraise different courses of action
- estimate and prepare quotations, etc.

Spreadsheets are particularly useful to observe changes to a model through calculations known as 'what if', e.g. 'what would be the effect on sales if prices were increased by, say, 3%, 3.5%, 4% etc?'. Spreadsheet packages also have the facility to produce graphics.

SSAP 1: see *accounting for associated companies*

SSAP 2: see *disclosure of accounting policies*

SSAP 4: see *accounting for government grants*

SSAP 5: see *accounting for value-added tax*

SSAP 6: see *extraordinary items* and *prior year adjustments*

SSAP 8: see *taxation under the imputation system*

SSAP 9: see *stocks and long-term contracts*

SSAP 10: see *statements of source and application of funds*

SSAP 12: see *accounting for depreciation*

SSAP 13: see *accounting for research and development*

SSAP 15: see *accounting for deferred tax*

SSAP 17: see *accounting for post-balance-sheet events*

SSAP 18: see *accounting for contingencies*

SSAP 19: see *accounting for investment properties*

SSAP 20: see *foreign currency translation*

SSAP 21: see *accounting for leases and hire-purchase contracts*

SSAP 22: see *accounting for goodwill*

SSAP 23: see *accounting for acquisitions and mergers*

SSAP 24: see *accounting for pension costs*

SSAP 25: see *segmental reporting*

staff appraisal aims to assess staff within the grading of their job. An immediate superior is required to put a value on specified qualities of each employee. Such a scheme would have a direct bearing on promotions and inter-departmental transfers.

stakeholders: people and organisations that stand to gain or lose by the activities of a business. The stakeholders contribute directly in some way to the success or failure of the business. Stakeholders in a business include:

- owners (shareholders)
- management
- workforce
- customers
- suppliers
- lenders
- banks
- community

Social accounting recognises that businesses have a responsibility to the stakeholders.

standard costing sets levels of costs and revenues which ought to be achievable when reasonable levels of performance are used, together with efficient working practices, to manufacture a product. It deals with costs and revenues that ought to occur. It is a carefully prepared prediction of what should happen to individual costs and revenues if everything goes according to plan.

Standard material cost, standard labour cost and standard overhead cost are compared with actual material cost, actual labour cost and actual overhead cost. Any differences between standard cost and actual cost is called a *variance.*

For worked examples of the calculation of total variances and sub-variances, see *direct labour variance*, *direct material variance, sales variance* and *overhead variance.*

standard hour measures the quantity of work that can be achieved at a standard level of performance in one hour. A standard hour may be 12 standard units, that is, a manager will expect a worker to produce 12 standard units of output in one hour's work.

standard minute measures the quantity of work that can be achieved at a standard level of performance in one minute. If a standard hour were 12 standard units, then a standard minute would be 0.2 standard units per minute.

standard setting is undertaken when a standard cost system is introduced into a manufacturing business. The cost accountant needs to prepare standards for materials, labour and overheads. Information with regard to quantities will be needed from the production departments. Specifications will be given on:

Materials	Labour	Overheads
type	grade	production methods
quantities	numbers	sequence of operations
		machines required
		tools required

The prices will be determined by:

buyers personnel absorption rates
trade union

standing orders: payments made automatically by a bank on behalf of customers. They are for set figures and may be paid on a weekly, monthly or annual basis by the bank. If the amount to be paid is likely to be variable then a direct debit arrangement with the creditor and bank is a more appropriate method of payment.

statement of account summarises the transactions that have taken place between a supplier and a customer, generally over an agreed period (usually one month). All *invoices* sent to the customer, all monies received plus *discounts allowed* and all returns are individually itemised on the statement.

The statement of account is a copy of the customer's account in the supplier's *sales ledger*. The customer checks the statement against the supplier's account in the *purchase ledger*. If there is a difference then remedial action can be taken by the party who has made the error. Any corrections are recorded on the next statement.

statement of affairs is identical to an opening *balance sheet*. It is prepared for a business that does not keep a full set of accounting records. Technically, the statement cannot be called a balance sheet (a sheet showing balances) since, by definition, the business does not have any ledger balances – it does not have *ledgers* because it has *incomplete records*.

statements: methods used to convey information. They are often asked for in examination questions. Candidates should be aware that statements can be presented in many different guises:

- a *profit and loss account* is a statement
- a statement may be written
- a computation of a change in profits can be a statement.

Choose the most appropriate way that you think will convey the information required clearly to a reader, but use the heading outlined in the question.

Statements of Standard Accounting Practice (SSAP) are guidelines issued by the major accounting bodies with regard to the manner and methods in which certain financial transactions are recorded and communicated to interested parties. See the appropriate SSAP for recognised treatments.

stepped costs remain fixed until a certain level of business activity is reached. Costs then rise to a higher fixed level and remain there until the next level of activity requiring a change is reached.

Worked example: Hanif owns a small engineering business which manufactures electrical generators. The maximum output is limited to 1000 generators per week. Hanif employs quality controllers on weekly contracts. They can inspect 250 generators per week. Each quality controller earns £300 per week.

Required:

A graph showing the budgeted costs of employing quality controllers.

Solution:

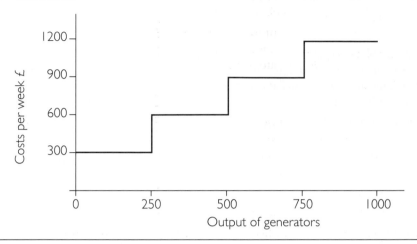

---

stewardship: the term applied to the responsiblity that managers have for the management of resources within a business on behalf of the owners. An accountant must report periodically the state of affairs of the business to the owners.

stock is goods for resale, raw materials, components or *work in progress* held by a business that have not been disposed of during the financial year.

stock account records receipts and issues of stock showing clearly the balance of stock held. There is a different stock account for each different raw material and each different stock item carried in the business.

If all the transactions in every stock account are totalled, they should agree with the total figures in the stores account. The stores account is, in essence, a stock control account which records all receipts of all stocks and all issues of all stocks to the various departments.

Description					Number			
Stock	Minimum				Maximum			
levels	Reorder level				Reorder quantity			
Date Detail	Stock level		Stock issue		Balance		Allocated stock	Free stock
	Quantity	£	Quantity	£	Quantity	£	Quantity	Quantity

The stock account can be maintained by using any of the recognised *methods of stock valuation* such as LIFO, FIFO and AVCO.

stock control is necessary to make sure that the correct levels of stock are maintained. Holding excessive stock is costly because:

- money must be spent to acquire the stock
- stocks represent idle money
- stocks may deteriorate or be stolen

Insufficient stock can result in:

- lost orders
- loss of bulk order discounts
- greater administration costs

stock exchange: the marketplace where stocks and shares are bought and sold. Much of the business of the stock exchanges is to deal in secondhand shares and government securities.

stock ledger: the book containing all the stock accounts.

stock losses: stock that has been stolen. Such losses are often not apparent until the year end if a periodic inventory system of stock valuation is taken.

To calculate the amount of stock that has gone missing during the financial year, a *trading account* is prepared using the figures that ought to apply and this is compared with the actual figures. The difference in closing stocks is assumed to be the stock that has been stolen.

Worked example: Helen Shaw owns a beauty salon. Several boxes of expensive make-up have been stolen during the year, but she is unsure of the exact value of the stolen goods.

Make-up in stock at 1 June 19*6 was £387. Make-up in stock at 31 May 19*7 was £450. Purchases of make-up during the financial year were £18 221. Sales of make-up during the year amounted to £26 781.

All make-up sold in the salon carries a mark-up of 50%.

Required:

Calculate the amount of stock stolen from Helen's salon.

Solution:

Trading account for the year ended 31 May 19*7

		Actual figures £		As they should be £
Sales		26 781		26 781
Less cost of sales				
Stock 1 June 19*6	387		387	
Purchases	18 221		18 221	
	18 608		18 608	
Less stock 30 May 19*7	450		754	
Stolen goods	304			
Cost of sales		17 854		17 854
Gross profit		8 927		8 927

We can calculate the gross profit by taking 33.1/3% of sales, so cost of sales must be £17 854. By deduction, the closing stock should be £754, but we are told that the make-up in stock was valued at £450. We can therefore assume that goods to the value of £304 had been stolen.

---

stockmarket: see *stock exchange*

stock outs: occasions when certain stocks are required for production purposes but stores or suppliers are unable to supply at that time.

stock record card records changes in levels of stock of each type of raw material or component held by a business. An appropriate entry is made on the card recording each movement of stock.

A stock record card is very similar to a *stock ledger* account, the only difference being that the stock record card does not usually show the prices of stock receipts and stock issues. The allocated stock column shows stock that is not available for issue because it has been earmarked for a job that has not yet started and is therefore not available for issue. The source documents are:

- stock received: goods received notes
- stock issued: material/component requisition note

stock reorder level indicates to the stock controller when it is necessary to reorder certain raw materials or components. The stock reorder level should ensure that the business always has sufficient stocks to meet demands from the production department.

The calculation to determine the reorder level is:

FORMULA: maximum usage × maximum lead time

Worked example: a manufacturing business has a maximum usage of 2500 units of component ATX/51 per week. The supplier of the component has a maximum lead time of 5 weeks.

Required:

Calculate the reorder level for component ATX/51.

Solution:

reorder level = maximum usage × maximum lead time
= 2500 × 5
= 12 500 units

To avoid cash being tied up in holding unnecessarily high levels of stock, many businesses will set a maximum level of stock to be held at any one time. The calculation to determine the maximum levels of stocks to be held is:

$$\text{FORMULA: } \text{reorder level} - \left(\text{minimum usage} \times \text{minimum lead time} \right) + \text{reorder quantity}$$

Worked example: the reorder level for component ATX/51 is 12 500 units. The business has a minimum usage of 650 units per week. The minimum lead time is 3 weeks. The reorder quantity is 10 000.

Required:

Calculate the maximum level of stocks of ATX/51 to be held at any one time.

Solution:

maximum level of stock to be held:

reorder level − (minimum usage × minimum lead time) + reorder quantity

    12 500   − (650   ×   3   ) +   10 000

= 12 500   −   1950   +   10 000

= 20 550 units of ATX/51

Minimum levels of stock to be held will allow the stock controller to avoid running out of stock. The calculation to determine the minimum levels of stocks to be held is:

FORMULA: $\text{reorder level} - (\text{average usage} \times \text{average lead time})$

Worked example: the reorder level for component ATX/51 is 12 500. The average usage is 1575 units per week. The average lead time is 4 weeks.

Required:

Calculate the minimum level of stocks of ATX/51 to be held.

Solution:

minimum level of stock to be held:

reorder level − (average usage × average lead time)

    12 500   − (850   ×   4   )

= 12 500   −   6300

= 6200 units of ATX/51

In order to ensure that a business never runs out of stock, a safety stock level should be maintained. Safety stocks are also known as buffer stocks. If the business using component ATX/51 in the worked examples above required a buffer stock of 2000 units, the minimum level of stocks to be held would increase to 11 100 units.

stocks and long-term contracts SSAP 9 states that stocks should be valued at the lower of cost or net realisable value. This is the overriding principle in the valuation of stocks.

Cost is the normal business expense incurred in bringing the goods (or service) to its present location and condition. This includes the historic cost of purchase, import duties, carriage charges, handling charges and any other costs which can be attributed to the product. *Trade discount* should be deducted.

Net realisable value is the actual or estimated selling price, less any costs incurred in getting the goods into a saleable state, including marketing, selling and distribution costs.

ISLE COLLEGE
RESOURCES CENTRE

These same principles apply to the valuation of *work in progress*, except for *long-term contract work in progress*.

The standard accepts FIFO, AVCO and standard cost (so long as it bears a reasonable relationship to actual costs) as bases of valuation. It does not accept LIFO, base stock or replacement cost (unless it is the best measure of net realisable value and this is less than cost).

Work in progress and manufactured goods should be valued at total production cost not *prime cost*. Long-term contracts should be valued at cost, plus any attributable profit, less any *progress payments* received and receivable and any foreseeable losses.

SSAP 9 also requires that all stocks should be valued as separate articles as far as this is possible, and the aggregate of the lower of cost or net realisable value for each article is taken as the value of stock.

stocks and shares: the generic term covering all *ordinary shares, preference shares, loan stocks* and *debentures.*

stockturn: see *rate of stockturn*

stock turnover: see *rate of stock turnover*

stock valuation: see *methods of stock valuation*

straight-line method of calculating depreciation is calculated by spreading the net cost of purchasing a *fixed asset* over its expected economic life (any anticipated residual value should be deducted from the initial cost to arrive at the net cost). Intuitively, this is the method that most people would choose as a method of depreciating fixed assets. It is also called the equal instalment method.

Worked example: Litt Ltd purchases a machine at a cost of £120 000. It is expected to have a useful economic life of 4 years. It can then be sold for £20 000 for scrap.

Required:

Calculate the annual depreciation charge using the straight-line method.

Solution:

$$\text{straight-line method} = \frac{\text{cost} - \text{scrap value}}{\text{years of use}}$$

$$= \frac{£120\ 000 - £20\ 000}{4}$$

$$= £25\ 000 \text{ per annum}$$

---

straight piece work: see *piece work*

strategic planning: formulation of a long-term plan of action which, when in place, will help an organisation to achieve the long-term objectives identified by the senior management team. Also known as corporate planning.

structural changes in partnerships: changes to a *partnership agreement* which can take the form of:

- the *admission of a new partner*

- the retirement or death of an existing partner (see *partnership retirement*)
- an agreed change in the *profit sharing ratios* of the partners

In each of these cases, one partnership ceases to exist when the change takes place, and immediately after the change a new partnership starts up. This means that when the structural change takes place there must be a revaluation of the business assets and liabilities so that the 'old' partner(s) are credited with their dues.

subjectivity: the use of personal judgements or assumptions rather than facts. This must be avoided in the writing up of the *books of account* and when preparing financial statements. Accounting is concerned only with those facts that can be given a monetary value (see *money measurement concept*).

To avoid individual bias in the accounting world, many areas have been standardised by the issue of:

- *Statements of Standard Accounting Practice*
- *Financial Reporting Standards*

subsidiary books: see *purchase day book, purchase returns day book, sales day book, sales returns day book, journal* and *cash book*

subsidiary budgets: the departmental and functional budgets which are collated by the budget officer and summarised into the master budget.

subsidiary company has more than 50 per cent of its *ordinary shares* held by a *holding company*. For example, Sayret Ltd has an issued share capital of 620 000 ordinary shares of 50 pence each. Likfor plc acquires 312 000 of Sayret's ordinary shares for £923 760. Since more than 50 per cent of Sayret Ltd's ordinary share capital is now owned by Likfor plc, Sayret Ltd is a subsidiary company and Likfor plc is the holding company. If Likfor plc purchased the remaining 308 000 ordinary shares in Sayret Ltd, Likfor plc would hold all the voting shares in Sayret Ltd. Sayret Ltd would become a wholly owned subsidiary company of Likfor plc.

The *Companies Act 1985* gives the following definition: 'a company is a "subsidiary" of another company, its "holding company", if that other company:

- holds a majority of the voting rights in it; or
- is a member of it and has the right to appoint or remove a majority of its *board of directors*; or
- is a member of it and controls alone, pursuant to an agreement with other shareholders or members, a majority of the voting rights in it; or
- if it is a subsidiary of a company which is itself a subsidiary of that other company'.

subsidiary undertakings FRS 2 refers to undertakings rather than companies because the standard deals with unincorporated bodies as well as *limited companies*.

sunk costs: costs which have occurred some time ago and any future decisions taken by the business will not incur those costs again. In the process of decision making, they are *irrelevant costs*.

For example, a business may incur market research costs in order to determine whether or not to produce a new product. Whether the business goes ahead with production of the new product or not, the expenditure has been incurred. The market research costs are a sunk cost and should now be disregarded when costing out the budget on which the decision will be based.

superannuation: a pension.

super profits: the excess profits earned by a business after an imputed *return on capital employed* and an imputed wage have been deducted. They are sometimes used as a basis for valuing the *goodwill* of a business.

Worked example: Lesley is a self-employed builder. Her annual net profit is £48 000. She has £85 000 capital invested in the business. She could earn £14 000 working for another building firm.

Required:

Calculate Lesley's annual super profits.

Solution:

	£	£
Annual net profits		48 000
Less imputed earnings in other employment	14 000	
Less imputed interest on capital employed	4 250	18 250
Annual super profits		29 750

The rate of interest chosen was 5% but this would clearly depend on the alternative investment opportunities available to Lesley at the time.

To value Lesley's goodwill, £29 750 might be multiplied by some agreed figure. If Lesley and the purchaser agreed, goodwill might be valued at 2 years' purchase of super profits, i.e. £29 750 × 2 = £59 500.

---

suspense account is used to balance a *trial balance*. It is a temporary account where the difference is held until errors are located and corrected.

In the real world, errors may not be found. If the difference in the suspense account is not material then the error can be written off, unless there are suspicious circumstances involved. £200 difference would be material for some small businesses, so every effort would be made to find and correct the error(s). £2000, on the other hand, could be an insignificant amount for a large multinational company and may therefore be written off.

Worked example: Tracy Kennedy extracted a trial balance from her ledgers at the close of business on 31 August 19*7. The trial balance totals failed to agree. The debit side of the trial balance exceeded the credit side by £491. During September 19*7 Tracy found the following errors:
1 The advertising account had been undercast by £100.
2 A cheque received from Jibe & Co. for £345 had been posted to the debit of Jibe & Co.'s account in the sales ledger.
3 Discounts allowed, £54, had been posted to the credit of the discount received account as £45.
4 Goods returned by Gerat plc, £87, had been completely omitted from the books of account.

Required:

i) journal entries necessary to correct the errors
ii) the suspense account used to correct the errors

Solution:

i) Journal

	Dr £	Cr £
Advertising	100	
Suspense		100
Suspense	690	
Jibe & Co.		690
Discount received	45	
Discount allowed	54	
Suspense		99
Returns inward	87	
Gerat plc		87

ii)

Suspense

	£		£
Jibe & Co.	690	Trial balance difference	491
		Advertising	100
		Discount received	45
		Discount allowed	54
	690		690

Note:

The trial balance difference is entered in the suspense account on the same side as the difference in the trial balance.

SWOT analysis might be part of a business's long-term planning process. The analysis seeks to identify:

- strengths
- weaknesses
- opportunities
- threats

to the achievement of the strategic plan. Management should then implement actions which will maximise the strengths and opportunities identified, while efforts are made to minimise the weaknesses and threats.

A four-box format makes the analysis a useful visual aid for discussion purposes:

strengths	weaknesses
opportunities	threats

systems analyst specialises in analysing a process such as stock control to see if it can be done more efficiently and effectively using a computer program.

T

table A: model *Articles of Association* for a *limited company*, as set out in the *Companies Act 1985*.

table B: model *Memorandum of Association* for a *limited company*, as set out in the *Companies Act 1985*.

tactical planning plans how resources will be utilised in an organisation in order to achieve specific objectives in the most efficient and cost-effective way.

take-home pay: see *net salary*

takeover occurs when one business acquires a controlling interest in another. In the case of a *limited company*, the bidder has to purchase more than 50 per cent of the issued ordinary share capital. (See *accounting for subsidiary companies FRS 2, acquisitions and mergers FRS 6, consolidated profit and loss account* and *consolidated balance sheet*.)

tangible fixed assets are physical assets such as:

- land and buildings
- plant and machinery
- fixtures and fittings
- office equipment
- motor vehicles

taxation: see *income tax* and *corporation tax*

taxation under the imputation system SSAP 8 requires that a company's *profit and loss account* should show separately:

- the charge for UK *corporation tax* on the income for the year
- transfers to and from *deferred taxation* account
- tax attributable to franked investment income
- irrecoverable *ACT*
- relief for overseas taxation
- relieved and unrelieved overseas taxation
- cash dividends paid or payable
- dividends received plus related tax credit
- unfranked receipts and payments should be included gross

Tax liabilities should be shown in the *balance sheet* under the heading:

Creditors: amounts falling due within one year
Other creditors including taxation and social security

The liability is for *mainstream corporation tax* for the period. ACT payable on proposed dividends must be shown under this heading.

tax avoidance: trying to pay as little tax as possible by using legal tax loopholes.

tax deductible are legitimate expenses that can be deducted from income or profits before tax is calculated.

tax evasion: illegal avoidance of paying tax.

tax liability: individuals who are resident in the UK are liable to pay tax on income no matter where it is earned. Non-residents can be liable to pay UK tax on income if it is derived from the UK.

tax point is the time when goods and services are said to be supplied for the purposes of calculating *value-added tax*. It is generally the date of issue of the VAT invoice. If a VAT invoice has not been issued within fourteen days of despatch of the goods, the tax point is the date on which the goods were despatched.

tenders are submitted by suppliers to a client showing what is included in the terms of the contract, how much the contract will cost and how long the contract will take. The client will decide which tender to accept based on the criteria laid down in the initial invitation for tenders.

time rate: the amount of pay to be earned for one hour's work, e.g. £6.40 per hour.

time-related pay schemes calculate a worker's gross pay by multiplying the hours worked in a week (as recorded on the *clock card*) by the agreed time rate for each hour.

Worked example: an employee works for 38 hours. The hourly rate of pay is £8.00 per hour.

Required:

Calculate the employee's gross weekly wage.

Solution:

gross weekly wage = hours worked × time rate = 38 × £8.00 = £304

---

time sheet (or job card) records the number of hours an employee spends on each task during each working day. The total hours recorded on the time sheet should correspond with the hours shown on the *clock card*. Any difference between the two is idle time (unproductive time). Idle time might be due to:

- the time taken to get from the time recorder to the workstation
- machine breakdown
- delay in receiving raw materials or components
- maintenance of machinery

Idle time means lost production while overheads are still being incurred. Managers must be aware of the extent of idle time in order to be able to take steps to reduce it as far as is practicable.

time value of money means that money received or paid in the future has not the same value as money paid today. Ask yourself, would you rather win £100 000 on Saturday night's national lottery, or £100 000 on the lottery in 2047? Would you rather settle a £100 debt today or in 15 years' time? The concept is used in capital investment appraisal techniques.

total cost is composed of all *variable costs* + all *fixed costs*.

total factory cost is composed of:

> FORMULA: factory direct costs + factory indirect costs + factory overheads

These are all brought together when a business prepares a *manufacturing account*.

trade creditors are debts owed to suppliers of goods for resale. They are shown on a *balance sheet* under the heading of *current liabilities*. They may simply be called 'creditors' while amounts owing for services are shown as *accrued expenses*.

trade debtors: amounts owed to a business by credit customers who have not yet settled their account. They are shown in the *balance sheet* as *current assets*. Very often they are simply shown as debtors. Amounts owed for services paid in advance are shown as *prepayments*.

trade discount: an amount allowed as a reduction in price when goods are supplied to other businesses. Trade discount is not allowed when the goods are sold on to the general public. Purchases are recorded in the *books of account* net of trade discount.

For example, if you or I purchase a bathroom suite it may cost £750. When Mr Tapp the local plumber purchases the same type of bathroom suite to install in a customer's bathroom, he might only pay £500. The difference is £250 trade discount. VAT is calculated on the net amount of Mr Tapp's purchase, i.e. on £500.

trade investments consist of small holdings of issued shares in other companies (less than 20 per cent). They are held to:

- earn *dividends*
- appreciate, ultimately giving a capital profit
- gain a foothold in another company as a possible start to gaining control in the future

trading account compares the value of sales at cost price with the actual value obtained from customers. The main activity of a trading business is to purchase goods and sell them on at a higher price. The difference between sales and the cost of the same sales is *gross profit*.

The trading account was traditionally the warehouse account and included in its format certain warehouse expenses. The majority of trading organisations now have limited warehousing space, so examination questions now rarely test the treatment of these expenses. However, the following worked example does include warehouse rent so that the reader can see where and how any warehouse expenses are dealt with.

Worked example: Rosemary Butt owns a hardware shop. The following balances have been extracted from her books of account at 30 April 19*7:

	£
Purchases	47 659
Sales	89 655
Returns inward	411
Returns outward	871
Carriage inward	544
Carriage outward	769
Warehouse rent	4 000
Stock 1 May 19*6	2 451
Stock 30 April 19*7	2 769

Required:

A trading account for the year ended 30 April 19*7 for Rosemary Butt.

Solution:

Rosemary Butt trading account for the year ended 30 April 19*7

	£	£	£
Sales			89 655
Less returns inward			411
			89 244
Less cost of sales			
Stock 1 May 19*6		2 451	
Purchases	47 659		
Carriage inward	544		
	48 203		
Less returns outward	871	47 332	
		49 783	
Less stock 30 April 19*7		2 769	
		47 014	
Plus warehouse rent		4 000	51 014
Gross profit			38 230

Carriage outward is a revenue expense that is shown on the profit and loss account.

---

trading assets: also known as *current assets*.

transfers between ledgers are recorded in the journal, for example:

Journal

		Dr	Cr
		£	£
Dretly	PL 26	410	
Dretly	SL 57		410

Debit balance in Dretly's account in the sales ledger set off against his account in the purchases ledger.

---

trend analysis is used to analyse the results of a business over a number of years. This technique is usually used over a five- or ten-year time scale. The main advantage is that it is easy to get a general picture of the trends in items highlighted in the accounts. The main disadvantage is that the figures may not be adjusted to take into account price inflation.

trend extrapolation seeks to predict future results by reference to the trends observed in past results. For example, examine the following turnover figures:

	£000
19*3	128
19*4	140
19*5	156
19*6	132
19*7	180

Apart from 19*6, the trend is that turnover is increasing at around 10 per cent per annum. If we extrapolate the trend to 19*8, we would expect turnover to be around £200 000.

trial balance: a summary of all balances extracted from all the *ledgers* of a business. It is used as an arithmetic check on the accuracy of the entries in the whole *double-entry bookkeeping* system. If the trial balance totals agree it does not necessarily mean that the system is error free. There are errors which will not be revealed by extracting a trial balance. (See *errors not affecting the balancing of the trial balance*.)

true and fair view: the *directors* of a *limited company* must produce a *profit and loss account* that shows a true and fair view of the company's results, and a *balance sheet* that shows a true and fair view of its financial position. One of the directors must sign the balance sheet, indicating that they have fulfilled this responsibility.

The *auditors* have to verify that the accounts show a true and fair view before the accounts are presented to the *shareholders* at a general meeting. When the accounts are adopted by the shareholders they can be filed with the *Registrar of Companies*.

unavoidable costs are incurred by businesses whether business activity takes place or not.

uncalled capital: see *called-up capital*

under-absorption of overheads occurs when fewer units of a product are produced than was predicted in the budget. This means that not all the expected overheads are recovered. For an example, see *over-absorption of overheads*.

underwriting: the acceptance of a business risk in return for a fee. Lloyd's of London has a worldwide reputation for accepting insurance risks of all kinds.

Merchant banks form a syndicate which guarantees that a share issue will be completely sold by agreeing to purchase all the shares which are not subscribed to by the general public.

undistributed profits: profits which have been retained within a business. They increase the *profit and loss account* balance in the books of a *limited company*, so the profit and loss account is an aggregate of all previous years' *undistributed profits*. The profit and loss account is a *revenue reserve*; it is available to issue cash *dividends*. The undistributed profits belong to the *ordinary shareholders*.

unfavourable variances occur when actual results are worse than the results predicted in a budget. If the *variance* has reduced the profit that was predicted in the budget, the variance is said to be an *adverse variance*. If, however, the variance increases the profit that was predicted in the budget, then the variance is favourable (see *favourable variances*).

uniform business rate: a form of local taxation levied on business properties.

unit cost: the average of all the costs involved in the production of one unit of a good or service. Unit cost is calculated by:

$$\text{FORMULA: unit cost} = \frac{\text{total production costs}}{\text{number of units produced}}$$

It is used in *process costing* where it would be impractical to try to find the cost of one small unit of production. Imagine trying to allocate, *apportion* and then absorb all the costs involved in the production of a child's lollipop retailing at 5 pence, or a cylinderhead gasket for a Ford Fiesta.

Unit costs could be enrolled students in a college, a keg of beer in a brewery, bed occupation in a hospital or a kilowatt hour (kWh) in electricity generation.

unpresented cheques: cheques that have not yet been cleared and debited to the business account at a bank. They occur because of the time delay between the writing of a cheque (when it is also entered in the *bank column* of the business *cash book*) and the cheque being entered on the bank statement by the bank. An example of an unpresented cheque is one that has been paid to a supplier, but who for some reason has not yet paid the cheque into his/her bank account; or it has been paid into the supplier's bank account and the cheque is still in the bank cheque clearing system. (See *bank reconciliations*.)

unrealised profit: see *realised profits* and *provision for unrealised profits*

unsecured creditor: a person or business who is owed money but has no security from the debtor for the debt.

unsecured loan: a loan that has been made without security. (See *secured loans.*)

unsocial hours payment: see *shift work*

users of financial reports are generally, but not always, interested in the survival of a business and its ability to generate profits and cash. The usefulness of the financial reports depends on the ability to compare the results with other businesses and earlier years. This means that the users are reliant on the reports being prepared with a consistent approach to all the *accounting concepts and conventions.*

The users of financial reports include:

- management
- auditors
- Inland Revenue
- Customs and Excise
- employees
- trade unions
- debtors
- creditors
- bank managers and other providers of finance
- researchers
- press
- pressure groups
- students

Competitors will use the accounts as a means of gaining information which might benefit them in their fight for a greater market share. (See *ratio analysis.*)

ISLE COLLEGE
RESOURCES CENTRE

valuation of stock: see *methods of stock valuation*

value added: *CIMA* defines value added as 'sales value less the cost of purchased materials and services. This represents the worth of an alteration in form, location or availability of a product or service'. Also known as *added value*.

value-added statement shows the value added to the goods and services acquired by an organisation in order to generate its sales revenue. The statement also shows how the value added has been distributed among the employees, the *shareholders* and other providers of finance, how much has been paid to the government in taxes and how much has been retained in the business.

In recent years, some limited companies have incorporated a value-added statement into their annual *published accounts*. Here is an example of a value-added statement:

Trasker plc value-added statements for the years to 28 February

		19*6		19*7
		£000		£000
Turnover		4754		6187
Purchases of materials and services		2358		3078
Value added		2396		3109
Applied as follows:				
To pay employees		1546		1873
To pay suppliers of capital				
interest on loans	23		28	
dividends to shareholders	80	103	90	118
To pay government – corporation tax		216		345
Io provide for maintainance of assets				
and expansion of business				
depreciation	42		48	
retained profits	489	531	725	773
Value added		2396		3109

value-added tax (VAT): a tax levied on the final consumer of goods and services. With the exception of certain services that are exempt, all business transactions are subject to VAT. Each time value is added in a stage of production, the tax is added and charged to the business undertaking the next stage of production. Each business can claim back from Customs and Excise the tax paid, with the exception of the final consumer who bears the tax based on the final invoice price.

variable costs: costs which change in direct relation to levels of business activity.

variable overhead absorption rate: the means by which the variable factory overheads are absorbed into the product cost(s). The variable factory overheads might be absorbed in a labour-intensive business by use of budgeted *direct labour* hours:

FORMULA: $\dfrac{\text{budgeted variable overheads}}{\text{budgeted direct labour hours}}$

In the case of a capital-intensive industry, the calculation could be:

$$\text{FORMULA: } \frac{\text{budgeted variable overheads}}{\text{budgeted machine hours}}$$

variance analysis investigates differences that occur when actual costs are different from *standard costs*. It enables managers to identify problem areas which need investigating in order that remedial action can be taken.(See *standard costing*.)

variances arise when there is a difference between actual and budgeted figures. Variances are reported to heads of department and highlight departures from budgets. They are often used as a measure of managerial effectiveness. (See *direct material variance, direct labour variance, sales variance, sales margin variance, overhead variance*.)

VAT: see *value-added tax*

VAT account in general ledger shows the *VAT* charged by suppliers (input tax) on the debit side of the account and VAT charged to customers (output tax) on the credit side of the account. At the end of the quarter, when the VAT return is sent to the Customs and Excise, the account will show a debit balance if inputs have been greater than outputs, or a credit balance if the outputs are greater than inputs. The debit balance will be wiped out when the cheque is received from the Customs and Excise. The credit balance will disappear when the business settles the liability with the Customs and Excise.

If there is a balance on the VAT account in the *general ledger* at the end of the *accounting period*, it will be shown on the business *balance sheet* as either a *current asset* (debit balance) or a *current liability* (credit balance).

VAT invoice: an *invoice* that details the *VAT* included in a transaction. It is essential if a registered business wishes to claim relief from the VAT paid to suppliers. A copy of the invoice must be retained for possible inspection by the Customs and Excise. A VAT invoice shows:

- invoice number
- tax point
- supplier's name, address and VAT registration number
- customer's name and address
- description of the goods supplied in sufficient detail for identification purposes
- rate of VAT applicable to each type of good referred to on the invoice
- total amount of the invoice payable excluding VAT
- amount of cash discount to be allowed, if any
- total amount of VAT chargeable

VAT payment: the payment of VAT collected by a business to the Customs and Excise. It should be made one month after the relevant quarterly period.

VAT returns: a record of the VAT involved in the transactions undertaken by a business. They are submitted to the Customs and Excise for a quarterly period.

vertical financial analysis considers only one year's set of financial statements. All the components of the financial statements are expressed as a percentage of a selected figure. For example, all the items in the *profit and loss account* can be expressed as a percentage of turnover. All *balance sheet* items might be expressed as a percentage of, say, capital employed.

Worked example: the following is the trading and profit and loss account for the year ended 30 June 19*7 for Tony Jones Ltd:

		£000
Turnover		1678
Less cost of sales		748
Gross profit		930
Less expenses		
distribution costs	189	
administration costs	320	
		509
Net profit on ordinary activities		421

Required:

A vertical financial analysis of the trading and profit and loss account for the year ended 30 June 19*7 for Tony Jones Ltd, using turnover as the basis of calculation.

Solution:

Tony Jones Ltd vertical financial analysis of the trading and profit and loss account for the year ended 30 June 19*7:

		£000	%
Turnover		1678	100.0
Less cost of sales		748	44.6
Gross profit		930	55.4
Less expenses			
distribution costs	189		11.2
administration costs	320		19.1
		509	30.3
		421	25.1

This type of analysis is also known as common size statements. The advantages of vertical analysis include:

- businesses of different size can be compared
- identifies changes in expenses relative to turnover (or significant changes in structure of balance sheet)
- since figures are based on only one year's figures, inflationary distortions are eliminated

Disadvantages of vertical analysis:

- when making *inter-firm comparisons*, care must be taken to compare like with like
- size of business is ignored, but this is important in analysing performance

vertical ledger accounts: many businesses record entries into the *ledger* using a vertical layout. The presentation is similar to that seen on a bank statement. The accounts generated by computer are often in this format.

This is a copy of Tracy Minall's account in Hilary's sales ledger using a traditional layout and a vertical layout:

Tracy Minall			
7 Jan Cash	150	3 Jan Purchases	174
28 Jan Rets	23	16 Jan Purchases	98
31 Jan Bal c/d	99		
	272		272
		1 Feb Bal b/d	99

Tracy Minall			
	Dr	Cr	Bal
3 Jan Purchases		174	174
7 Jan Cash	150		24
16 Jan Purchases		98	122
28 Jan Returns	23		99

vertical presentation of final accounts is widely used today. It is probably easier for the lay person to understand a set of *final accounts* presented in this way rather than in the traditional horizontal format used in the past. The vast majority of *limited companies* use a vertical presentation when publishing their *annual reports and accounts*.

A vertical presentation of a *profit and loss account* could look like this:

John Lumley trading and profit and loss account for the year ended 31 October 19*7

	£	£	£
Sales			173 502
Less returns inward			1 497
			172 005
Less cost of sales			
Stock 1 November 19*6		8 467	
Purchases	93 551		
Less returns outward	4 792	88 759	
		97 226	
Less stock 31 October 19*7		10 005	87 221
Gross profit			84 784
Add discount received		512	
commission received		750	1 262
			86 046
Less expenses			
Discount allowed		2 918	
Rent and rates		7 500	
Wages		46 853	
Gas and electricity		4 710	
Printing, stationery and advertising		5 636	
Insurances		4 981	
Depreciation office equipment	2 300		
vehicles	7 500	9 800	82 398
Net profit			3 648

wage methods of calculation: see under various methods. Examples include the *Halsey premium bonus scheme, piece work,* etc.

warehouse costs: costs incurred in the holding of goods. They are a *trading account* expense. Warehouse expenses are found in the *general ledger.* At the end of the *accounting period* these *nominal accounts* are closed by transferring the balance to the business *trading account.*

Worked example: Tom Damansara opened a mini-market on 1 August 19*6. During the year ended 31 July 19*7, the following expenses had been incurred in running his warehouse:

Warehouse rent paid on 3 August 19*6: £4500; warehouse rent paid on 17 February 19*7: £4500.

Warehouse insurance paid on 1 August 19*6 for period 1 August 19*6 until 31 December 19*6: £670; warehouse insurance paid on 2 January 19*7 for the year ended 31 December 19*7: £1200.

Required:

The warehouse rent account and the warehouse insurance account showing clearly the transfer to the trading account for the year ended 31 July 19*7.

Solution:

Warehouse rent				
19*6	£		£	
3 Aug Cash	4500			
19*7		19*7		
17 Feb Cash	4500	31 Jul Trading account	9000	
	9000		9000	

Warehouse insurance				
19*6	£	19*6	£	
1 Aug Cash	670			
19*7		19*7		
2 Jan Cash	1200	31 Jul Trading account	1370	
		31 Jul Bal. c/d	500	
	1870		1870	
1 Aug Bal. b/d	500			

On the trading account there will be two debit entries immediately after the cost of sales figure for: warehouse rent – £9000; warehouse insurance – £1370.

Under the heading 'current assets' in Tom Damansara's balance sheet will appear: Insurance prepaid: £500

---

wastage makes up the major source of material losses in a manufacturing business. Wastage has no value – it cannot be sold. Scrap does have a value and produces some revenue for the business.

weighted average cost method of stock valuation (AVCO): see *methods of stock valuation*

wholly owned subsidiary company: see *subsidiary company*

winding up: the term used when a business goes out of existence (see *bankruptcy*). The winding-up procedure, when a company goes into *liquidation,* is a complex subject. The major concern is that during the winding-up process everyone involved should be treated in the fairest way possible.

work certified: an interim valuation of work done on a *long-term contract*. The interim valuation is undertaken by a professional valuer. The valuation then forms the basis upon which progress payments are made by the customer. It would be very unfair to expect the contractor to wait until the *contract* was completed before any payment was made; conversely it would be equally unfair to expect the customer to pay the whole amount at the start of the contract. Part payments based on work certified is a compromise which should suit both parties.

working capital: see *net current assets*

working capital cycle: the time taken between making payment for goods taken into stock and the receipts of cash from the customers for the sale of the goods. The shorter the time between the business laying out the cash for the purchase of stock and the collection of the cash for the sales of the stock, the better for the business.

The cycle is calculated by adding the *rate of stock turnover* (in days) to the *debtors' payment* (collection) *period* (in days), and deducting the *creditors' payment period* (in days).

Worked example: the following is the trading account of Sandra Neal for the year ended 31 May 19*7:

	£	£
Sales		970 365
Less cost of sales		
Stock 1 June 19*6	40 132	
Purchases	437 561	
	477 693	
Stock 31 May 19*7	42 462	435 231
Gross profit		535 134

Additional information:
All purchases and sales are on credit.
Debtors at 31 May 19*7   76 438
Creditors at 31 May 19*7   36 281

Required:

Calculate Sandra Neal's working capital cycle.

Solution:

stock turnover in days	35	$\dfrac{\text{cost of sales}}{\text{average stock}}$ = 10.54 times per year
debtors' collection period in days	29	$\dfrac{\text{debtors} \times 365}{\text{credit sales}}$
	64	
creditors' payment period in days	31	$\dfrac{\text{creditors} \times 365}{\text{credit purchases}}$
working capital cycle in days	33	

The shorter the cycle, the lower the value of working capital to be financed by other sources. The cycle can be reduced by:

- increasing the rate of stock turnover by reducing the levels of stock held
- speeding up the rate at which debtors pay
- taking longer to pay creditors

working capital ratio: see *current ratio*

work in progress: stocks of partly finished goods. In any manufacturing business there will be three distinct types of stock:

- stocks of raw materials and components waiting to go through the production process
- stocks of finished goods waiting to be despatched to the customer
- stocks of goods that are only part way through the production process – work in progress

In a manufacturing business's *final accounts*, work in progress is treated like any other type of stock. *Opening stock* is added and *closing stock* is deducted.

Total *production cost* in a *manufacturing account* is made up of *prime cost* plus factory overheads. Opening work in progress is added to this figure, and closing work in progress is deducted. The result is the amount to be transferred to the *trading account*.

Worked example: James John owns a manufacturing business. The following information relates to his financial year end 30 April 19*7:

	£
Prime cost	506 781
Factory overhead costs	307 374
Work in progress 1 May 19*6	15 889
Work in progress 30 April 19*7	18 550

Required:

A summarised manufacturing account for the year ended 30 April 19*7 for James John.

Solution:

James John manufacturing account for the year ended 30 April 19*7

	£
Prime cost	506 781
Factory overheads	307 374
	814 155
Add work in progress 1 May 19*6	15 889
	830 044
Less work in progress 30 April 19*7	18 550
Cost of goods manufactured transferred to trading account	811 494

---

work not yet certified: similar to *work in progress* in a manufacturing business. As a *contract* progresses there will be work completed that a valuer has not yet been asked to certify. The contractor will make a valuation of this work at the financial year end and carry it forward in the *contract account* to start the next financial period's contract account.

zero-based budget questions each activity as if it were new and before any resources are allocated towards it. Each plan of action has to be justified in terms of total costs involved and total benefits to accrue, with no reference to past activities.

HINTS ON EXAM SUCCESS

The most obvious advice here is to be well-prepared for the day of the examination. The most critical factor in order to ensure this is a thorough revision programme. Revision must be started in plenty of time to allow you to identify any aspects of your syllabus that you do not fully understand. If you have done this early enough, you will have plenty of time to work through the sections where you are weak and also to ask for further help and guidance from your tutor if necessary. Do not underestimate the benefits of an early start to your revision. You will be made aware of all your examination dates months in advance, but beware, because it is amazing how they 'creep up' on you and suddenly they are only a week away. If you push them to the back of your mind, there is a danger that your revision will take the form of a panic attack!

Revision is helped by a revision plan or timetable. This can be as simple as a list of topics that you can tick off when you have read through your notes, and perhaps tick again when you have worked through some questions, e.g.

Read notes	Re-write notes in brief	Test with past questions
Concepts		
Partnerships		
Club accounts		
Stock valuation		
Social accounting		

By doing this you can see that you are making progress. I recommend this kind of planning and record-keeping because at some time during revision many students experience the feeling that they are 'not getting anywhere' or that they 'will never understand this', etc. If you have a checklist like the one above you can look at it and see that you have made progress. Look at how many topics you have ticked off and hopefully reassure yourself that your revision programme is well underway. Of course, this list will not help if you have not started work on it!

Try to work out which time of day suits you best to do your revision. If you are still at school or college try to make the best possible use of your free time. Most importantly, try to develop a routine for your studies; it then becomes much easier to discipline yourself to get down to work.

Students can revise effectively in many different ways. If you begin to lose your concentration during one of your revision sessions try switching to another method – a change is as good as a rest! You must take regular breaks too. Some revision methods are:

- read aloud
- ask a friend to question you
- try test questions
- summarise your explanations/answers
- try to answer questions within a limited time
- try explaining a topic to someone who does not study accounting – if you do not feel that you could do this then perhaps you need to study that topic a little more

Some people revise to music and your tutors will probably tell you to use whichever method suits you best, but remember that you have to complete your examination under examination conditions, which do not include music, so please make sure that you are able to concentrate under those conditions too.

Another way in which you can improve your chances of success is by making yourself familiar with the terms that examiners might use in your examination papers and therefore how they will expect you to respond. What follows is not an exhaustive list of terms but it includes the ones most commonly used, together with an explanation of the type of approach you will expected to take.

Advise: this instruction usually requires you to consider information given in a question or calculated by yourself and then to use this in order to arrive at a business decision. This can be based on financial and/or non-financial considerations.

Analyse: this word will be used when a descriptive answer is required. You will be expected to give as many aspects of the topic in question as possible, bearing in mind that you must retain focus on the question. You should provide an argument which outlines the potential advantages and disadvantages of a given situation or decision.

Assess: this instruction is asking you to weigh up information both for and against a stated action or situation. It requires you to give an evaluation (justified conclusion).

Calculate: find the answer mathematically without necessarily preparing a detailed statement. For example, you might be asked to calculate the profits of a business. This can be done by making a comparison between the opening and closing capitals and then making an adjustment to take into account any capital introduced into the business during the year and any drawings made by the proprietor(s) during the year. A detailed profit and loss account is not required, but do remember to show your workings.

Comment: weigh the results and evidence given or calculated in the first part(s) of a question in order to reach your conclusions. When such an instruction is given the examiner expects you to demonstrate a deeper understanding of the topic in question. Your comments must be consistent with your results.

Comment critically: means weigh up the pros and cons of the information given or deduced in a question in order to reach your conclusion. Remember that a critique considers the positive aspects of a problem as well as the negative aspects.

Define: give an explanation of the word or term given in the question. Remember that an example is not an explanation, although it may earn you further development marks after you have provided your definition.

Describe: means provide a detailed outline of the steps involved in a financial transaction or the characteristics of a financial document.

Discuss: means that both sides of a problem have to be outlined and considered before you reach a conclusion. It is important that you reach a conclusion based on your discussion and one which is consistent with the information that you present.

Draft: a preparatory statement or document which may need to be altered later in the light of further information becoming available.

Evaluate: requires you to consider all the information given in the question and to reach a decision based on the facts outlined. This requires a personal judgement so do not be afraid to express your own opinion.

Examine: you will be required to reach a conclusion based on the facts relevant to the situation given in the question.

Explain: this term is designed to give you the opportunity to show that you have developed a clear understanding of the facts outlined in the question. You can do this by giving a clear and precise definition and then enlarging on points made. A relevant example may help you to gain further marks. Once again, it must be emphasised that an example is not an explanation in itself but it can help to add some clarity to your answer.

Explain the difference between: this type of answer requires you to compare alternatives; it does not require you to reach a conclusion or to make a recommendation. However, you must make comparisons rather than just make two lists.

If a question asks you to explain the difference between preference shares and ordinary shares you could say that preference shares pay a stipulated dividend whereas ordinary share dividends may vary from year to year. Notice the use of the word 'whereas' to show that you are considering the differences.

Extract: to show the appropriate part of a financial statement. For example, you might be asked to calculate a stock figure and then show how it would appear in the balance sheet. Your answer could look something like this:

    Balance sheet extract as at 31 October 19*7
    Current assets
    Stock   £32 900

Note the use of the word 'extract' in the heading.

Formulae: same as model.

Identify: to name examples asked for in the question. Generally, your answer would take the form of a list.

Illustrate: means to use an example taken from the information given in the question or derived from your own answer and to explain its relevance within the question.

List: itemise the components briefly without any attempt to explain.

Model: generally, another name for the formulae that you have used to calculate your answer. When calculating ratios you should always show the model that your calculations are based on, e.g:

$$\text{mark-up} = \frac{\text{gross profit}}{\text{turnover}} \times 100$$

Outline: to give a brief explanation. Candidates are often unsure how much to write when given this instruction; the length of response should always be governed by the mark allocation.

Prepare: present the required answer from the information given in the question.

Quality of language: from 1998 onwards some marks will be awarded in A-level examinations for spelling, punctuation and grammar. Candidates will need to demonstrate the ability to present ideas and information in an appropriate manner and demonstrate that they can argue with clarity and in a logical structure.

Statement: a presentation of the relevant facts in a format suitable for the reader. The format could be a memorandum, or it could take the form of a report, but do not fall into the trap of thinking that statements are necessarily written presentations – they can take the form of a revenue statement or a series of adjustments to a draft profit figure. Remember that the term 'statement of affairs' has a presentation very similar to the conventional balance sheet.

Recommend: after considering all the facts outlined in the question and/or your answer, you must advise on a course of action, e.g. 'based on the information outlined above I would advise Rebecca to invest in Gavington plc'.

Reservations: the examiner wishes you to outline any doubts that you may have on the course of action determined after due consideration of the facts outlined in the question.

State your assumptions: this phrase allows you to tell the examiner why you have pursued a certain line of thought in your answer. Your actions must be based on a logical line of thought to gain marks.

REVISION LIST

This appendix identifies the most popular examination topics. To use it, select a topic that you wish to revise and look up the terms listed. This may lead you to cross references which will build up to give a comprehensive answer.

When answering any written section of the paper, always make a plan as this will ensure that you do not repeat yourself and thus waste time. It will also allow you to marshall your points into a logical, sensible format.

Always identify the point you wish to make, explain it in general terms and then apply the point to the question being asked.

The topics outlined below are the elements commonly examined in most accounting examinations.

1 Concepts

Accruals concept
Business entity concept
Consistency
Dual aspect concept
Going-concern concept

Materiality
Money measurement concept
Prudence
Realisation concept

2 Marginal costing

Break-even analysis
Break-even charts
Break-even point
Contribution
Contribution pricing
Contribution/sales ratio

Fixed costs
Limiting factor
Make or buy decisions
Penetration pricing
Special-order pricing
Variable cost

3 Basic bookkeeping

Bad debts
Balance sheet
Bank reconciliation statement
Books of prime entry
Control accounts
Correction of errors
Extended trial balance
Manufacturing accounts
Profit and loss account

Provision
Provision for bad debts
Provision for depreciation
Provision for discounts
Reserves
Suspense accounts
Trading account
Trial balance

4 Partnerships

Garner v Murray (1904)
Goodwill
Partnership Act 1890
Partnership agreements
Partnership capital account
Partnership current account
Partnership dissolution

Partnership profit and loss appropriation accounts
Partnership salaries
Realisation account
Retiring partner
Structural changes

5 Limited companies

Auditors' report
Bonus shares
Capital reserves
Called-up capital
Calls in advance
Calls in arrears
Current assets
Debentures
Directors
Directors' report
Fixed assets
Forfeiture of shares

Format 1 and 2 layouts
Issue of debentures
Issue of ordinary shares
Paid-up share capital
Preference shares
Provisions
Published accounts
Redemption of shares
Reserves
Revenue reserves
Rights issue

6 Incomplete records

Adjustment account
Club accounts
Income and expenditure account
Life membership

Receipts and payments
Single entry bookkeeping
Statement of affairs
Subscription account (see club accounts)

7 Cash flow statements

Bonus shares
Cash and cash equivalents

FRS 1
Revaluation reserve

8 Standard costing

Direct labour variances
Direct material variances
Flexible budgets
Management by exception
Overhead variances
Sales variances

Standard hour
Standard minute
Standard setting
Variance analysis
Variances

9 Ratio analysis

Credit control	Profitability ratios
Gearing	Users of financial statements
Liquidity ratios	Working capital cycle

Formulae for the calculation of accounting ratios:

Acid test ratio
$$\frac{\text{current assets} - \text{stock}}{\text{current liabilities}}$$

Creditors' payment period
$$\frac{\text{creditors} \times 365}{\text{credit purchases}}$$

Current ratio
$$\frac{\text{current assets}}{\text{current liabilities}}$$

Debtors' payment period
$$\frac{\text{debtors} \times 365}{\text{credit sales}}$$

Dividend cover
$$\frac{\text{profit after tax and interest}}{\text{ordinary dividend paid}}$$

Dividend yield
$$\frac{\text{dividend per share} \times 100}{\text{market price per share}}$$

Earnings per share (EPS)
$$\frac{\text{earnings in pence}}{\text{number of issued ordinary shares}}$$

Gearing
$$\frac{\text{fixed cost capital} \times 100}{\text{total capital}}$$

Interest cover
$$\frac{\text{profits before interest and tax}}{\text{interest payable}}$$

Margin
$$\frac{\text{gross profit} \times 100}{\text{sales}}$$

Mark-up
$$\frac{\text{gross profit} \times 100}{\text{cost of sales}}$$

Net margin
$$\frac{\text{net profit} \times 100}{\text{sales}}$$

Price/earnings ratio (P/E)
$$\frac{\text{current market price of a share}}{\text{earnings per share}}$$

Rate of stock turnover
$$\frac{\text{cost of sales}}{\text{average stock held}}$$

Return on capital employed (ROCE)
$$\frac{\text{profit before interest and tax} \times 100}{\text{capital employed}}$$

Return on owner's equity
$$\frac{\text{net profit before interest and tax less preference dividends} \times 100}{\text{issued ordinary share capital plus all reserves}}$$

revision list